Competition Law in Argentina

Second Edition

Marcelo den Toom

This book was originally published as a monograph in the International
Encyclopaedia of Laws/Competition Law.

General Editors: Roger Blanpain, Frank Hendrickx
Volume Editors: Francesco Denozza, Alberto Toffoletto

Published by:
Kluwer Law International B.V.
PO Box 316
2400 AH Alphen aan den Rijn
The Netherlands
Website: www.wklawbusiness.com

Sold and distributed in North, Central and South America by:
Wolters Kluwer Legal & Regulatory U.S.
7201 McKinney Circle
Frederick, MD 21704
United States of America
Email: customer.service@wolterskluwer.com

Sold and distributed in all other countries by:
Turpin Distribution Services Ltd.
Stratton Business Park
Pegasus Drive, Biggleswade
Bedfordshire SG18 8TQ
United Kingdom
Email: kluwerlaw@turpin-distribution.com

DISCLAIMER: The material in this volume is in the nature of general comment only. It is not offered as advice on any particular matter and should not be taken as such. The editor and the contributing authors expressly disclaim all liability to any person with regard to anything done or omitted to be done, and with respect to the consequences of anything done or omitted to be done wholly or partly in reliance upon the whole or any part of the contents of this volume. No reader should act or refrain from acting on the basis of any matter contained in this volume without first obtaining professional advice regarding the particular facts and circumstances at issue. Any and all opinions expressed herein are those of the particular author and are not necessarily those of the editor or publisher of this volume.

Printed on acid-free paper

ISBN 978-90-411-8257-9

This title is available on www.kluwerlawonline.com

© 2016, Kluwer Law International BV, The Netherlands

All rights reserved. No part of this publication may be reproduced, stored in a retrieval system, or transmitted in any form or by any means, electronic, mechanical, photocopying, recording, or otherwise, without the prior written permission of the publisher.

Permission to use this content must be obtained from the copyright owner. Please apply to: Permissions Department, Wolters Kluwer Legal & Regulatory U.S., 76 Ninth Avenue, 7th Floor, New York, NY 10011-5201, USA. Website: www.wklawbusiness.com

Printed and Bound by CPI Group (UK) Ltd, Croydon, CR0 4YY.

Competition Law in Argentina

The Author

Prof. Dr Marcelo den Toom (born 19 November 1968) obtained a degree in law (1993) from the University of Belgrano in Buenos Aires. He attended the University of Illinois in 1992 and graduated as Master of Laws from the University of Michigan in 1997. He has been professor of corporate law at the National University of Buenos Aires (Argentina) and is currently professor of competition law at Universidad Austral (Argentina). He is current Vice-Chair and past Chair of the Competition Law Commission of *Colegio de Abogados de la Ciudad de Buenos Aires* and is current Co-Chair of the Antitrust Committee of the Section of International Law of the American Bar Association. He is admitted to practice by the bars of the cities of Buenos Aires (1994) and New York (2000). He is currently a partner at M. & M. Bomchil in Buenos Aires, where he heads the Competition Law practice. He is a former foreign associate at Haynes & Boone (Houston office) and Skadden, Arps, Slate, Meagher & Flom (New York office).

He has published different works on corporate, commercial and antitrust issues, and is the author of the Argentine chapters of *Getting the Deal Through: Merger Control* (2000–2015), *Getting the Fine Down: Cartels 2001* (both works published by Global Competition Review), *International Mergers: The Antitrust Process* (Sweet & Maxwell, 2001–), *Merger Control Worldwide and Anti-Cartel Enforcement* (Cambridge University Press, 2004– and 2009–, respectively), *Antitrust Issues in International Intellectual Property Licensing Transactions* (American Bar Association, 2012) and *Global Legal Insights – Cartels* (Global Legal Group, 2013–).

The author wishes to thank Agustina Laboureau, Lucía Grima Wencelblat, Agustina Morán and Cecilia del Barrio Arleo for their cooperation in the research required for the first edition of this work.

The Author

Table of Contents

The Author	3
List of Abbreviations	11
General Introduction	13
§1. GENERAL BACKGROUND	13
I. Geography	13
II. Population and Economy	13
III. Language	14
IV. Political System	14
V. Judicial System	15
§2. ECONOMIC SYSTEM	16
§3. LEGAL SYSTEM	17
§4. HISTORICAL BACKGROUND OF ANTITRUST LAW	18
Part I. Structure of Antitrust Law and Its Enforcement	25
Chapter 1. Sources of Antitrust Law	25
§1. NATIONAL SOURCES	25
§2. INTERNATIONAL SOURCES	27
§3. SECONDARY SOURCES	29
I. Regulations and Guidelines	29
§4. SOURCES' RELATION AND HIERARCHY	31
§5. ROLE AND AUTHORITY OF PRECEDENTS	32

Table of Contents

Chapter 2. Scope of Application — 33

§1. Territorial Reach — 33
§2. Special Sectors — 34
§3. State-Owned Enterprises and Public Utilities — 35
§4. Sensible Effect and *De Minimis* — 36

Chapter 3. Overview of Substantive Provisions — 37

§1. Restrictive Agreements — 37
§2. Dominant Undertakings — 37
§3. Concentrations — 39
§4. Other Prohibitions — 43
§5. Tests of Illegality — 43
  I. Per Se Prohibitions and Naked Restraints — 43
  II. Balancing Tests — 44
  III. Merger Tests — 45

Chapter 4. Overview of Main Notions — 47

§1. Undertaking — 47
§2. Relevant Market — 48
§3. Market Power/Dominant Position — 49
§4. Agreements and Concerted Practices — 50
§5. Restriction of Competition — 51
§6. Monopolization and Abuse of Dominance — 52
§7. Concentrations — 55
§8. Joint Ventures — 56

Table of Contents

Chapter 5. Consequences of Violations — 58

§1. ADMINISTRATIVE ENFORCEMENT — 58
    I. The Antitrust Authorities — 58
        A. Formation, Composition — 58
        B. Investigating Powers — 60
        C. Adjudicating Powers *(Ascertaining and Sanctioning)* — 62
        D. Other Institutional Tasks *(Consultancy to Parliament/ Government)* — 62
    II. Government Direct Enforcement Activities — 64
    III. Other Administrative Agencies Applying Antitrust Rules — 64
    IV. Administrative Fines — 65
    V. Administrative Injunctions and Other Restrictive Orders — 67
    VI. Interim Measures — 70

§2. CIVIL ENFORCEMENT — 70
    I. Competent Civil Courts — 70
    II. Sanctions — 74
        A. Nullity — 74
        B. Damages — 75
        C. Interim Measures — 76

§3. CRIMINAL ENFORCEMENT — 78
    I. Criminal Sanctions for Antitrust Violations — 78
    II. Other Application of Criminal Law to Relevant Conducts — 78
    III. Role of Prosecutors — 79
    IV. Competent Criminal Courts — 80

Part II. The Application of the Prohibitions — 83

Chapter 1. Restrictive Agreements — 83

§1. HORIZONTAL AGREEMENTS — 83
    I. Cartels — 83
        A. Price-Fixing — 83
        B. Market/Client Allocation — 87
        C. Production/Innovation Limitation — 92
        D. Group Boycott — 94
        E. Collusion on Other Objects — 97
    II. Information Exchange Practices — 98
    III. Cooperation Agreements — 99
        A. Research and Development — 99
        B. Specialization — 100
        C. Standardization — 100
        D. Joint Production/Purchasing/Selling — 100

Table of Contents

§2. VERTICAL AGREEMENTS	102
I. Distribution	102
A. Exclusive Distributorship	102
B. Exclusive Dealing	105
C. Selective Distribution	106
D. Franchising	106
II. Technology Licensing	107
A. Patent Licensing	107
B. Trademark Licensing, Know-How and Trade Secret Licensing	110

Chapter 2. Dominant Undertakings' Prohibited Practices   111

§1. EXPLOITATIVE PRACTICES	111
I. Excessive/Unfair Pricing	111
II. Discrimination	113
§2. EXCLUSIONARY PRACTICES	114
I. Predation	114
II. Tying	116
III. Rebates	120
IV. Refusal to Deal	121
V. Price Squeeze	124

Chapter 3. Concentrations   126

§1. HORIZONTAL MERGERS	126
§2. VERTICAL MERGERS	140
§3. MARKET/PRODUCT EXTENSION MERGERS	141
§4. PURE CONGLOMERATE MERGERS	141
§5. JOINT VENTURES	143

Part III. Administrative Procedure   145

Chapter 1. Administrative Investigations   145

§1. INITIATIVE	145
I. General Sectors Inquiries	145
II. Ex Officio Investigations	153
III. Complaints	153
§2. POWERS	153
I. Requests for Information	153

Table of Contents

II. Investigating and Search Powers	154
III. Cooperation with Other State Institutions	155

§3. RIGHT OF DEFENCE — 155
    I. Content and Notification of Opening Decisions — 155
    II. The Proceedings: Hearings, Access to File, Briefs — 156
    III. Statement of Objections — 158
    IV. Final Hearing and Decision — 158

Chapter 2. Voluntary Notifications and Clearance Decisions Merger Control — 161

§1. PRELIMINARY FILING OBLIGATIONS — 161
    I. Criteria and Thresholds — 161
    II. Turnover Calculation — 161
    III. Market Share Calculation — 164
    IV. Other Relevant Notions — 166

§2. STRUCTURE OF PROCEEDINGS — 166
    I. Preliminary Assessments and Full Investigation — 166
    II. Time Framework — 167
    III. Right of Defence — 171

§3. CLEARANCE AND CONDITIONAL CLEARANCE — 172
    I. Conditions and Undertakings — 173
        A. Content — 173
        B. Timing — 176

§4. RELATIONS WITH OTHER MERGER CONTROL AUTHORITIES — 177
    I. Other Authorities within the Local Jurisdiction — 177
    II. International Coordination — 177

Chapter 3. Challenging of the Administrative Decision — 178

§1. COMPETENT COURTS — 178

§2. TIME LIMITS — 180

§3. SCOPE OF JUDICIAL REVIEW — 182

Selected Bibliography — 183

Index — 185

Table of Contents

List of Abbreviations

ACE	*Agrupación de Colaboración*
ADLA	Anales de Legislación Argentina
AVC	Average Variable Cost
BO	Boletín Oficial de la República Argentina
CDC	Committee for the Defence of Competition
CFed. Bahía Blanca	Cámara Federal de Apelaciones de Bahía Blanca (Prov. de Buenos Aires)
CFed. Com. Riv.	Cámara Federal de Apelaciones de Comodoro Rivadavia (Prov. del Chubut)
CFed. Paraná	Cámara Federal de Apelaciones de Paraná (Prov. de Entre Ríos)
CFed. Posadas	Cámara Federal de Apelaciones de Posadas (Prov. de Misiones)
CFed. Rosario	Cámara Federal de Apelaciones de Rosario (Prov. de Santa Fe)
CNCiv. Com. Fed.	Cámara Nacional de Apelaciones en lo Civil y Comercial Federal
CNCiv. Com. y ContAdm. R.C.	Cámara Nacional de Apelaciones Civil, Comercial y Contenciosoadministrativa de Río Cuarto (Prov. de Córdoba)
CNCom	Cámara Nacional de Apelaciones en lo Comercial
CNCont. Adm. Fed.	Cámara Nacional de Apelaciones en lo Contenciosoadministrativo Federal
CNCP	Cámara Nacional de Casación Penal
CNG	Compressed Natural Gas
CNPenal Económico	Cámara Nacional de Apelaciones en lo Penal Económico
Const. Arg.	Constitución de la Nación Argentina

List of Abbreviations

Corte Sup. Just. Santa Fe	Corte Suprema de Justicia de Santa Fe
CCC	Código Civil y Comercial de la Nación
CPCCN	Código Procesal Civil y Comercial de la Nación
CPN	Código Penal de la Nación
CPPN	Código Procesal Penal de la Nación
CSJN	Corte Suprema de Justicia de la Nación
ECJ	European Court of Justice
ED	Revista 'El Derecho'
EDA	Revista 'El Derecho Administrativo'
HR	House of Representatives
JA	Revista 'Jurisprudencia Argentina'
Juzg. Fed. Salta	Juzgado Federal de Salta
Juzg. Nac. de Prim. Inst. en lo Com.	Juzgado Nacional de Primera Instancia en lo Comercial
LL	Revista 'La Ley'
LLC	Revista 'La Ley. Córdoba'
LLO	Revista 'La Ley Online'
LPG	Liquefied Petroleum Gas
MCA	Mercosur Competition Agreement
OECD	Organisation of Economic Co-operation & Development
UNCTAD	United Nations Conference on Trade and Development

General Introduction

§1. GENERAL BACKGROUND[1]

I. Geography

1. The Republic of Argentina[2] is located in the Southern and Western Hemispheres. Its relative position in South America gives the country a diversity of land and culture. From the Antarctic regions in the south to the forested jungle regions in the north, from the ocean coastline on the Atlantic to the rugged mountain regions in the west, and bordering five other countries, Argentina provides an important cultural and economic connection for all of South America.[3] It is the second-largest country in South America and eighth in the world by land area and the largest among Spanish-speaking nations.

2. Argentina's continental area is 2,766,890 square kilometres (1,068,300 sq miles), covering the area between the Andes mountain range in the west and the southern Atlantic Ocean in the east and south. Argentina borders Paraguay and Bolivia to the north, Brazil and Uruguay to the northeast, and Chile to the west and south.

II. Population and Economy[4]

3. The first inhabitants of the present Argentine territory were indigenous people who congregated in tribes and developed their respective cultures to different extents. In the fifteenth century, the Spanish conquerors brought their own customs and values, thus generating a cultural convergence of everlasting dimensions, not without pain in some cases and cooperation in others. Spain established a permanent colony on the site of Buenos Aires in 1580, and the Viceroyalty of the Río de la Plata was created in 1776.

4. This area was largely a country of Spanish immigrants and their descendants, known as *criollos*, and others of native cultures. A wave of foreign investment and

---

1. This section follows the content of points I and II of the work entitled *Doing Business in Argentina*, which was edited by the author. Please refer to said country report at www.bomchil.com.
2. Please refer to www.argentina.gob.ar/advf/descargas/about_english.pdf.
3. *Ibid*.
4. *Ibid*.

immigration from Europe after 1870 led to the development of modern agriculture and to a near-reinvention of Argentine society and economy, leading to the strengthening of a cohesive State.

5. The last census carried out in 2010 reported 40,091,359 inhabitants, a 7.5% increase from 2001.

6. Argentina benefits from rich natural resources (including land suitable for livestock and crops, fisheries, oil, natural gas, gold, silver, potassium, manganese and many other minerals), a highly literate population, an export-oriented agricultural sector and a diversified industrial base. Argentina is one of the world's major agricultural producers; produce includes honey, soybeans, sunflower seeds, maize and wheat. In 2014, agricultural output accounted for 9% of the GDP and over 40% of all exports. Soy and its by-products, mainly animal feed and vegetable oils, were major export commodities, amounting to over a quarter of all exports. Wheat, maize, sorghum and other cereals totalled 8.8%, while beef, leather and dairy amounted to slightly above 5% of total exports.[5]

III. Language

7. Spanish is the official language in the Argentine Republic. The vast majority of the population is Roman Catholic.

IV. Political System

8. Argentina is a Presidential Republic. The political system is formed by the three traditional branches: the Judicial, the Legislative and the Executive.

9. The Legislative Branch is the Congress, formed by the House of Representatives (HR) and the Senate. The primary function of the Congress is to pass, amend, revoke and repeal laws. The Executive Branch is made up of the President, the Vice-President, the Chief of the Ministerial Cabinet, Ministers, and other officers and directors of administrative agencies. The President is the head of the State.

10. The President serves a four-year term and may be re-elected for only one consecutive term. Election is by universal suffrage (electors must be over 16 years). HR members are elected for a four-year term, half being elected every two years. Each province elects two Senators for the majority party and one for the minority party, all of them serving for a six-year term. Senators and HR members are elected by direct vote.

---

5. Instituto Nacional de Estadísticas y Censos, Exportaciones por complejos exportadores, Año 2014 (available at www.indec.mecon.ar).

General Introduction

11. The country is divided into a Federal Capital (the city of Buenos Aires) and twenty-three provinces. Each province has its own Governor, legislature and judiciary.

V. Judicial System

12. The National Supreme Court of Justice (the 'Supreme Court') is at the highest level of the Argentinean judicial system. It exercises ordinary – general – appellate jurisdiction, special appellate jurisdiction, and exclusive and original jurisdiction.

13. General appellate jurisdiction is exercised when matters have been previously treated by First and Second Instance Courts. Said matters are those governed by the National Constitution and federal laws, such as issues related to international treaties, admiralty and maritime jurisdiction.

14. Special appellate jurisdiction is exercised through what is commonly referred to as 'constitutional control', since the Supreme Court has been endowed with the power to control legal rules and administrative acts.

15. The Supreme Court's exclusive and original jurisdiction involves all matters related to ambassadors, ministers and foreign consuls and those involving a province.

16. With the exception of exclusive and original jurisdiction cases, Supreme Court rulings are issued on appeal and after a specific petition has been filed (the latter being applicable to all matters brought before Judicial Courts). Likewise, the Supreme Court is only allowed to pass judgment on concrete litigation. Should this litigation be a collective action, the effects of the res judicata shall affect all the persons in the same situation even when they were not a party to said litigation.

17. Jurisdiction over matters in the city of Buenos Aires can be federal or 'national'.

18. Federal jurisdiction deals with cases based on federal matters referred to by the National Congress, like trademarks, maritime law, patent or competition law matters. However, national jurisdiction examines cases related to non-federal matters, like torts, contractual relationships, bankruptcy, commercial papers or company law.

19. There is also a general jurisdiction which has been vested in provincial courts and involves matters ruled by laws dictated by both national and local Congresses.

20. Moreover, alongside the aforementioned tribunals in the provinces presiding over ordinary matters, there are also tribunals having jurisdiction over controversies involving federal matters (i.e., federal jurisdiction).

21. Regarding subject-matter jurisdiction, most courts preside over specific issues (i.e., civil, commercial, criminal, labour, etc.).

22. The procedure applicable before most of the aforementioned courts is written and may involve any of the following stages: complaint, answer, defences to the complaint, counterclaim, evidence stage and final ruling; whereas criminal proceedings are generally comprised of two stages, a probable cause-type proceeding followed by an oral trial before a three-judge court.

§2. ECONOMIC SYSTEM

23. Contemporary Argentina can be regarded as having a mixed economy, with varying degrees of market intervention.

24. When President Carlos Menem took office in 1989, the country had piled up huge external debts, inflation had reached 200% per month, and output was plummeting. To combat the economic crisis the government embraced free market policies by opening of the national economy, privatizing most State-owned enterprises and, largely, dismantling the State as an economic agent. In 1991, the Government implemented radical monetary reforms which pegged the Peso to the US Dollar (Convertibility Law[6]) and limited the growth in the monetary base by law to the growth in reserves. Inflation fell sharply in subsequent years.[7]

25. However, these measures ultimately did not yield the expected results, the country entered recession around 1998 that ended in a major banking crisis in 2002 with the devaluation of the national currency by around 200% and its ensuing social impact.

26. Post-crisis administrations have once again expanded the State's role in the economy and undone some of the changes implemented during the 1990s, like nationalizing the pension fund system, flag carrier and major oil and gas company. Tariffs of privatized companies were frozen for several years, and competition mechanisms introduced in their regulatory frameworks replaced by direct regulation. Foreign exchange became tightly regulated, international trade – both inbound and outbound – subject to numerous restrictions, and areas of domestic trade were

---

6. Law No. 23,928 (28 Mar. 1991 [27104] BO) established a fixed exchange rate between the local and the US currency, at a rate of 1 (one) US Dollar per 10,000 Australes, which were afterwards replaced by a new currency, the Peso, also of a fixed rate of USD 1.
7. Julio Godio, *The Argentine Anomaly: from Wealth through Collapse to Neo-Developmentalism* Friedrich-Ebert-Stiftung (FES) ed., 2004).

affected by price controls. However, the new Administration that took office in December 2015 is undoing several of those changes.

§3. LEGAL SYSTEM

27. Following its Roman Law tradition, Argentina's legal system is based on codification, that is, an organic collecting and re-stating of the law of a particular branch of law in a single legal document. A Code's characteristics generally are:

(i) *Unity*: unifies all rules concerning a particular branch of law.
(ii) *Exclusivity*: must contain all existing rules on the matter in force.
(iii) *Systematization*: the subject matter of the code is presented in an organized manner.

28. Because of the federal system adopted by the Constitution, two legal systems coexist side by side; the national, originated in the National Government, and the provincial, whose legislative power derives from each province.[8]

29. The political organization of Argentina is based on a federal representative and republican structure of government. Each province has its own Constitution, through which it ensures the administration of justice and the municipal autonomy of its territory, regulating the scope and reach of the institutional, political, administrative, economic and financial order. Provinces elect their authorities: governor, legislators and other officials. Through their local institutions, they issue their local laws. They are also entitled to enter into international treaties, provided that those treaties are not incompatible with the national foreign policy, and that they do not affect the powers vested in the National Government or the national public credit. Likewise, they can enter into partial treaties in order to administer justice, pursue economic interests and carry out common use works with the prior authorization of the National Congress.[9]

30. The National Constitution has demarcated the powers of both public authorities (national and local). The National Constitution is the fundamental law of the State, which organizes the form of government, powers and duties of both rulers and ruled. All other laws and also provincial constitutions must adjust to the National Constitution.[10] Regulatory decrees are regulations enacted by the President (at the national level) or the governors (at the provincial level) to facilitate and clarify law enforcement, so they are conditioned by them, and shall not alter their spirit with regulatory exceptions.[11]

---

8. Jorge Joaquin Llambías, Tratado De Derecho Civil Parte General, Tomo 1 (Lexis Nexis, Abeledo – Perrot ed., 2007) at 53.
9. Constitución Argentina [Const. Arg.] Art. 1.
10. Const. Arg., Art. 5.
11. *See* Llambías, *supra* n. 8.

31. Article 75 paragraph 22 of the 1994 National Constitution[12] establishes that, as a general rule: (i) international treaties are of a higher hierarchy than laws, and (ii) human rights related treaties and conventions expressly mentioned in that article have constitutional hierarchy.

§4. HISTORICAL BACKGROUND OF ANTITRUST LAW[13]

32. Congressional discussion for the passing of an antitrust law dates back to 1909, with a bill prohibiting trusts and concerted actions regarding cattle-raising activities. The bill was inspired by the Sherman Act, and cited specific US cases on related markets.

33. In 1913, as a consequence of a Congressional debate over the effects of a meat trust, members of the HR presented several antitrust bills, some directly referring to the meat problem and others of a more general scope. In order to review and improve them, the HR named a special commission, which ultimately presented three bills, one of which prohibited any contract or combination having the object of artificially altering the prices of items of mass consumption and essential goods and the second dealt with cattle-raising and agricultural markets. The first of such bills was approved by the HR, but not the Senate.

34. In 1918, on occasion of the discussion of an export tariff bill, several members of the HR once again proposed the appointment of a commission to (a) investigate the then existing trusts of, inter alia, flour, sugar, wine, oil and meat; and (b) draft one or more antitrust bills.

35. It is interesting to note that, even when the bills proposed by the referred to commission two years later were inspired in the Sherman Act, they also specifically intended to deal with several of the presumed anticompetitive conducts which the commission had been entrusted to investigate.

36. One of four such bills was formally presented before the HR, which approved it in July 1921. The bill was considered by the Senate in May 1922 and, with some amendments, reverted to the HR, which accepted only few of those amendments and passed a new bill in April 1923. In July of the same year, the Senate insisted on its original amendments by the vote of two-third of its members, but the HR, with a similar majority, insisted on its wording, and the law was finally passed with the number 11,210, named 'Law for the Repression of Speculation and Trusts'.[14]

---

12. Const. Arg., Art. 75 para. 22.
13. This section was based on the following sources: Hernan Abel Pesagno, Experiencia De La Ley Nº 11.210 (Ideas ed., 1944) and Enrique Gil, Represion De La Especulación y Trusts (Talleres Gráficos de la Penitenciaria Nacional ed., 1929).
14. Law No. 11,210, 28 Aug. 1923 [1920–1940], ADLA, 110.

General Introduction

37. Law 11,210 was a purely criminal law, exclusively enforced by the courts. Its two main provisions were the following:

> Section 1. Every agreement, pact, combination or concentration or merger of capitals leading to the establishment or aid of a monopoly and its profits in one or more branches of production, land, or water transport, or domestic or foreign commerce, in one or several cities or in the entire national territory, shall be a crime.
>
> Section 2. It shall be considered as an act of monopoly or leading to the same, to be sanctioned by the law, those acts that, without representing a technical or economic progress, arbitrarily increase the profits of those performing them, with no proportion to the capital effectively used, and those acts impairing or with the aim of impairing the conditions of free competition to other living or juridical persons as regards production and in domestic trade vis-à-vis foreign trade, and in particular:
>
> 2.a) the intentional destruction of products by any means and at any stage of its manufacturing or production, by producers, businessmen or traders, with the aim of provoking a price increase and without those actions being justified by governmental authorization.
>
> 2.b) the abandonment of plantations, the cease of production of industrial facilities, generating facilities, quarries, mines or any other productive establishment, when such abandonment is due to indemnifications paid to their owners.
>
> 2.c) agreements to allocate a city, region, province or any part of the territory as exclusive sale or purchase market for certain products and to the benefit of certain persons or companies, with the aim of suppressing competition and producing an increase or decrease in prices or imposing a fix price of purchase or sale.
>
> 2.d) hoarding, excluding from the market by any means, or agreeing not to sell, with the aim of provoking a price increase of essential goods destined to the food, clothing, housing and heating areas.
>
> 2.e) agreements or acts to limit production or manufacturing of one or more items with the purpose expressed in Section 1 hereof.
>
> 2.f) the wilful sale of goods or rendering of services on a regular basis below price, without those items being damaged or on sale, provided that such conduct have as its object the prevention of free competition.
>
> 2.g) agreements demanding a buyer not to purchase other sellers.
>
> 2.h) agreements imposing a reseller a certain resale price.
>
> 2.i) that a same person be director of different companies, or administrator or manager of one of them and director of other or others of the same market, when such relation may lead to a monopoly or to a restriction of competition.
>
> 2.j) any direct or indirect guaranty to be provided by industrialists to storekeepers for merchandise provided to workmen of the former.

38. As anticipated, the extensive description of specific prohibited conducts in section 2 was to a large part due to the results of the investigative commission. For example, section 2.a) intended to tackle situations like the wilful destruction of grapes in the province of Mendoza in order to sustain high wine prices; the prohibition to close a competing business in exchange for an indemnification was included to deal with cases such as those in the lime business in the province of Córdoba, etc. Other provisions, such as those of section 2.j), had minor contacts with antitrust law.[15]

39. The enforcement of law 11,210 proved to be a failure. In fact, in almost half of the period in which the law was in force, the courts debated which the correct scope of prohibited acts was. The issue in question was whether sections 1 and 2 of the law contemplated different conducts, in which case section 1 applied to concerted actions and section 2 to general acts of monopolization or attempts of monopolization or, on the contrary, whether the provisions of section 2, and in particular its first part (which required that acts be made with the intention to arbitrarily increase profits, and that those profits have no proportion with the investment effectively made) had also to be met in all cases to find an infringement.

40. The first of such interpretations, which better reflected the intention of the legislator, was consistently applied as from 1934. However, until the law was abrogated in 1946, only sixteen cases had been decided by the courts and, most importantly, only one conviction had been accomplished.

41. By 1946, under the first administration of President Juan Perón, discussions for the abrogation of Law 11,210 ensued. The congressional debate pointed to the main focus of the reform, consistent with the weaknesses of Law 11,210: a very brief statute of limitations (two years) that prevented most courts to pass timely judgments, the lack of interim measures and the fact that courts were sometimes ill-prepared to investigate economic crimes.

42. The new law, which was passed in September 1946 under the number 12,906 and named 'Law for the Repression of Monopolies and Trusts',[16] was structured under the following guidelines or purposes:

(i) to establish the true meaning of the crimes set forth in sections 1 and 2 of Law 11,210;
(ii) to distinguish local from interstate monopoly;
(iii) to improve the drafting of the former law;
(iv) to establish the jurisdiction of federal courts for federal crimes;

---

15. They were intended to prevent a rather common practice in industrial establishments located in isolated areas whereby employees were forced to accept part of their salaries in coupons that could be redeemed by merchandise in 'company stores' which, in their capacity of monopolists, charged higher prices.
16. Law No. 12,906, 22 Feb. 1947 [15704] BO.

General Introduction 43–48

(v) to empower a new administrative agency to control and investigate monopoly practices;
(vi) to apply sanctions consisting of fines as well as imprisonment terms; and
(vii) to extend the statute of limitations.

43. Section 2 of Law 12,906 still included a list of practices that were considered as 'acts of monopoly' or 'leading to a monopoly', which for the most part replicated those of section 2 of Law 11,210, with the notable exception of the inclusion of tying practices (section f) and, quite extraordinarily, business combinations (section m).[17]

44. However, the law created the National Office of Antitrust Investigations (*Oficina Nacional de Investigaciones Antimonopolistas*), which was granted several of the empowerments that would later be included in Law 22,262 (the 'Former Competition Act'),[18] with one important exception: the National Office of Antitrust Investigations did not apply administrative sanctions, but rather acted as a prosecutor of criminal actions before the courts.

45. Law 12,906 had a similar or poorer enforcement track record than its predecessor. Legal authors[19] are of the view that this was mainly due to a lack of: (a) conviction by the new agency of the illegality of the practices prohibited by the law; (b) proficiency of the judiciary in the investigation of economic crimes; and (c) an active role granted to the plaintiff in the administrative proceeding. In addition, and this has been a constant in the history of Argentinean antitrust law, the recurrent economic crises that have hit the country have led to the application of interventionist measures such as price controls, which obviously directly oppose the principles of competition.

46. In spite of the foregoing, Law 12,906 remained in force for thirty-four years, until it was abrogated by the Former Competition Act in 1980.

47. The Former Competition Act innovated in several areas. Mostly influenced by EC law, it divided prohibited practices into two groups: general anticompetitive acts and abuses of dominant position, this last prohibition replacing the earlier prohibition to 'acts of monopoly', sometimes loosely used by Laws 11,210 and 12,906.

48. Another administrative agency was created, named the National Commission for the Defence of Competition (*Comisión Nacional de Defensa de la Competencia* or 'CNDC'). The CNDC was entrusted with the carrying out of administrative proceedings which, unlike those of Law 12,906, were not only

---

17. Section (m) considered as illegal *the direct or indirect acquisition by a physical or juridical person of all or part of the shares or capital interests of another juridical person, when such acquisition has the object to form a monopoly, restrict or suppress competition or eliminate competitive prices for consumers or users.*
18. Law No. 22,262, 6 Aug. 1980 [24474] BO.
19. Guillermo Cabanellas De Las Cuevas (h), Derecho Antimonopólico y De Defensa De La Competencia, Tomo 1 (Heliasta ed., 2005) at 89 to 95.

directed to the filing of a criminal action but also to the application by a Secretary of State of separate administrative sanctions, including fines, cease-and-desist orders, requests to dissolve and liquidate investigated companies, etc.

49. All kinds of concerted actions were considered crimes and thus subject to potential criminal sanctions. As in the case of Law 12,906, once the administrative proceeding that declared the existence of a concerted action had been closed, the Secretary of State was empowered to file a criminal action before a criminal court.

50. Even when no criminal sanctions were applied under the Former Competition Act, numerous investigations were closed by the CNDC in the nineteen years of its enforcement.[20] Given that the Former Competition Act bears many similarities with the competition law in force and that the case law derived there from is still applied today, we will refer to the Former Competition Act in several sections in this report.

51. The 1990s brought about a radical change in the role of the State in the economy in Argentina, mostly as a consequence of the privatization process that encompassed many formerly State-owned companies.

52. Early in the decade, Congress showed concern on the impact of transferring to the private sector the substantial market position held by most of the privatized companies. Merger control (understood as a process whereby certain mergers were required to obtain administrative approval to be valid and not the general prohibition of certain mergers as anticompetitive acts, as was provided for in Law 12,906) was then deemed a necessity, and a new bill was approved by the HR in 1994.[21] However, it was not considered by the Senate and thus lost parliamentary status. Similar bills were introduced in the House in 1996 and 1998, without success.[22] New bills introduced in 1998[23] (the 'Antitrust Law Bills') were finally seriously considered the following year, a few months before the presidential elections.

53. From the review of the parliamentary debate of the Antitrust Law Bills, it stems that the main driving force underlying its approval by the HR and its swift consideration by the Senate was to control the sale of oil and gas company YPF – the then largest company in Argentina – by making the application of the law retroactive. As Repsol's tender offer for the shares of YPF was launched on the same day, the bill was considered by the Senate, its approval became a matter of national interest:

> We propose that the law enters into force as from January 1st; maybe someone else proposes another date. We have no doubt that these actions are directed to

---

20. Without considering the enforcement of the numerous pending cases as of the date of enactment of the Competition Law, which according to its provisions have to be decided in accordance with the Former Competition Law.
21. House of Representatives, Bill No. 0001-D-93.
22. House of Representatives, Bills No. 0630-D96, 1026-D.1996, 3645-D-96 and 0466-D-98.
23. House of Representatives, Bill No. 0311-D-98 and 0426-D-98.

General Introduction

avoid, precisely, the formation of the greatest monopoly in Argentine history, that is, the sale of YPF to Repsol. We have no doubts that there has not been in Argentine history a precedent of an economic concentration as serious as the one we are examining now. And what a coincidence! We are trying to pass this law – it almost seems a paradox – practically at the same time in which said monopolistic transaction is taking place.[24]

54. The second reason most cited by members of Congress in support of the new law was the need to create an independent antitrust agency, in view of what was perceived as an excessive dependence of the CNDC to the Federal Government.

55. There was also a clear intention to subject competition laws to the review of commercial courts rather than criminal ones – as was the case with the Former Competition Law – and prioritize the application of fines, for which purpose clearer guidelines were provided.

56. It is also worth mentioning that the original House bill intended to exclude the media from the application of competition laws insofar as freedom of speech could be compromised. This anomaly was corrected at the Senate.

57. The bill, as amended by the Senate, was returned to the HR, which accepted some of the amendments and insisted on the original wording of the bill by super majority vote. The bill was then sent to the consideration of the Executive Power, which partially vetoed the bill.

58. The Presidential veto[25] reached mainly two areas of the bill: merger control and judicial review.

59. As regards the former, section 8 originally included a market share threshold of 25% the relevant market for merger control purposes, which was seen as inconvenient due to the fact that such a determination was precisely the task of the authorities.

60. The Executive disagreed with the proposal to extend the application of civil procedural law principles in detriment of criminal law ones, which was seen as more adequate to the consideration of the subject-matter of the law. It thus vetoed section 24 item o), which allowed the parties to reach agreements with the authorities on the conducts being investigated, section 53, which appointed the civil and commercial courts of the city of Buenos Aires to hear on appeal decisions issued by the

---

24. Statements by Sen. Antonio Berhongaray, 29th meeting, 11th ordinary session (23 Jun. 1999), File CD 50/99 (available at www.senado.gov.ar). In May 2012, the Argentine Congress passed a law expropriating Repsol's shares in YPF.
25. Decree No. 1019, 16 Sep. 1999 [29233] BO, 7.

competition authorities, and section 56, which provided for the subsidiary application of the CPCCN in all matters not expressly contemplated in the Act.

61. Almost a year later, the HR approved the objections of the Executive[26] and forwarded the Act for the consideration of the Senate, which failed to consider it, thus confirming the vetoed language.

---

26. House of Representatives, 25th reunion – 15th ordinary session, 7 Sep. 2000.

Part I. Structure of Antitrust Law and Its Enforcement

Chapter 1. Sources of Antitrust Law

§1. NATIONAL SOURCES

62. Consumers' rights are specifically protected under section 42 of the 1994 Federal Constitution, which provides that public authorities:

> shall provide for the defence of competition against any kind of market distortions, the control of natural and legal monopolies, the control of quality and efficiency of public utilities and the creation of consumer and user associations.[27]

63. Competition law is embodied under Competition Act 25,156 (the 'Competition Act')[28] as regulated by Decree 89/2001[29] (the 'Regulation') and amended by Decree 396/01[30] (the 'Decree') and Law 26,993 of 2014 (the '2014 Amendment').[31]

64. The Competition Act was enacted on 25 August 1999, passed into law on 16 September 1999 and entered into force on 1 October 1999. It replaces the Former Competition Act.

65. The original wording of the Competition Act has sixty-one sections, divided into ten chapters, as follows:

– Chapter I: *Prohibited agreements and practices.* Sets forth the substantive test and includes a non-exhaustive list of anticompetitive practices.
– Chapter II: *Dominant position.*
– Chapter III: *Economic concentrations and mergers.* Includes a mandatory merger control regime.

---

27. Const. Arg., Art. 42.
28. Law No. 25,156, 20 Sep. 1999 [29233] BO, 5.
29. Decree No. 89, 30 Jan. 2001 [29577] BO, 1.
30. Decree No. 396, 5 Apr. 2001 [29623] BO, 2.
31. Law No. 29,993, 19 Sep. 2014 [32972] BO, 1.

- Chapter IV: *Authority*. Creates the National Tribunal for the Defence of Competition (the 'Tribunal') as the sole authority in charge of the application of a Competition Law, and describes its empowerments.
- Chapter V: *Budget*. Contemplates how the Tribunal will be financed.
- Chapter VI: *Proceeding*. Deals with the administrative proceeding for the investigation of anticompetitive practices.
- Chapter VII: *Sanctions*. Lists applicable sanctions and includes guidelines for the application of fines.
- Chapter VIII: *Appeals*. Indicates which decisions might be subject to appeal, provides for the term and procedure of the appeal and identifies the competent courts to hear on the case.
- Chapter IX: *Statute of limitations.* Indicates the applicable statute of limitations and how the term is interrupted.
- Chapter X: *Transitory and complementary provisions*. Includes some additional complementary provisions as well as explains how the transition between the Former Competition Act and the Competition Act should be implemented.

65.1. The main changes introduced by the 2014 Amendment are as follows:

Elimination of the Tribunal

Any reference to the Tribunal – originally created by the Competition Act as an independent competition agency but never established by the Executive – was deleted. The enforcement of the Competition Act was entrusted to an authority to be appointed by the Executive, and the CNDC relegated to an advisory role. The dual agency structure set forth by Former Competition Act whereby a Secretary of State (lately, the Secretariat of Trade, the 'Secretariat') acted as enforcement authority with the assistance of the CNDC, continued, albeit as anticipated concentrating most of the empowerments in a political rather than technical agency (the confirmation of the Secretariat as enforcement agency was implemented by Decree 718 issued on 27 May 2016). The elimination of the Tribunal is relevant on at least the following issues:

(a) The enforcement authority will continue under the scope of the Executive, thus altering the principles of agency autonomy and independence fostered by the original wording of the Competition Act.
(b) In principle, the Secretariat will be fully entitled to undertake most of the tasks originally entrusted to the Tribunal. This situation may grant legitimacy to certain decisions adopted in the past by the Secretariat, like e.g., injunctions issued during the course of investigations or merger reviews, which until the present date were generally revoked by the courts as they were considered reserved to the Tribunal.
(c) In addition, the 2014 Amendment (i) includes, within the enforcement authority's powers, the possibility of encouraging '*consensual solutions between the parties*', a possibility that was allegedly de facto available but had no statutory recognition; and (ii) eliminates the possibility for the enforcement authority to have its own budget and set fees for proceedings brought under its scope (such as in the case of merger filings).

Part I, Ch. 1, Sources of Antitrust Law   65.2–67

Creation of specialized courts and amendment of appeal process

The 2014 Amendment creates the National Court of Appeals in Consumer Protection Matters, with jurisdiction in the City of Buenos Aires, as appeal court on competition matters in replacement of the Federal Civil and Commercial Court of Appeals and the Federal Court of Appeals in Economic Crimes. According to the 2014 Amendment, this new Court of Appeals should become operational in a term of 180 days as from the publication of the Amendment, but such a Court of Appeals has not been formed as of the date of this report. Also, as regards the appeal process: (a) the term to file appeals to final decisions of the enforcement agency is reduced from fifteen to ten working days; and (b) appeals against the imposition of fines no longer will have suspensory effect, being compulsory to file evidence of the deposit of the payment of the fine jointly with the appeal brief under penalty of immediate dismissal, with exception of cases in which there is a risk of irreparable damage to the appellant.

Amendment of supplementary regulations

The supplementary application – for all matters not expressly contemplated in the Law – of the CPN and CPPN was replaced by that of the Administrative Procedures Law No. 19,549 and its regulations.

65.2. Even when the changes reproduced above clearly cannot be seen as an improvement of competition policy in Argentina, the new Administration that took office in December 2015 has publicly reported that it will introduce a new bill amending the Competition Act, in which case may of those changes will cease having effects.

§2. INTERNATIONAL SOURCES

66. With the signing of the Mercosur Competition Protocol in 1996 (the 'Protocol'), Argentina formally committed to adopting a policy in harmony with the competition policies of the Mercosur region. The Protocol created a supranational body, the Committee for the Defence of Competition (CDC), with enforcement powers in matters referred to it by the national competition agencies of the member countries.[32] In addition, as a result of meetings held in Buenos Aires during the first semester of 2002, the Technical Committee concluded the regulation of the Protocol, which was approved within Mercosur during the second half of 2002 (the 'Protocol Regulation').

67. The Protocol never entered into force, as it was only ratified by Brazil[33] and Paraguay.[34]

---

32. Org. Econ. Co-operation & Dev., *Competition Law and Policy in Argentina – A peer review – 2006*, 37 (available at www.cndc.gov.ar/peer/peer_review_eng.pdf).
33. Legislative Decree No. 6 (15 Feb. 2000).
34. Law No. 4956 (25 Jun. 2013).

68. Due to lack of progress in the implementation of the Protocol, on 16 October 2003, Argentine and Brazilian then Presidents, Néstor Kirchner and Luiz Inácio Lula da Silva, signed a cooperation agreement upon the Brazilian President's visit to Buenos Aires (the 'Bilateral Agreement'). The purpose of the Bilateral Agreement was, inter alia, to: (i) agree on the notification of conducts being investigated and mergers being filed with the competition agency of one of the countries to the agencies of the other country, if the relevant conduct or merger is relevant to or may have contacts with the latter country; (ii) exchange information on competition matters and policies; and (iii) promote technical cooperation. The Bilateral Agreement was ultimately approved in 2008[35] and 2010[36] in Brazil and Argentina, respectively, and thus is in force. The CNDC reported that the first case of cooperation under the Bilateral Agreement took place on 16 June 2011.

69. At a regional level and while the scope of the Protocol was being redefined, the Mercosur Member States entered into two Understandings, which cover similar issues to the Bilateral Agreement, to wit:

(i) the Understanding on Cooperation between Competition Defence Authorities of Member States of the Mercosur for the Enforcement of National Competition Laws, adopted by Decision 4 of the Common Market of the Mercosur Council on 7 July 2004 and incorporated into Argentine law by Resolution 100/2004 of the Secretariat of Technical Coordination on 18 August 2004; and
(ii) the Understanding on Cooperation between Competition Defence Authorities of Member States of the Mercosur for the Control of Economic Concentrations at a Regional Level, adopted by Decision 15 of the Common Market of the Mercosur Council on 20 July 2006. This Understanding has still not been incorporated into Argentine law.

70. Ultimately, the Protocol was abrogated in 2010 by the Mercosur Competition Agreement (the 'MCA').[37] The MCA, which has still to be ratified by all Member States, is much more modest in its objectives, which are the following:

(i) promote cooperation and coordination among Member States in the application of national competition laws within Mercosur;
(ii) provide mutual assistance in competition policy issues; and
(iii) as regards the application by Member States of their own competition laws, assure a careful examination by them of their relevant reciprocal interests.

71. The above goals are to be achieved through the following actions:

– A consultation process, whereby a national authority of a Member State may communicate with that of another regarding acts impacting on competition or

---

35. Legislative Decree No. 264 (18 Sep. 2008).
36. Law No. 26,622 (7 Sep. 2010 [31981] BO).
37. While Directive 15/11 of the Mercosur Commerce Commission (Mercosur/CCM/Dir. No. 15/11, 19 Jun. 2011) abrogated the Protocol Regulation.

Part I, Ch. 1, Sources of Antitrust Law

economic concentrations occurring in the latter Member State's jurisdiction that may also affect the consulting party's jurisdiction. The opinions in this regard expressed by the consulting party must be carefully examined by the other party, but are not binding on it.
– Coordination among national competition authorities, taking into consideration their prospective results, the possibility of accessing to additional information, reduction of enforcement costs and timing issues.
– Technical cooperation and information exchange, in the form of training, exchange of staff, academic activities, counselling, etc.
– Notification of enforcement actions taken by a national competition authority that may be relevant or affect any other Member State.

72. Technical Committee No. 5 of the Mercosur Commerce Commission is the body in charge of implementing joint actions on the area of competition law. For example, its working agenda for 2010 included items such as the review of the Protocol, resumption of negotiations with the European Union with the aim of reaching a biregional agreement, provision of technical assistance to Paraguay in the approval of its antitrust law, strengthening of the relationship with organizations like the Organisation of Economic Co-operation & Development (OECD) and United Nations Conference on Trade and Development (UNCTAD), identification of business sectors which could present common competition issues at a regional level, implementation of leniency programmes for the fight of cartels, implementation of the Understandings referred to above, training of public officials, competition advocacy and furtherance of cooperation activities.

72.1. On 15 September 2014 the CNDC entered into a Cooperation Agreement with Spain's *Comisión Nacional de los Mercados y la Competencia*. The Agreement mostly covers technical cooperation and training issues.

72.2. Also, in 2015 the CNDC participated in the third regional COMPAL programme along with Bolivia, Chile, Colombia, Costa Rica, República Dominicana, Ecuador, El Salvador, Guatemala, Honduras, México, Nicaragua, Paraguay, Perú, and Uruguay. This programme, implemented by the UNCTAD, has established as its targets the: (i) strengthening of regional cooperation, (ii) support to the activities that competition and consumer authorities deploy in the private sector and the creation of mechanisms for the private sector to voluntarily comply with competition policy and consumer protection rules.

§3. SECONDARY SOURCES

I. Regulations and Guidelines

73. The Competition Act is regulated by the Regulation, which complements slightly more than half (32) of its sections, in basically three main areas: merger control, procedure and appeals.

74. Section 99, item 2 of the Federal Constitution[38] provides that the powers of the President of Argentina to issue instructions and rules necessary for the enforcement of the laws of the Nation (i.e., through decrees) must be exercised '*without altering their spirit with regulatory exceptions*'. When regulatory decrees exceed the scope of the law, they may be deemed unconstitutional.

75. These concerns have been raised in connection with the aforementioned last two areas regulated by the Regulation. Chapter VI of the Regulation empowers an agency not created by the Competition Law, the Secretariat of Defence of Competition and the Consumer (as of the date of this report, the Secretariat of Trade, the 'Secretariat') with a prosecutorial role that was not contemplated in the Competition Act. In addition, as will be seen below, the selection of the Federal Civil and Commercial Courts as those having jurisdiction to hear on appeal on competition cases in the City of Buenos Aires has, in some cases, been declared unconstitutional.

75.1. As from the passing of the 2014 Amendment, several sections of the Regulation – e.g., those regulating the empowerments of the Tribunal – no longer apply. Given that the new Administration that took office in December 2015 has publicly reported that it will introduce a new bill amending the Competition Act, it is expected that when that occurs the Regulation will be replaced by a new one that is consistent with the newly passed law.

76. The Decree, still in force, amended the Competition Act by virtue of the provisions of Law 25,414 of 29 March 2001,[39] which granted the Executive Power extraordinary legislative empowerments up to 1 March 2002. In particular, Article 1, section II e) empowered the President to abrogate or amend federal laws only in case they impaired the competitiveness of the national economy, while Article 1, section I f) of the same law empowered the President to amend statutes affecting the operation of public agencies.

77. Under that scenario, the Decree amended the Competition Act by eliminating the ARS 2.5 billion worldwide threshold for mandatory merger notifications, included a *de minimis* exemption to notifications and, generally, streamlined the merger control procedure.

78. Resolution 40/2001 of the former Secretariat for the Defence of Competition and the Consumer (Resolution 40)[40] describes the procedure for the notification of economic concentrations, basically including:

(i) basic definitions necessary to understand the scope of the standard template notification forms included therein;
(ii) the first and second stage notification forms, named forms 1 and 2; and

---

38. Const. Arg., Art. 99.
39. Law No. 25,414, 30 Mar. 2001 [29620] BO, 1.
40. Secretaría de Defensa de la Competencia y del Consumidor, Resolution No. 40 (26 Feb. 2001).

Part I, Ch. 1, Sources of Antitrust Law

(iii) a 'fast-track' procedure for the analysis of economic concentrations which, as will be seen below, is rarely followed by the CNDC.

79. Resolution 164/2001 on the Guidelines for the Control of Economic Concentrations and the Economic Concentrations Notification Rules (the 'Guidelines')[41] issued by the former Secretariat for Competition, Deregulation and Consumer Defense adopted a series of non-binding guidelines to be followed by the CNDC in the analysis of economic concentrations to be notified pursuant to the Act.

80. Finally, Resolution 26/06 of the former Secretariat of Technical Coordination[42] amended the procedure applicable for the issuance of Advisory Opinions,[43] by:

(i) making them binding;
(ii) providing that the Secretariat of Technical Coordination (currently, the Secretariat) will adjudicate decisions in such an area, being the role of the CNDC limited to issuing non-binding opinions to the Secretariat; and
(iii) providing for the possibility to appeal such decisions.

§4. Sources' Relation and Hierarchy

81. The Federal Constitution tops the hierarchy, followed by the Competition Act, Resolution and Decree, resolutions of the Secretariat and those of the CNDC. As will be explained in further detail below, as a matter of procedure the CNDC carries out investigative tasks, issuing non-binding recommendations to the Secretariat, which is the adjudicatory authority.

82. Neither the CNDC nor the Secretariat is bound by their past decisions, although they tend to follow them in case the circumstances of a particular case are substantially similar.

---

41. Secretaría de Defensa de la Competencia y del Consumidor, Resolution No. 164 (30 Nov. 2001) [29786] BO.
42. Secretaría de Coordinación Técnica, Resolution No. 26 (24 Jul. 2006).
43. An Advisory Opinion is an opinion issued by the Secretariat – after receiving the recommendation of the CNDC – on whether a certain concentration presented by the parties before the agencies requires a mandatory notification or not. The request for an Advisory Opinion suspends the notification deadline. Resolution No. 26/2006 provides for a 'fast-track' procedure, whereby: (i) the CNDC must make any follow-up questions within five days after receipt of the original request; (ii) the parties must answer such questions within five days; (iii) the CNDC must then issue its recommendation to the Secretariat within ten days from the original request; and (iv) the Secretariat must decide within five days of the recommendation of the CNDC. Those terms are in practice not strictly followed by the authorities, as repeated information requests are generally made by the CNDC, thus extending the overall review period.

§5. Role and Authority of Precedents

83. Precedents are only one of the sources of law in Argentina. As a principle, Argentine courts are not legally obliged to follow them in their judgments, but they do so because of the persuasive force stemming from the resolutions adopted therein.

84. This rule is particularly observed with Supreme Court case law, by virtue of its role of last interpreter of the law attributed by the Constitution. In such a role, the Supreme Court has repeatedly ruled that lower courts and administrative authorities have a moral and even institutional duty of harmonizing their decisions with the ones passed by the former in similar cases.[44]

85. Precedents are legally binding only when all Chambers of certain Appeal Courts agree (unanimously or by majority) on the solution to be provided to a certain matter. In that case, the legal interpretation established by means of the plenary decision is compulsory for the former and even for the lower courts of that same jurisdiction. Hence, judges of both instances are obliged to adapt their decisions to said legal doctrine without prejudice of expressing their personal opinion on the case at dispute. Plenary precedents remain binding until they are replaced by a new plenary decision on the same subject.

86. Due to the unlimited scope of judicial review of decisions of the CNDC and Secretariat, the same principles apply to them. In practice, however, given the greater technical expertise of the agencies on competition law matters, most judicial precedents affecting them relate to procedural issues.

---

44. 'Rodríguez Blanco de Serrao, I.C.', 304 Fallos 898 (1982).

Chapter 2. Scope of Application

§1. TERRITORIAL REACH

87. Section 3 of the Competition Act provides that the law applies to all individuals or entities, public or private, for profit or not-for-profit, carrying out economic activities in all or part of Argentina, ' ... as well as those carrying out economic activities outside the country, insofar as their acts, activities or agreements may produce effects in the national market'.

88. The effects test put forward in section 3 has mostly been cited to develop a certain administrative case law for application to merger transactions when the target company does not have a physical presence in Argentina. In a series of Advisory Opinions,[45] the CNDC stated that such mergers only have effects if target's Argentinean sales were 'substantial' and 'made on a regular basis' in the three years preceding the merger being reported. As to the meaning of the term 'substantial', the CNDC has generally been of the view that sales below 5%–15% of the relevant market/total imports of the relevant products should not meet this test and thus should not require notification, although those percentages were set aside by more recent Advisory Opinions, which now require a case-by-case analysis in all cases.[46] As will be seen below, this test appears to still be used in spite of the *de minimis* exemption introduced by the Decree.

89. Very occasionally, the effects test has been raised by the CNDC to justify an enforcement action in conducts taking place outside Argentina. An example of this has been portrayed in the probe against a number of companies of the Monsanto Group.[47]

90. The case involved the filing of lawsuits by certain Monsanto companies in some EU jurisdictions, aimed at obtaining samples of different soy and soy by-products shipments from Argentina in order to determine whether the crop effectively contained a certain gene which was subject to Monsanto patent rights in foreign jurisdictions, but not Argentina, where Monsanto lacked such rights.

---

45. 'Productos Roche S.A.Q. e I.', Comisión Nacional de Defensa de la Competencia, Advisory Opinion No. 44 (23 May 2000), 'Thomson CSF', Comisión Nacional de Defensa de la Competencia, Advisory Opinion No. 52 (10 Jul. 2000), 'International Paper Company', Comisión Nacional de Defensa de la Competencia, Advisory Opinion No. 65 (25 Sep. 2000), 'Alcan Aluminium Limited', Comisión Nacional de Defensa de la Competencia, Advisory Opinion No. 68 (6 Oct. 2000), 'Tyson Foods Inc. e IBP Inc.', Comisión Nacional de Defensa de la Competencia, Advisory Opinion No. 99*bis* (27 Feb. 2001) and 'Suzano Petroquímica S.A.', Comisión Nacional de Defensa de la Competencia, Advisory Opinion No. 211 (28 Sep. 2005), among others.
46. 'Siderar S.A.I.C., Prosid Investments S.C.A., Ternium Investments S.A.R.L., Confab Industrial S.A. y Otros s/ Consulta Interpretación Ley N° 25.156 (OPI N° 215)', Secretaría de Comercio Interior, Resolution No. 59 (26 Jun. 2012).
47. 'Secretaría de Agricultura, Ganadería, Pesca y Alimentos' (complaint against Monsanto Company and Monsanto Argentina S.A.), Comisión Nacional de Defensa de la Competencia, File S01:0047160/2006 (30 Oct. 2006).

91. As per the request of the Secretary of Agriculture, Cattle-Raising, Fishing and Food, the CNDC opened an investigation, as it deemed Monsanto's judicial claims to be potential anticompetitive practices consisting of the abusive and illegitimate exercise of legal procedures aimed at affecting competition (a type of sham petitioning).

92. Although the scrutinized practices were carried out by Monsanto outside Argentina, the CNDC considered itself as having jurisdiction over the matter due to the impact the conduct might have had on the local market pursuant to section 3 of the Competition Law.

93. It is worth noting that the decision to open the investigation was successfully appealed by Monsanto.[48] The Court of Appeals dissented with the CNDC on a number of grounds, including with the fact that the conducts carried out by Monsanto outside Argentina could reasonably be argued as having effects in our country.

§2. Special Sectors

94. Foreign investors are generally subject to the same regulations as local investors regarding the purchase of companies and going concerns, in the sense that they are not required to obtain specific governmental approval or register their capital. However, there may be some restrictive or sensitive areas where national security or public interest issues are involved.

95. For example, Law 25,750[49] limits an investor's participation in media companies that are currently under Argentine ownership to 30% of the economic and political rights of the local company. This limit may be increased in case of countries which have reciprocity rules towards Argentina. In the same direction, Law No. 26,737 and Decree No. 274/2012[50] provide for certain restrictions in the foreign ownership of rural land.

96. In addition, economic concentrations of firms acting in regulated markets such as banking, insurance, energy and telecommunications require (to both foreign and local investors alike) the approval of the corresponding regulatory agencies in addition to that of the Secretariat. Section 16 of the Competition Act expressly contemplates the obligation of the CNDC to require the regulator to give its opinion on the impact of the merger in the relevant market and its compliance with the regulatory framework within three days of the initial filing. This notification does not suspend the review period. The regulator must answer within fifteen days. As is

---

48. 'Monsanto Company s /Apel. Resol. Comisión Nac. De Defensa de la Competencia' and 'Monsanto Argentina SAIC s/ Apel. Resol. Comisión Nacional de Defensa de la Competencia', CNCiv. Com. Fed., Sala III [2009-C] LL 61 (2008).
49. Law No. 25,750, 7 Jul. 2003 [30186] BO, 1.
50. Law No. 26,737, 28 Dec. 2011 [32305] BO, 13. Decree No. 274/2012, 29 Feb. 2012 [32347]BO, 1.

Part I, Ch. 2, Scope of Application

usual with competition law practice in Argentina, this procedure is rarely followed by the authorities as contemplated in the law, the CNDC or Secretariat usually suspending the review term until the regulator issues its opinion.[51]

97. The Competition Act abrogated all competition empowerments that any earlier legislation – mainly in regulated sectors – granted to regulatory agencies (section 59), which means that no such regulators can investigate and sanction anticompetitive conducts[52] and review mergers. Of course, this provision does not prohibit regulatory frameworks to be designed with competition concerns in mind, as limitations such as those preventing vertical integration of companies involved in different segments of the industry existing in the electricity and gas regulations.[53]

98. From a practical perspective, and even though the Competition Act does not provide for the protection of non-competition issues like investment or labour, certain areas, in particular in regulated markets, may in practice be subject to a more stringent analysis which may unveil some of those concerns, evidencing the need to harmonize the potentially diverging goals of the Competition Act and other regulations.

§3. STATE-OWNED ENTERPRISES AND PUBLIC UTILITIES

99. There is no exemption from the Competition Act to State-owned enterprises insofar as they act in commerce (section 3). Public utilities, if natural monopolies, are generally subject to specific regulation, their capability of affecting price and quantity being then totally eliminated or greatly reduced. This has been the case in Argentina with most formerly State-owned enterprises that were privatized in the 1990s (i.e., natural gas, electricity, water and sewage and telecommunications), their regulatory frameworks establishing a maximum price or 'price cap' system whereby the regulator set forth maximum prices for a specific period, adjustable as per the increase in the retail price index. Maximum prices were set assuming an average efficiency standard and taking into account that the utility had to cover the costs of supply of the services and amortizations and obtain a reasonable profit. More efficient utilities obtained a higher profit. At the end of each period, the regulator had to review the maximum price, so as to transfer the operating efficiencies to the consumer.

---

51. This interpretation has been deemed illegal by the courts. *See*, e.g., 'AEI Utilities SL y otros s/ apel. resol. Comisión Nacional de Defensa de la Competencia', CNCiv. Com. Fed., Sala I (20 Oct. 2011).
52. For example, ss 19 and 74 of Law No. 24,065, the Electricity Act of 1991 (16 Jan. 1992 [27306] BO, 30), respectively: (i) prohibited 'unfair trade' acts (possibly meaning acts in restraint of competition) and abuses of dominant position, and provided that affected parties could resort directly to the courts under the Former Competition Act, without the need of the administrative procedure before the competition authorities to be first followed; and (ii) granted the electricity regulator authority to decide on anticompetitive conducts.
53. *Ibid.*, at Ch. VII and Ch. VIII of the Natural Gas Act of 1992 (12 Jun. 1992 [27407] BO, 30).

§4. SENSIBLE EFFECT AND *DE MINIMIS*

100. As will be seen below, the substantive test of the Competition Act, as applied by the CNDC, requires a sensible effect on the market, in the way of increased prices or reduced output by means of the exercise of market power.

101. In the area of merger control, such an effect is reached by the application of only local turnover thresholds and certain exemptions to notifications, most notably the 'first landing exemption' (acquisition of a single Argentinean company by a single foreign company which previously did not have assets in Argentina) and a *de minimis* exception (based on the value of the target's assets located in Argentina and the price paid for them). Transactions having little or no effects on competition are generally reported only through the filing of a Form 1. Resolution 40, as anticipated, contemplated a fast-track procedure to expedite the review period from the standard forty-five business days provided for in the Competition Act to 15, 35 or 45 business days, depending on the complexity of the transaction. In practice, however, none of the reduced periods is followed by the CNDC, thus becoming customary that reviewing periods of even simple transactions may take well over two years.

102. In the area of antitrust investigations – particularly those initiated as a consequence of a third-party complaint – a claim having prima facie little or no effects on competition generally represents no obstacle for the CNDC to pursue proceedings, although very rarely concludes with a sanction being applied.

Chapter 3. Overview of Substantive Provisions

§1. RESTRICTIVE AGREEMENTS

103. There is no express prohibition for restrictive *agreements* under the Competition Act, in spite of the name of Chapter I thereof (Prohibited Agreements and Practices). Section 1 broadly forbids ' ... acts or conducts, however carried out, related with the production and exchange of goods and services, with the object or effect of limiting, restricting, falsifying or distorting competition or access to the market ... provided that injury to the general economic interest may result as a consequence thereof'.

104. Section 2, which includes a non-exhaustive list of prohibited practices, indirectly refers to restrictive agreements in several of its paragraphs, such as: price-fixing (item a), market-division (item b), bid rigging (item c), restriction of innovation or investments (item d) and group boycott (item e).

105. In addition, sections 300, item 1 and 309 item 1 (a) of the CPN[54] sanction with imprisonment from, respectively, six months to two years and one year to four years, price-fixing agreements involving, respectively, goods and securities. As will be seen below, those provisions have almost never been enforced in Argentina.

§2. DOMINANT UNDERTAKINGS

106. As was the case with anticompetitive acts, section 1 of the Competition Act prohibits:

> acts or conducts, however carried out, related with the production and exchange of goods and services, ... resulting in abuses of dominant position, provided that injury to the general economic interest may result as a consequence thereof.

107. Section 4 of the Competition Act defines one or more persons as having 'dominant position' when:

> for a certain type of product or service is the only offeror or consumer within the national market or within one or several parts of the world or, even when is not the sole offeror or consumer, is not exposed to substantial competition, or when due to the degree of vertical or horizontal integration, such party can determine the economic viability of a competitor, to its detriment.

108. In addition, section 5 of the Competition Act provides that the following facts must be considered to conclude that a dominant position exists:

---

54. Código Penal de la Nación [Criminal Code, CPN], Law No. 11,179, 3 Nov. 1921 [8300] BO (text consolidated in 1984, *as amended*).

(i) The degree of substitution of the relevant good or service, the conditions of such substitution and time required to perform it.
(ii) The existence of legal barriers of entry.
(iii) The existence of market power on the side of the offeror and the consumer.

109. The amendments to the original definition of the term 'dominant position' included in the Former Competition Act[55] introduced by section 4 of the Competition Act cannot be seen as improvements, given that both the reference that a person may be dominant in Argentina if it is so in other countries, as well as focusing on the status of a competitor rather than competition, seem incorrect from a legal and economic perspective.

110. In the 1983 *Industrias Welbers* case[56] the National Court of Appeals in Economic Crimes defined dominance, following the 1978 European Court of Justice (ECJ) opinion in *United Brands*,[57] as:

> the situation enabling a company to behave independently, act without regards to its competitors, buyers or suppliers due to its market position, possession of technical know-how, raw materials or capital, which allows it to impose prices or control a significant part of the production or distribution of the relevant products.

111. The above definition indicates that a finding of dominance is made on a case-by-case basis, and that market shares may or may not be the deciding factor.

112. For example, in the *Ifrisa* case[58] YPF, an oil and gas company, was deemed dominant in the retail gas market due to a market share of 65%. However, in the 1999 *YPF* case[59] the company was considered dominant in the bulk liquefied petroleum gas (LPG) market with a participation of only 55%, although complemented with a number of additional factors like participation in the upstream market, its storing capacity, vertical integration, etc. As anticipated in an economic report published by the CNDC in 1997[60] (hereinafter, the '1997 Report'):

> Many times the term dominant position is assimilated to high market shares of a company or group of companies in a market. This relation, however, is valid

---

55. Which stated in its s. 2 that 'a) A person has dominant position in a market when, for a certain product or service, is the only offeror or consumer within a national market or, when not the only one, is not exposed to substantial competition. b) Two or more persons have dominant position in a market when for a certain product or service there is no substantial competition between them, or substantial competition vis-a-vis third parties, in all the national market or a part thereof'.
56. 'S.A. Industrias Welbers Ltda.', CNPenal Económico, Sala II [v.107] ED, 459 (1983).
57. *United Brands v. Commission of the European Communities*, ECJ [1978] ECR 207.
58. 'Ifrisa S.R.L.' (complaint against YPF S.A. and Ecsal S.A.), Secretaría de Comercio, Resolution No. 106 (12 Apr. 1982).
59. 'YPF S.A.', Secretaría de Industria, Comercio y Minería, Resolution No. 189 (22 Mar. 1999).
60. *Breve análisis económico de la ley argentina de defensa de la competencia* [Brief Economic Analysis of the Argentine Antitrust Act] (1997), www.mecon.gov.ar/cndc/memorias/memoria97/docu1.htm.

Part I, Ch. 3, Overview of Substantive Provisions

only in those cases where such participation allows the occurrence of a specific conduct, whereby the company or group of companies having the same may – through it – influence the decisions of its competitors. This situation can occur in cases where a market share is relatively independent from pricing policies and related instead to the exclusive possession of certain resources (i.e. oil & gas reservoirs, transport or communications networks, installed production or storage capacity, etc.). These obstacles then act as barriers of entry to other competitors and obstacles for the expansion of the sales of existing competitors, and consequently are the true originators of the existence of a dominant position, rather than market shares themselves.

113. By the same token, a relatively high market share alone does not grant a finding of dominance if it does not affect the ability of competitors to offer substantial competition, as both the *Sociedad Argentina de Distribuidores Independientes de Tabaco*[61] and *Cámara Argentina de Distribuidores y Autoservicios Mayoristas*[62] cases illustrate.

114. As regards the requirement of independent behaviour leading to a finding of dominance, the *Industrias Welbers*[63] court was of the view that said conduct in itself was important, and did not require that the relevant company also had an absolute dominion of the market.

§3. CONCENTRATIONS

115. Section 6 of the Competition Act provides that:

[A]n economic concentration is understood as the acquisition of control over one or more enterprises through any of the following acts:

(a) mergers;
(b) transfers of going concerns;
(c) the acquisition of ownership or any right over shares or capital participations or debt instruments of any type granting rights to be converted into shares or capital participations or to have any type of influence over the decisions of the issuer, when such acquisition grants the acquirer control or substantial influence over the same;
(d) any other act or agreement transferring de facto or de jure to a person or economic group the assets of a company or granting them a determining

---

61. 'Sociedad Argentina de Distribuidores Independientes de Tabaco' (complaint against Massalin Particulares S.A.), Secretaría de Defensa de la Competencia y del Consumidor, Resolution No. 281 (4 Dec. 2000).
62. 'Cámara Argentina de Distribuidores y Autoservicios Mayoristas' (complaint against Luncheon Tickets S.A.), Secretaría de la Competencia, la Desregulación y la Defensa del Consumidor, Resolution No. 14 (31 Jan. 2003).
63. 'S.A. Industrias Welbers Ltda.', *supra* n. 56.

influence in the passing of decisions of the ordinary or extraordinary administration of a company.

116. 'Control' can be characterized as the right to conduct an undertaking's business strategy by any means (corporate, contractual or otherwise), and thus is generally achieved through the acquisition of equity participations in an undertaking granting a majority vote in board and partners or shareholders meetings, or by the acquisition of the undertaking's assets, as in a transfer of going concern. Acquisition of minority participations may also grant de facto control if the remaining holdings are dispersed.

117. The definition of 'substantial influence', however, has been assimilated by the CNDC to that of 'decisive influence' of European Union legislation,[64] and thus refers to the situation which allows an undertaking to influence or alter an undertaking's business or competitive strategy, in particular in the context of minority participations granting veto rights (where it is also named 'negative control'):[65]

> The analysis regarding whether an acquisition entails an acquisition of control or substantial influence over a target enterprise requires the consideration of several factual and legal circumstances.
> […]
> [I]nsofar as the voting rights granted do not refer to the commercial policy and its direct consequence, that is, the competitive strategy, such rights are not consider suitable to grant its holder the control over an enterprise.
> […]
> [C]omparative case law and, in particular, European case law, … understands that veto rights granting control refer to strategic decisions of the commercial policy of an enterprise, that is, decisions and issues such as the budget, the list of activities, business plan or appointment of key executives. On the contrary, veto rights generally granted to minority shareholders for the purpose of protecting their financial interests as investors do not give rise to control.

118. The term 'determining influence' has also been interpreted by the CNDC as bearing a similar meaning to that of 'substantial influence',[66] although it is worth noting that, in spite of the statutory language, one of the situations contemplated in section 6 d) of the Competition Act (influence over acts of the 'extraordinary administration' of an undertaking) contradicts with the definition of 'substantial influence' accepted by the CNDC which, as seen above, sets aside the acquisition of rights by

---

64. 'Ente Provincial Regulador Eléctrico de Mendoza s/ consulta interpretación Ley 25.156', Comisión Nacional de Defensa de la Competencia, Advisory Opinion No. 124 (6 Jul. 2001), paras 32–42.
65. Ente Provincial Regulador Eléctrico de Mendoza s/ consulta interpretación Ley 25.156', *supra* n. 64, Comisión Nacional de Defensa de la Competencia, Advisory Opinion No. 9 (date unavailable) and 'Oleoducto Trasandino Argentino S.A. (Opi 77) s/ consulta interpretación Ley 25.156', Comisión Nacional de Defensa de la Competencia, Advisory Opinion No. 180 (31 Oct. 2003), among others.
66. 'Telefónica de España, Olimpia y Otros s/ diligencia preliminar Art. 8 de la Ley 25.156', Comisión Nacional de Defensa de la Competencia, Resolution No. 4 (9 Jan. 2009), 51.

Part I, Ch. 3, Overview of Substantive Provisions 119–120

minority shareholders for the purpose of protecting their financial interests – such as mergers, dissolutions, etc. – which are precisely matters dealt with in extraordinary shareholder meetings under Argentine corporate law.

119. It is important to point out, however, that in spite of references to EU legislation,[67] section 6 c) of the Competition Act refers to 'substantial' and not 'decisive' influence, the former term suggesting a lower threshold than the latter[68] and possibly providing more flexibility on the side of the agency when confronted to a particular case.

120. The foregoing has been made very clear in *Telefónica de España, Olimpia y otros*.[69] The case involved the acquisition of control over Telecom Italia (and indirectly over Telecom Argentina, 50% owned by it) by a joint venture, in which Telefónica – which local subsidiary was Telecom Argentina's main competitor – was the main shareholder. The CNDC concluded that certain provisions contained in the governing documents of the joint venture granted Telefónica substantial influence over Telecom Argentina, to wit:

(i) The fact that Telefónica was the only shareholder who had paid a premium for its shares.[70]
(ii) The provision reserving to Telefónica the role of sole telecommunications operator in the joint venture.[71]
(iii) Certain references in the joint ventures documents that: (a) the Telefónica and Telecom Italia groups would be managed independently, 'with the exception of the rights and obligations of the parties stemming from the agreements';[72] (b) Telefónica would voluntarily abstain from voting in Telecom Italia if such decisions relate with jurisdictions in which regulations would prevent such voting right of Telefónica;[73] and (c) the investment in Telecom Italia had been made with a 'strategic purpose', and consequently the parties would favour any strategic initiative carried out by the managements of Telefónica and Telecom Italia.[74]
(iv) Certain rights granted to Telefónica in case of blockage.[75]

---

67. 'Ente Provincial Regulador Eléctrico de Mendoza s/ consulta interpretación Ley 25.156', n. 63 and 'Oleoducto Trasandino Argentino S.A. (Opi 77) s/ consulta interpretación Ley 25.156', Comisión Nacional de Defensa de la Competencia, Advisory Opinion No. 180 (31 Oct. 2003), among others.
68. Although it could be argued that, given that s. 6 (d) of the Competition Act refers to 'determining' influence, apparently similar in meaning as the term 'decisive', it would be illogical for the Competition Act to include two different standards and thus the one posing the higher evidentiary standard should be applied.
69. *Supra* n. 66.
70. *Ibid.*, at 59.
71. *Ibid.*, at 59–61.
72. *Ibid.*, at 55, 69–88.
73. *Ibid.*, at 55, 69–88.
74. *Ibid.*, at 69–82.
75. *Ibid.*, at 93–96.

121. Generally speaking, it could be argued that the authorities will be prepared to expand the meaning of the term 'substantial influence' when the transaction, if confirmed as an economic concentration, would raise competition concerns. Of particular interest is the case of an acquisition of a minority interest in a competitor, leading to potential transfers of confidential information. As the *Telefónica de España* case illustrates:

> Effects on competition can also be produced if the rights of acquirer over a corporate structure allows it to decide on its *own* behaviour (even when it *does not* decide on the conduct of the target person), on the basis of information acquired through the exercise of those rights.
> From an antitrust standpoint, said act would achieve the structural effect on competition characterizing economic concentrations.[76]
> […]
> [T]his Antitrust Commission considers, in the context of the transaction under review, that there are sufficient elements to classify this transaction under the merger control provisions of Law 25,156, such as … *the possibility of the same* [Telefónica] *accessing non-public information* from its main competitor in Argentina, Telecom Argentina, related with its commercial, technological and business strategy.[77] (emphasis added)

122. As seen above, in *Telefónica de España*, the CNDC considered several issues in addition to the possibility of exchanging confidential information in order to conclude on the existence of substantial influence by Telefónica. It remains to be seen how it would examine a minority acquisition in a competitor without the 'aggravating circumstances' considered in that case. In the author's opinion, such situation should not be covered by the merger regulations but rather as a potential anticompetitive conduct, that is, requiring proof of the information exchange and its effects on the relevant market.

123. An economic concentration is found not only in cases where a change is produced in the party exercising exclusive or joint control, but also in changes from sole to joint control and vice versa. However, a transaction whereby neither party acting individually nor any two or more parties acting jointly – pursuant to a shareholders or voting agreement – exercise such control, will normally not be considered as subject to notification.[78]

124. As regards the definition of the term 'assets' referred to in item d) of section 6 of the Competition Act, the CNDC has long been of the view that only assets from which an independent turnover can be derived from, associated with a distinct clientele, are included. The list of such assets has been expanded over the years to

---

76. *Supra* n. 66, at 46.
77. *Ibid.*, at 144.
78. 'Ibero-American Media Partners II Ltd. y El Sitio Inc. s/ notificación Art- 8 Ley 25.156', Comisión Nacional de Defensa de la Competencia, Resolution dated 28 Dec. 2001.

include, inter alia, certain manufacturing supply agreements,[79] trademarks,[80] oil exploration licenses,[81] purchase orders,[82] programming agreements[83] and Transitory Union of Enterprises (*Unión Transitoria de Empresas* or UTEs).[84]

§4. OTHER PROHIBITIONS

125. There are no prohibitions other than those mentioned above.

§5. TESTS OF ILLEGALITY

I. Per Se Prohibitions and Naked Restraints

126. There are no 'per se' prohibitions under the Competition Act. In spite of the reference to acts with anticompetitive 'object', in all cases the law requires that an injury to the 'general economic interest' may occur. The potentiality to affect the general economic interest should be interpreted as requiring the relevant party/ies to have considerable market power, because absent the same consumer welfare could not be affected. In turn, in most cases the relevant market and position of the party/ies in it should be defined to conclude on the existence of market power. This position, more or less explicitly, has been followed by the CNDC even in the case of hard-core cartels, maybe with the exception of a case in the LPG market[85] where the agency, upon gathering evidentiary elements pointing to the finding that the involved companies had engaged in collusive conduct, recommended to the Secretariat the imposition of fines without further enquiring on the market structure and the potential harm to general economic interest.

127. The definition of 'general economic interest', however, has changed over the years.

128. The Statement of Reasons of the Formal Competition Act did not define it, but rather pointed out that it could be affected when the 'proper functioning of a market' was prevented, adding that '*conducts that may seem anticompetitive but that are truly beneficial for the community*' were legal. This definition prompted some authors to assimilate the meaning of the terms 'general economic interest'

---

79. Comisión Nacional de Defensa de la Competencia, Advisory Opinion No. 83 (27 Dec. 2000).
80. Comisión Nacional de Defensa de la Competencia, Advisory Opinion No. 84 (10 Jan. 2001).
81. Comisión Nacional de Defensa de la Competencia, Advisory Opinion No. 98 (15 Feb. 2001).
82. Comisión Nacional de Defensa de la Competencia, Advisory Opinion No. 102 (18 Mar. 2001).
83. Comisión Nacional de Defensa de la Competencia, Advisory Opinion No. 161 (30 May 2002).
84. Comisión Nacional de Defensa de la Competencia, Advisory Opinion No. 191 (18 Aug. 2004). Please *see* para. 175 *infra*.
85. 'Ref. Eleva Denuncia', Secretaría de Comercio Interior, Resolution No. 32 (20 Oct. 2006). This decision was reversed by the Courts, as explained in n. 87 below.

with 'proper functioning of the market'.[86] To determine whether the latter had been affected, according to those authors, a rule of reason approach had to be followed, in order to compare the restrictive aspects of the conduct with the potentially pro-competitive ones, and then sanctioning only those cases in which the former exceeded the latter.

129. The 1997 Report adopted an economics-based definition that, with some changes, has been applied ever since and adopted by the courts. The report assimilated the term 'general economic interest' with that of economic efficiency, that is, the sum of consumer surplus (the difference between what the consumer would pay for a relevant product or service and what he or she effectively pays) and the producers surplus (the economic benefit obtained by them from the sale). Thus a conduct would be anticompetitive if it has the potential to reduce the total surplus of a certain relevant market.

130. Even when a few cases followed the total surplus approach,[87] as will be seen below the interpretation of the term by the CNDC shifted from total to consumers' surplus, mainly due to the impact on merger control.

131. As noted above, section 1 of the Competition Act also prohibits acts which 'object' is or may be the restriction of competition. This reference, extracted from European law and absent in the Former Competition Act, could be regarded as leading to the application of a per se standard for certain types of anticompetitive practices such as cartels. However, the fact that in all cases the potential to produce a detriment to the general economic interest must be determined, and that the interpretation of such term requires an effects-based approach, has in practice prevented the enforcement of conducts solely based on their illegal object.

II. Balancing Tests

132. As anticipated in section I above, the Statement of Reasons of the Former Competition Act, which is valid to interpret the Competition Act as well, did provide for a balancing test, weighing the potential anticompetitive and pro-competitive effects of the conduct.

133. In the case of horizontal agreements, the lack of provisions as to what may justify an otherwise illegal collusive conduct makes the application of an effects-based test consistent with a per se approach, with the difference that, at a minimum,

---

86. Otamendi, Jorge, *El interés general y la eficiencia económica en la ley de defensa de la competencia*, LL [1999-F], 1087.
87. *See*, e.g., 'Federación de Clínicas, Sanatorios, Hospitales y Otros Establecimientos Privados de la Provincia de Buenos Aires' (complaint against Roux-Ocefa S.A., Productos Farmacéuticos Fidex S.A. and P.L. Rivero y Cia. S.A.I. y C.', Secretaría de Industria, Comercio y Minería, Resolution No. 211 (26 Mar. 1998).

Part I, Ch. 3, Overview of Substantive Provisions 134–135

under the Competition Act proof of market power – i.e., the potential to affect the general economic interest – should be found.[88]

III. Merger Tests

134. Section 7 of the Competition Act sets forth the substantive test for economic concentrations, which is similar to the one used in the first part of section 1: concentrations which object or effect be or may be to restrict or distort competition, if as a consequence thereof the general economic interest may be affected, are prohibited.

135. As further explained by the Guidelines:

> A concentration may affect the general economic interest when it creates or strengthens market power in a way sufficient to restrict the offer and increase the price of the good being commercialized. This is because all the units of a good being consumed in a competitive market economy generate a net positive social value. Society values those units that are consumed more than it takes to produce them; otherwise, the goods would not be consumed, given that the price that consumers would be willing to pay for them (which reflects the value given by them) would be lower than the price demanded by the producers (which, in a competitive environment, reflects the cost of producing the good). Likewise, when the offer of a good is restricted due to the exercise of market power, units which in the past generated a net positive social value cease to be consumed, and as a consequence thereof society as a whole is harmed.
>
> However, there are cases in which a concentration strengthens a firm's market power, but simultaneously generates efficiency gains such that the price ends up being lower than that enforced before the transaction. In these cases it is considered that the transaction does not affect the general economic interest.
> […]
> With the aim of determining if the market power of the companies involved in a concentration increases as a consequence thereof, the evaluation will be mainly oriented to the competition developed through prices. Specifically it will aim to determine if the prices will be higher as a consequence of the concentration.
>
> For simplification purposes, these guidelines will refer to the impact of concentration on market prices. However, when the transaction is unfolded in a market in which competition does not express mainly through prices (markets in which competition is achieved through product variety, innovation, services related with the products or the quality of the product, among other possibilities) the impact of the concentration over variables which may be representative of the benefits derived from a competitive process will be evaluated.

---

88. The departure by the CNDC from this requirement was one of the reasons for the annulment of the cartel decision in 'Shell Gas S.A. y Totalgaz Argentina S.A.', CSJN S. 808 XLIV, 2010.

Mentioned below are two typical hypotheses in which, as a consequence of the concentration, the possibility of exercising market power to the detriment of consumers is harmed:

– When, as a consequence of the transaction, the companies involved in the concentration unilaterally exercise or strengthen its market power. In this case, the companies involved may influence over prices and quantities sold in the market. The companies will have the possibility of increasing their benefits through the increase of prices of the relevant product.
– When, as a consequence of the concentration, conditions are generated through which, through coordination with the remaining companies participating in the market, the companies involved in the transaction experience the possibility of exercising market power. The concentration will not necessarily allow the companies to unilaterally increase the prices in the relevant market. However, as a consequence of the reduction in the number of competitors, the concerted fixing of prices in the relevant market is facilitated. This concerted price fixing (tacit or express) depends on the specific conditions of each market. Consequently, for each concentration the conditions of the relevant market facilitating the design and successful implementation of concerted price fixing strategies must be analyzed.

136. The early guidelines for the control of economic concentrations, approved by Resolution 726/99 of the Secretariat of Industry, Commerce and Mining,[89] fully embraced the total surplus standard by stating that the generation or increase in market power of the merging companies had to be balanced with whatever economic efficiencies the merger might create, which ' … *could be used in other productive activities and, consequently, have a positive value for society*'.

137. However, the Guidelines – which replaced those approved by Resolution 726/99 – mostly concentrate on the effect of the merger on prices and only accept efficiencies if they: (i) cannot be achieved without the concentration; (ii) can be at least partially transferred to consumers as lower prices or increased product variety, thus rejecting the total surplus standard mentioned above; and (iii) do not consist on cost reductions originating from transfers among two or more economic agents.[90] This change has not only affected merger review but, as anticipated, anticompetitive practices as well, as it has been recognized in important cases such as *YPF*,[91] even when it could be argued that the term 'general economic interest' was introduced in Argentine law as referring to, at least, economic efficiency.[92]

---

89. Resolution No. 726, Secretaría de Industria, Comercio y Minería (29 Sep. 1999), [29240] BO, 32.
90. Guidelines, Annex I, s. VI.
91. 'Yacimientos Petrolíferos Fiscales Gas S.A.', 325 Fallos 1702 (2002).
92. Note that the Statement of Reasons of the Former Competition Act suggested the application of a balancing test of a *community-wide* scope.

Chapter 4. Overview of Main Notions

§1. UNDERTAKING

138. As regards the enforcement of anticompetitive acts, the law applies to any person, individuals and legal entities alike, for profit or not-for-profit, State or privately owned, domiciled in Argentina or abroad, with the only requisites that:

(i) the infringing acts be produced by such while acting in commerce, as opposed to, for example, a decision issued by a certain governmental agency within its powers which, notwithstanding its anticompetitive object or effect, will not violate the Competition Act; and
(ii) the conduct has effect in Argentina.

139. As discussed in *Advance Comunicaciones*,[93] undertakings that form part of the same business group must be considered as a single undertaking for purposes of the Competition Act, and as a consequence thereof no collusive conduct between companies subject to common control can occur, and the abusive conduct of two such companies should be considered within a single finding of dominance. This last situation was found in the *Monsanto* case mentioned in paragraphs 89–93 above, where the CNDC suggested that the legal actions filed by Monsanto group companies outside Argentina were aimed at completing a certain abuse of dominance with effects in Argentina (Monsanto's local subsidiary been made part of the proceedings), and in *Terminal Salta/La Veloz del Norte*,[94] where, following the provisions of section 4 of the Competition Act, an exclusionary abuse of dominance was found due to the monopoly power of a bus terminal operator and – precisely – its vertical integration with a bus company.

140. As referred to in paragraph 330 below, professional associations have been the focus of many CNDC enforcement actions, where the conduct at issue has generally been regarded as an abuse of dominance by a single entity more than a concerted action by its members, probably due to practical considerations.[95]

---

93. 'Advance Comunicaciones S.A., Telecom Soluciones S.A., Startel S.A., Telefónica de Argentina S.A. y Telecom Argentina Stet-France Telecom S.A. s / infracción Ley 25.156', Comisión Nacional de Defensa de la Competencia, Resolution No. 442 (20 Feb. 2004).
94. 'Terminal Salta S.A. y La Veloz del Norte S.A. s/ infracción Ley 25.156', Secretaría de Comercio Interior, Resolution No. 7 (7 Feb. 2011).
95. 'Incidente de verificación de cumplimiento de sanciones definitivas en autos principales Círculo Odontológico Regional de Venado Tuerto S/ infracción Art. 1 Ley 22.262', Secretaría de Comercio Interior, Resolution No. 86 (11 Jul. 2008); 'Medinea S.A. y Asociación de Clínicas y Sanatorios de El Dorado s/ Infracción Ley 22.626', Secretaría de Comercio Interior, Resolution No. 7 (Dic.16, 2008) and 'Círculo Médico de Catamarca y Obra Social de Empleados Públicos de Catamarca s/ infracción a ley 25.156', Secretaría de Comercio Interior, Resolution No. 479 (3 Dec. 2010), among others. But *see*, e.g., 'Investigación de oficio de los abonos de la televisión paga', Comisión Nacional de Defensa de la Competencia, File No. S01:0021390/2010 (C.1321), where both a trade association and its numerous members were made part of the proceedings.

§2. RELEVANT MARKET

141. This term is of paramount importance for the application of the Competition Act, mostly because the CNDC generally does not use alternative methods for determining the existence of market power.

142. It was first introduced by Resolution 726/99 which, as explained above, was replaced by the Guidelines.

143. The relevant product market is defined as that including:

> [A]ll such goods and/or services that are considered as substitute by the consumer, given the characteristics of the product, its price and purpose of its use. If the good produced by the merging companies is substitutable by other goods, then the market power of the same will be limited by the conduct of consumers. Those companies will not be able to unilaterally increase the price of its products without noting a significant loss of consumers to other alternative goods. In conclusion, goods that are substitutable between them compete to attract consumer demand, and so it is correct to include them in the same market.

144. The Guidelines go on to provide a non-exhaustive list of the factors that will be considered as indicative of the existence of potential substitutes, to wit:

(i) Evidence that consumers have shifted or may shift its consumption towards other goods as a consequence of a change in relative prices or other relevant variables (i.e., quality).
(ii) Evidence that producers prepare their business strategies on the assumption that substitution in the demand of different product as a consequence of changes in relative prices or other relevant variables exist.
(iii) Time and cost required to the consumer to shift its demand towards other goods.

145. The Guidelines then adopt the traditional definition of relevant product market as the ' … more reduced group of products regarding which a hypothetical monopolist of those products would find profitable to impose a small, albeit significant and non-transitory price increase'.

146. In the same direction, the relevant geographic market is defined as ' … the smaller region within which a sole provider of a product would find profitable to apply a small, albeit significant and non-transitory price increase'.

147. For a more detailed analysis as to the role of the definition of relevant market in the merger control process, please refer to paragraph 633 below.

§3. MARKET POWER/DOMINANT POSITION

148. Market power is an economic term and has been defined as the ability of an undertaking to increase prices at a profit above the competitive level.[96] Given the innate undefined scope of legal terms such as 'act in restraint of competition', 'abuse of dominance' and 'general economic interest', the exercise of market power is generally favoured by the CNDC's staff of economists as a proxy for most acts that are considered anticompetitive under the Competition Act. In this connection, profit maximization is seen as the 'motive' leading companies to exercise its market power, and said exercise, when market power is substantial and in the case of single-firm conduct, as an abuse of dominant position.[97] By the same token, concerted practices have been defined as the joint exercise of market power by the companies participating in such acts.[98]

149. However, as seen above, in the area of merger control a finding of the creation or strengthening of market power is required to allow for the application of remedies.

150. The 1997 Report, summarizing economic theory, states that market power is measured through the application of the Lerner Index:

> Market power is commonly measured through the calculation of the inverse of the elasticity-price of its demand at the point where an undertaking maximizes its profits. This stems from the relationship existing between said concept and the optimal percentage separation achieved by a profit maximizing firm, which arises from the solving of a mathematical problem through which the quantity and price a firm finds most profitable are found,
> [...]
> Graphically represented, the idea is that companies facing more elastic (flat) demand do not find profitable to exceed significantly its marginal costs, and thus tend to behave in a way considerably similar to price taking companies. However, those facing more upward (inelastic) demand find that in order to maximize profits they must increase their prices substantially above their marginal costs, and thereby take advantage the fact that the quantity that is demanded to them is reduced relative little compared to price increases.[99]
> [...]

151. Even due to the evident difficulty in applying the foregoing economic concepts to particular cases with a substantial degree of certainty, the term 'market power' is used in a significant number of CNDC cases, as it helps the building of conclusions based on other economic definitions such as that of relevant market, for example. However, the reader should be aware that actual cases are decided on less

---

96. 1997 Report, s. 4, para. 3.
97. 1997 Report, s. 4, para. 4.
98. 1997 Report, s. 5, para. 4.
99. 1997 Report, s. 4, para. 5.

sophisticated yet easier to grasp issues such as market shares, competitive position of the relevant companies vis-à-vis its competitors, barriers of entry, etc.

151.1. As to other regimes, it is worth noting that recent telecom regulations define and to some extent regulate the exercise of market power in the following terms:

> 'Significant market power': The position of economic strength that allows the behavior of one or more providers to be, in an appreciable manner, independent from that of its competitors. This economic strength may be based on the market share in the relevant market/s, in the ownership of essential facilities, in the ability to influence in price formation or in the viability of its competitors, including all situations allowing or facilitating the exercise of anticompetitive practices by one or more providers based on, for example, its degree of vertical or horizontal integration. The specific obligations imposed to the provider with significant market power will be extinguished by resolution of the enforcement authority once conditions of effective competition exist in the relevant market/s. The enforcement authority will be empowered to declare at any time the existence of providers with significant market power in the services contemplated in the instant law in accordance to the procedure to be established by regulation.[100]

§4. AGREEMENTS AND CONCERTED PRACTICES

152. The Former Competition Act considered a number of practices as crimes insofar as they were 'concerted' or, in a few cases, a consequence of an 'agreement'. The definition of what exactly was a concerted practice is not easily found. Earlier decisions referred to it as a sort of 'prior understanding' by the parties,[101] and many cases, both old and new,[102] indistinctly refer to cartels as 'concerted practices'. A more recent decision, however, has more adequately defined the term as a type of tacit collusion *requiring a parallel action by relevant competitors of the investigated parties and the existence of sufficient facilitating factors for the occurrence and continuation of the practice*[103] or, as stated by the Appeal Court in *Loma Negra Compañía Industrial*, a practice aimed at eliminating the uncertainty as to the behaviour of competitors.[104] As was seen in paragraph 49 above, both agreements

---

100. Law No. 27,078 (16 Dec. 2014 [33034] BO 1, as amended.
101. 'Tejeduría del Chubut S.A.', CNPenal Económico, Sala II (22 Dec. 1990).
102. 'Repsol YPF Gas S.A. – Cooperativa de Obras y Servicios Publicos, Sociales y Viviendas El Bolson Ltda. (Coopetel Ltda.) – Totalgaz Argentina S.A. – Shell Gas S.A. s/infracción a la Ley 22.262', CF Gral. Roca [327] JA, 3723 (2004).
103. 'Asociación de Agencias de Viaje de Buenos Aires (AVIABUE)', CNDC report No. 356 (27 Aug. 2001), at VII (attached to Resolution No. 115 of the Secretariat of Competition, Deregulation and Consumer Defense (10 Sep. 2001).
104. 'Loma Negra Compañía Industrial S.A. y otros', CNPenal Económico, Sala B, LL 2008-E, 394, at 57. For example, this court was of the view the lack of exploitation of 100% of total installed capacity by some cement companies, coupled with the implementation of an information exchange system dealing with the amount of goods sold by each of them, amounted to a 'concerted practice'.

Part I, Ch. 4, Overview of Main Notions 153–157

and concerted practices were considered crimes and potentially subject to criminal penalties.

153. The Competition Act makes a discrete use of both the term 'concerted' and 'agreement' in section 2 – which enumerates a non-exhaustive list of potentially anticompetitive practices – but provides no guidance as to the meaning of those terms. In the few cartel cases issued under the Competition Act, they are used almost as synonyms.[105] Also, in practice, references to agreements or concerted practices are made depending on the availability of relevant evidence.[106]

154. It should be noted, however, that section 1 of the Competition Act, the main provision penalizing anticompetitive practices, makes no reference to agreements or concerted practices given that, as anticipated, its wording broadly requires the existence of *'acts or conducts'* in restraint of competition. Section 2 of the Competition Act, which provides a non-exhaustive list of conducts that may be deemed anticompetitive if found in violation of section 1, only refers to the word 'agreement' twice. It then follows that a concerted practice need not necessarily be an agreement to be found in infringement of the Competition Act.[107]

155. On a related matter, as anticipated in paragraph 105 above and will be seen with more detail in paragraph 269 below, Article 300, item 1 of the CPN sanctions price-fixing agreements exclusively in goods markets.

§5. RESTRICTION OF COMPETITION

156. As anticipated in Chapter 3 §1 and §2 above, acts in restraint of competition, along with abuses of dominance, are the two conducts included in section 1 of the Competition Act.

157. As appears from its wording, section 1 indistinctly employs the verbs 'limit', 'restrict', 'falsify' and 'distort' to refer to conducts which may negatively impact on the conditions of competition in a certain market. The exact meaning of each of them is not to be found in the Competition Act and is probably not very relevant, as the real key finding is whether, through any market conduct, there is a potential to impair the 'general economic interest', that is, as currently interpreted,

---

105. *'Having examined the evidence of the investigation, this National Commission considered that the investigated conduct, that is, the price agreement, had been proved and consisted in a concerted practice of the accused'*, 'Comerciantes de la Ciudad de San Carlos de Bariloche s/ infracción Ley 22.262', Secretaría de Cordinación Técnica, Resolution No. 101 (21 Nov. 2003).
106. For example, in 'Loma Negra Compañía Industrial S.A. y otros' case – *supra* n. 104 – the focus was on concerted actions and exchange of competitive information as an illegal conduct in itself, while in 'Oxígeno Liquido', Secretaría de la Competencia, la Desregulación y la Defensa del Consumidor, Resolution No. 510 (8 Jul. 2005) the CNDC and Secretariat mostly referred to the existence of an illegal agreement.
107. Please *see*, in this direction, Note 20 of the CNDC report attached to the administrative decision in 'Loma Negra Compañía Industrial S.A. y otros' -CNDC Report No. 513 (25 Jul. 2005), Secretaría de Coordinación Técnica, Resolution No. 124 (25 Jul. 2005).

affect prices and consumer choice. An example of the foregoing can be found in the wording of section 2, which refers to a list of practices commonly considered as anticompetitive as acts 'in restraint of competition', provided that they also fulfil the requirement of injury to the general economic interest.

158. The two-step approach followed by the Competition Act could be regarded as redundant, but also as ratification that some material effect on consumer welfare is required to turn an act illegal, thus ratifying that there are no 'per se' prohibitions under it.

159. It should be noted that the requirement of 'restriction of competition' does not necessarily apply to abuse of dominance conducts, which may be found to infringe the Competition Act through a direct exercise of market power (i.e., an exploitative abuse) which, at least literally would not represent a restriction of competition (in fact, such a conduct could attract competition in certain cases).

§6. Monopolization and Abuse of Dominance

160. The term 'monopolization' is not used by the Competition Act, which follows the EC terminology in that respect. Neither the existence of monopolies, nor acts tending to acquire such a market position through business acumen are prohibited. For references to the use of the term 'monopoly' in earlier antitrust laws, please refer to General Introduction – section 4 (Historical Background of Antitrust Law).

161. The Statement of Reasons of the Former Competition Act,[108] interpreting the comparative laws which inspired the latter,[109] simply defined 'abuse of dominance' as the *unilateral decisions adopted as a consequence of the possession of dominance.*[110] Given that the Former Competition Act required, as well as the Competition Act, that any abuse of dominance affect the 'general economic interest', it follows that such unilateral decisions must impact, directly or indirectly, on consumer or total welfare.

162. Given that the Former Competition Act defined the meaning of dominance but not abuse, early cases relied to that effect on some of the accepted foreign sources like the Treaty of Rome in cases that fit into one of the examples of former Article 86 thereof, as, for example, in *Industrias Welbers*,[111] that dealt with the practice of unfair pricing.

---

108. Available at http://www.mecon.gov.ar/cndc/memorias/memoria97/expo.htm.
109. Treaty Establishing the European Coal and Steel Community of 1951, Treaty of Rome of 1957 and Spanish Antitrust Act of 1963.
110. Statement of Reasons, s. III.1.
111. *Supra* n. 56.

Part I, Ch. 4, Overview of Main Notions

163. The 1997 Report, mostly written by economists, tried to subdue the inherent subjectivities of the legal term 'abuse of dominance' under the more familiar one of 'exercise of market power':

> The idea of the exercise of market power relates to decisions adopted by undertakings to increase their benefits through actions that influence market prices. Interpreted under a criminal law perspective, profit maximization would be the 'motive' leading undertakings to exercise their market power, and both terms can be assimilated to the abuse of dominant position.[112]

164. The foregoing economic interpretation of the term has been generally followed by the CNDC and the courts ever since.[113] Starting from the requirement of a dominant position – presumably one of substantial market power, and this part of the test is less mechanic and generally analysed on a case-by-case basis – any economic act of an undertaking in such condition which may: (i) affect competition and ultimately market prices through the exclusion of market participants; or (ii) directly affect consumer welfare, may be deemed an abuse of dominant position.[114]

165. Like its predecessor, the Competition Act did not define the concept of abuse. However, it did include in section 2 an indicative list of conducts, most of which, provided that the provisions of section 1 – potential impact on consumer welfare – are met, can easily be identified as examples of abuse of dominance, to wit:

(i) imposing obligations to produce, process, distribute, purchase or commercialize only a restricted or limited amount of goods, or render a restricted or limited number, volume or frequency of services (item b);
(ii) impeding, causing difficulty or obstructing the entry or stay of third parties in a market or excluding them from the same (item f);
(iii) fixing, imposing or applying, directly or indirectly, through an agreement with competitors or individually, by any means, prices and conditions for the purchase or sale of goods, the rendering of services or production (item g);
(iv) conditioning the sale of a good to the acquisition of another good or the use of a service, or condition the rendering of a service to the use of another service or the acquisition of a good (item i);
(v) conditioning the purchase or sale to the condition of not using, purchasing, selling or supplying goods or services produced, processed, distributed or commercialized by a third party (item j);
(vi) imposing discriminatory conditions for the acquisition or sale of goods or services without motives based on commercial usage and customs (item k);

---

112. 1997 Report, *supra* n. 97.
113. Of course, an abuse of dominance can be characterized as a type of 'abuse of rights' under civil law, as expressly recognized by s. 11 of the Código Civil y Comercial de la Nación [Civil and Commercial Code, CCC], Law No. 26,994, 8 Oct. 2014 [32985] BO 1.(CCC).
114. *Supra* n. 112.

(vii) unjustifiably denying the supply of concrete orders, for the purchase or sale of goods and services, made under prevailing market conditions (item l);
(viii) suspending the supply of a monopolistic service that may be dominant in the market to a supplier of public services or services of a public interest (item ll); and
(ix) selling goods or supplying services at prices lower than their cost, without reasons based on commercial usage and customs, with the aim of displacing competition in the market or damaging its brand image or patrimony or the value of the brands of its suppliers of goods and services (item m).

166. The foregoing list – which enumerates several of the anticompetitive conducts described elsewhere in this work – and relevant case law make clear that a dominant undertaking is imposed a stricter standard of behaviour than one that is not. As generally stated by the CNDC:

> [N]otwithstanding the fact that the intention of a dominant undertaking may not be to restrict competition through a certain practice, it should be noted that, as a consequence of its condition of dominant undertaking in a market, it bears a special responsibility of avoiding that its conduct may restrict competition. Because this outcome will result in the act, regardless of its intention, being considered prejudicial to the general economic interest and therefore in violation of Law 25,156.[115]

167. The distinction made in paragraph 164 above anticipated the two accepted main divisions of abusive conducts: *exclusionary* and *exploitative*.[116] As confirmed by the Supreme Court in the *YPF* case:[117]

> The court must define whether the conduct charged against the company may fit into the meaning of 'abuse of a dominant position in a market, so that detriment to the general economic interest may occur' (Section 1, last part, law 22,262). The aforementioned provision includes both practices carried out by those occupying a dominant position in a market, limiting restricting or distorting competition – i.e., acts raising entry barriers to competitors – as well as those other practices that, similarly to the former, impair the economic efficiency of a market through actions against social interest, as occurs when the offer of goods is unjustifiably reduced with the deliberate purpose of maintaining a specific price level. In those cases, the commercial strategy, more than using a simple dominance position to obtain market profits, abuses of such

---

115. 'Terminal Salta S.A. y La Veloz del Norte S.A. s/ infracción Ley 25.156', Secretaría de Comercio Interior, Resolution No. 7 (7 Feb. 2011).
116. Although some courts have become confused with the assimilation of abuse of dominance with the exercise of market power portrayed in the 1997 Report by considering that *only exploitative abuses*, that is, where a direct exercise of market power is involved, fit into the definition of abuse of dominance. *See*, i.e., 'Giangrossi Juan y otros s/denuncia', CNPenal Económico, Sala B (27 Mar. 2001) and 'Video Cable 6 S.A. y otros s/ infracción Art. 1 ley 22.262', CFed. Paraná (25 Aug. 2011).
117. *Supra* n. 91.

position, through artificially manipulating the offer making the market less efficient in terms of quantities and prices, with direct incidence in consumer welfare.

168. The limits that apply to the conduct of dominant undertakings have been more clearly defined in the case of exclusionary conducts: freedom to contract is very much curtailed, and fairness of treatment under objective criteria must be applied. This issue is more obscure as regards exploitative abuses, as will be seen in paragraph 397 below.

§7. CONCENTRATIONS

169. Section 6 of the Competition Act defines the term 'economic concentration' as the acquisition of control of one or more enterprises (undertakings), through any of the following acts:

(i) mergers;
(ii) transfers of going concerns;
(iii) the acquisition of any rights over shares or other capital participations, or debt instruments that may be converted into such, when the acquirer of said rights is granted the control or a substantive influence over the relevant enterprise;
(iv) any other agreement or act transferring de jure or de facto to a person or economic group the assets of an enterprise or granting such person or group a determining influence in the passing of resolutions of the ordinary or extraordinary management of a company.

170. As anticipated as from paragraph 115 above:

(i) 'Control' can be characterized as the right to conduct an undertaking's business strategy by any means (corporate, contractual or otherwise), and thus is generally achieved through the acquisition of equity participations in an undertaking granting a majority vote in board and partners or shareholders meetings, or by the acquisition of the undertaking's assets, as in a transfer of going concern. Acquisition of minority participations may also grant de facto control if the remaining holdings are dispersed.
(ii) 'Substantial influence' refers to the situation which allows an undertaking to influence or alter an undertaking's business strategy, in particular in the context of minority participations granting veto rights (where it is also named 'negative control').
(iii) 'Determining influence' has been interpreted by the CNDC as bearing a similar meaning to that of 'substantial influence'.
(iv) An economic concentration is found not only in cases where a change is produced in the party exercising exclusive or joint control, but also in changes from sole to joint control and vice versa. However, a transaction whereby neither party acting individually nor any two or more parties acting jointly –

pursuant to a shareholders or voting agreement – exercise such control, will normally not be considered as subject to notification.
(v) 'Assets' refers to assets of an undertaking from which an independent turnover can be obtained.

171. The subject of merger control will be examined in more detail below.

§8. JOINT VENTURES

172. A joint venture is analysed under different provisions, depending on its type.

173. A typical horizontal cooperation agreement will be examined under the standard of section 1 of the Competition Act, and thus will be valid insofar as it does not have as its object or effect the substantial restriction of competition and/or the exchange of sensitive competitive information.

174. A long-lasting cooperation agreement, aimed at the joint implementation of a common productive activity may adopt the form of a 'Cooperation Joint Venture' (*Agrupación de Colaboración* or ACE) under the CCC.[118] Said agreements are generally examined with more caution, and thus the CCC provides that a copy of the same must be forwarded by the Public Registry of Commerce to the CNDC.[119] Since the enactment of the Competition Act, however, Cooperation Joint Ventures may also be considered an economic concentration and thus subject to mandatory review if the thresholds are met,[120] provided that they meet the requirements to be considered a concentration, that is, that one or more of the joint venture partners acquire control or substantial influence over the assets contributed to the joint venture by one or more of the other partners.

175. Other types of cooperation agreements contemplated in the Companies Act, the UTE, suitable for the joint development or execution of a specific work, service or supply,[121] have also been considered by the CNDC as economic concentrations subject to its review.[122]

---

118. Sections 1453 to 1462. Under s. 1453 of the CCC, the purpose of an ACE is to set up a common organization with the aim of facilitating or developing certain stages of the commercial activity of its members or to perfect or increase the result of said activities.
119. Section 1455.
120. *See*, e.g., 'Cargill S.A.C.I. y Buyatti S.A.I.C.A. (c. 374) s/ notificación art. 8 de la Ley 25.156', Secretaría de la Competencia, la Desregulación y la Defensa del Consumidor, Resolution No. 11 (14 Jun. 2002).
121. CCC, s. 1463.
122. *See*, e.g., 'Petrolera TDF Company S.R.L., Petrolera LF Company S.R.L. y Pan American Fueguina S.A.S. s/ notificación artículo 8 Ley 25.156 (conc. 593), Secretaría de Comercio Interior, Resolution No. 19 (19 Mar. 2007) and 'YPF S.A. y otros', Secretaría de la Competencia, la Desregulación y la Defensa del Consumidor, Resolution No. 19 (7 May 2001).

Part I, Ch. 4, Overview of Main Notions

176. As anticipated, the formation of a joint venture, be it an ACE or a UTE, should only be included within the merger control provisions of the Competition Act if one or more of the parties contribute assets which at the time already independently generate turnover, and one or more of the remaining parties acquire some sort of control or significant influence over those assets.

177. By the same token, the acquisition of a stake in an existing joint venture must allow for at least a blocking vote on the passing of strategic company decisions to become an 'economic concentration'.

Chapter 5. Consequences of Violations

§1. Administrative Enforcement

I. The Antitrust Authorities

A. Formation, Composition

178. As of the date of this report, the enforcement authorities of the Former Competition Act, namely the CNDC and the Secretariat, apply the Competition Act.

179. The CNDC was created by the Former Competition Act. It is comprised by one President and four Commissioners, all of them appointed by the Executive Power. The term of office of the Commissioners is four years, while that of the President is, in principle, unlimited. Two of the four members have to be lawyers and two economics professionals. All of them must be at least thirty years old.

180. Resolution 70/2008 of the Secretariat[123] reorganized the CNDC as follows:

(i) dividing the agency in three departments: Technical, Administrative and Investigations and Audits;
(ii) appointing the two Commissioners who are legal professionals as First and Second Vice-President of the CNDC;
(iii) entrusting the First Vice-President with the responsibility of the Administrative department and the replacement of the President of the CNDC in case of absence or impediment;
(iv) entrusting the Second Vice-President with the responsibility of the Investigations and Audits department; and
(v) entrusting the President and Commissioners of the CNDC, by majority vote, with responsibility over the Technical department (which includes the legal and economics sections).

181. Both the President and the Commissioners may be removed from their office, by a special jury appointed by the Executive Power. To date, this procedure has not been applied.

182. The powers to adjudicate competition cases under the Former Competition Act were reserved to the Secretary of State, Commerce and International Economic Negotiations, a single-person office appointed by the Executive Power. The name of this Secretariat has changed over the years, to Secretariat of Industry, Commerce and Mining; Secretariat of Competition and Consumer Defence; Secretariat of Competition, Deregulation and Consumer Defence; Secretariat of Technical Coordination, Secretariat of Domestic Trade and ultimately Secretariat of Trade.

---

123. Secretariat of Domestic Trade, Resolution No. 70 (3 Jun. 2008) [31420] BO, 4.

Part I, Ch. 5, Consequences of Violations

183. The Competition Act, however, originally intended to replace the dual-agency system of the former Competition Act by the Tribunal, a single administrative authority. The Tribunal was created as an independent agency within the auspices of the Ministry of Economy, to be comprised by seven members, at least two of them lawyers and two economics professionals, with more than five years as such.

184. The appointment of the members of the Tribunal was to be made through a public process before a jury comprised of the Attorney General, the Secretary of Industry, Commerce and Mining (currently the Secretary of Domestic Trade), the Presidents of the Commerce Commissions of both Houses of Congress, the President of the National Chamber of Appeals in Commercial Matters and the Presidents of the National Law Academy and National Economics Sciences Academy. Their term of office was chosen to be six years.

185. By Resolution 29/02 of the Ministry of Production,[124] the rules of the public appointment procedure were approved; such process was publicly announced and the resumes of the candidates filed. Thereinafter the selection and appointment process stalled due to the inaction of the Executive Power, whose members not only comprised the jury but also presided over it.[125]

186. Over the years, the delay in the appointment of the members of the Tribunal led to a number of decisions by the CNDC and the Secretariat being challenged before the courts, on the basis that the CNDC, the Secretariat or neither of them was empowered to apply the Competition Act.

187. Truly, section 58 of the Competition Act provides that the public authorities appointed by the former Competition Act are empowered to apply the Competition Act until the Tribunal be formed. The issue was settled in a series of cases, most notably in re *Credit Suisse*,[126] where the Supreme Court stated that the dual-agency system created by the former Competition Act was still in force.

188. As will be seen below, in more recent cases where the courts have regarded certain CNDC or Secretariat decisions as arbitrary, a strong request was made to the Supreme Court to force the Government to create the Tribunal.[127]

189. It is now obvious that since the enactment of the Competition Act none of the successive Administrations has been interested in losing control of antitrust policy, particularly in the case of mergers.

---

124. Ministry of Production, Resolution No. 29 (18 Nov. 2002).
125. Decree 89/2001, s. 19, para. 4. The Executive Power is also empowered under the Competition Act to appoint the members of the Tribunal selected by the jury.
126. 'Credit Suisse First Boston Private Equity Argentina II y otros s/apel. resol. Comisión Nac. Defensa de la Compet.', 330 Fallos 2527 (2007).
127. 'Incidente de apelación contra Resolución SCI No. 483/09 (en autos principales: 'Pirelli & C S.p.A. y otros s/notificación art. 8 ley 25.156', CNPenal Económico, Sala A (1 Feb. 2010).

190. To partially tackle this concern, a former Minister of Economy filed in 2005 a bill proposing to form the Tribunal through the initial appointment of the five members of the CNDC, plus two others appointed by the Executive Power, as their initial members, their replacements then being selected by a jury.[128] The bill was never considered and lost parliamentary status. More recently high-level public officials have stated that the provisions of the Competition Act related to the formation of the Tribunal have been abrogated by the mere passing of time, without them being applied.[129] Ultimately and as anticipated, the Government's response to criticism was to submit a bill to amend the Competition Act, approved as the 2014 Amendment, which eliminated all traces of the Tribunal, consolidating the status quo ante.

B. Investigating Powers

191. Under the original wording of the Competition Act, investigating powers rested upon the Tribunal. Based on section 58 and the Supreme Court's *Credit Suisse* decision,[130] most of such powers rested upon the CNDC.

191.1. The 2014 Amendment eliminated all references to the Tribunal, and granted most of the empowerments originally contemplated to such new agency to a new enforcement authority to be created by the Executive.

192. Those empowerments are now listed under section 18, to wit:

(i) entrust the preparation of market studies and the pursuance of investigations(item a);
(ii) hold hearings, obtain testimony and order cross examinations (item b);
(iii) entrust the implementation of audits over books, documents and other documents (item c);
(iv) audit inventories, verify origin and costs of raw materials and other goods (item d);
(v) impose sanctions (item e);
(vi) advocate the study and investigation on competition matters (item f);
(vii) provide advice to the relevant agencies in the negotiation of treaties or international agreements on competition matters (item g);
(viii) organize the National Registry of Competition (item h);
(ix) promote and initiate legal actions (item i);
(x) suspend the legal terms of the competition proceedings by cause (item j);
(xi) access premises for inspection purposes with the relevant party's consent or with a court order, which will be requested to the competent judge, who shall decide the request within twenty-four hours (item k);

---

128. P.E. 426/05, National Senate (17 Aug. 2005).
129. Chief of Staff of Ministers, Report No. 76 to the House of Representatives, Nov. 2009, para. 87 (available at http://www.jgm.gov.ar/paginas.dhtml?pagina=56).
130. *Supra* n. 126.

Part I, Ch. 5, Consequences of Violations 193–194

(xii) request the competent judge on the issuance of interim measures, which decision shall be decided within twenty-four hours (item l);
(xiii) enter into agreements with provincial or municipal agencies for the setting up of premises to receive complaints on competition matters in the provinces (item m);
(xiv) foster consented agreements between the parties (item n);
(xv) enter into agreements with consumer associations for the promotion of the participation of such in competition and market transparency issues (item ñ).

193. On the other hand, section 20 of the 2014 Amendment reserved to the CNDC the following limited tasks, and only for as long as the new enforcement authority is not operational, that is, while the empowerments listed under section 18 are exercised by the Secretariat:

(i) conduct the market studies and investigations entrusted to it by the enforcement authority (item a);
(ii) issue non-binding opinions upon competition matters as regards laws, regulations and other administrative acts (item b);
(iii) issue recommendations of a general or sectorial nature (item c);
(iv) issue recommendations before the enforcement of sanctions (item d), and, generally;
(v) pursue the tasks entrusted to it by the enforcement authority (item e).

194. The improvisation behind the 2014 Amendment is best evidenced by the fact that because the new enforcement agency was not created until the issuance of Decree 718/2016 (which, as anticipated and due to the new Administration's intention to implement a complete amendment of the Competition Act, ultimately appointed the Secretary to at least maintain the *status quo ante*), the Secretariat had to temporarily assign many of its empowerments to the CNDC, the agency which existence was set to cease by the latest reform. Such assignment, implemented through Secretariat Resolution 359/2015[131] for a limited period and extended by Resolution of the Ministry of Production 2/2016[132] until 30 June 2016, includes the following tasks:

(i) handle presentations for merger control and anticompetitive conduct, the Secretariat deciding on the CNDC Commissioner to be appointed on each administrative file (item a);
(ii) handle all type of documents filed by the parties or third parties (item b);
(iii) hold hearings, obtain testimony and order cross examinations (item c);
(iv) request information to the parties or third parties (item d);
(v) issue and notify all types of mere procedural decisions (item e);
(vi) grant or deny access to administrative files and provide opinion on requests for confidentiality to the Undersecretariat of Domestic Trade (item f);

---

131. Secretaría de Comercio, Resolution No. 359 (7 Sep. 2015) [33211] BO 16.
132. Ministry of Production, Resolution No. 2 (17 Dec. 2015) [33278] BO 36.

(vii) issue request for information regarding merger notification forms 1, 2 and 3 (item g);
(viii) request additional information as regards a request for issuance of an advisory opinion (ítem h);
(ix) serve notice to parties accused of anticompetitive conduct in order for them to reply to the charges (ítem i);
(x) order and perform audits over books, documents and other documents, audit inventories, verify origin and costs of raw materials and other goods (item j);
(xi) serve the Statement of Objections (item k);
(xii) accept or deny evidence proposed by the parties (item l);
(xiii) produce relevant evidence (item m);
(xiv) close the evidentiary stage (ítem n);
(xv) foster consented agreements between the parties (item o);
(xvi) access premises for inspection purposes with the relevant party's consent or with a court order (item p); and
(xvii) carry out any other relevant act in the context of merger control, requests for advisory opinions or investigations proceedings (item q).

C. Adjudicating Powers (Ascertaining and Sanctioning)

195. As stated above, currently adjudicating powers rest on the Secretariat, which, in addition to the powers already mentioned, can and has instructed the CNDC to open investigations.

196. The vast majority of recommendations issued by the CNDC are followed by the Secretariat. This circumstance, however, must not be interpreted to mean that the Secretariat heavily relies on the opinion of the CNDC, at least not in sensitive cases – especially in the merger control area – where it is not uncommon for an informal agreement being reached between the CNDC and Secretariat before the former issuing its recommendation.[133]

D. Other Institutional Tasks (Consultancy to Parliament/Government)

197. As stated above, section 20 of the Competition Act provide for the power of the CNDC to perform market studies and investigations and issue recommendations on competition matters, including to, inter alia, the Executive and Congress.

198. Over the years, the CNDC has carried out certain sectorial investigations in areas such as fruit, pay-TV, steel, fertilizers, LPG and meat,[134] ex officio or as a result of a request from the Secretariat or some national or local public official. Even when the primary purpose of those studies is generally to investigate the conditions

---

133. Org. Econ. Co-operation & Dev., *Competition Law and Policy in Argentina – A peer review – 2006*, s. 3.3, 31 (*supra* n. 32).
134. Please refer to http://www.cndc.gov.ar/publicaciones_estudios.html.

Part I, Ch. 5, Consequences of Violations 199–202

of competition with a view to a potential application of the competition laws, sometimes it is used as a basis for subsequent regulation. An example of the foregoing can be found in the report on the LPG market,[135] which derived in the passing of industry-wide legislation that imposed maximum prices.[136]

199. Specific pro-competitive recommendations have been issued in markets such as petrol retailing (2000), LPG (2003), Natural Compressed Gas (2004) and mobile communications (2008), as will be mentioned in more detail below:

200. Petrol Retailing. In 2000, the CNDC undertook a comprehensive study of the market due to an apparent lack of competition, presumably caused by Repsol YPF's significant market participation and vertical integration. In particular, the investigation focused on the relationship between the petrol refiners and retailers, where the CNDC found that in spite of most of them being independently owned and operated the fact that they were linked to the refiner with long-term contracts represented a barrier of entry to other refiners. The recommendation of the CNDC, eventually implemented through Decree 1060/00,[137] was to limit the duration of new supply contracts to five years, and that refiners be limited to owning 40% of their retail network.

201. LPG subsidies. The CNDC issued a recommendation to the Ministry of Economy in connection with subsidies granted by the National Government and provincial authorities for the domestic consumption of LPG.[138] After stating that subsidies to consumers are at odds with efficient markets, the CNDC pointed out that subsidies in the LPG market had been granted to certain companies and not as a general measure. In particular, in the province of Rio Negro, Coopetel was the only cooperative that had received the relevant subsidy. The CNDC observed that, with this benefit, Coopetel could offer LPG at prices lower than those that would arise from a competitive process, thus causing serious distortions in the relevant market. In order to avoid these results, the CNDC recommended that benefits to consumption should be general, including all the companies participating in the relevant market.

202. Compressed Natural Gas (CNG). In this case, the competitive concern was raised due to the vertical integration between two gas producers, Repsol YPF and Petrobras, and its self-operated CNG retail stations (CNG being a common automobile fuel in Argentina), which could lead to potential discrimination to non-integrated retailers. The report ultimately did not include any specific recommendation, but pointed out the importance of closely monitoring the situation with a view towards preventing possible anticompetitive effects.

---

135. www.cndc.gov.ar/dictamenes/dictamen967.pdf.
136. Law No. 26,020, 8 Apr. 2005 [30628] BO 1.
137. Decree No. 1060, 15 Nov. 2000 [29526] BO 8.
138. This recommendation was made in the course of the investigation of the LPG cartel case referred to in para. 291 below.

203. Mobile communications. Upon performing an investigation originating from a complaint filed against mobile telephone companies in 2001,[139] the CNDC recommended the Communications Secretariat to refrain from inviting private participants to jointly propose the value of mobile termination charges so as to avoid the occurrence of opportunistic conducts.

II. Government Direct Enforcement Activities

204. The powers of the Secretariat encompass much more than the enforcement of the Competition Act. In the last few years, the Secretariat has become one of the most important government agencies, regulating many aspects of both domestic and international commerce by Argentine companies. In particular, increasing inflation rates led the Secretariat to adopt several interventionist measures that contradict competition policy. To name a few, the Secretariat prompted the adoption of price control agreements among competitors, both formally[140] and informally.[141] After the failure of those agreements was made evident, the Secretariat applied – directly or through the aid of other government agencies – direct measures including the imposition of maximum prices,[142] export or import restrictions or prohibitions[143] and the like. Few of the relevant sectors of the economy currently fall outside of the regulation of the Secretariat.

205. The wide support of the former Federal Government to those policies explains to a great extent the uncertain position that competition policies had in the political agenda.

III. Other Administrative Agencies Applying Antitrust Rules

206. Section 59 of the Competition Act abrogated all empowerments to apply competition law to agencies other than the CNDC and the Secretariat. This provision has particular effects in certain sectorial regulators, which pre-existing

---

139. 'Solicita avocamiento ante el nuevo aumento unilateral de la telefonía celular', File No. 064-006233/2001 of the Ministry of Economy. The complaint was filed by certain consumer associations against mobile communications companies.
140. For example, the 'Supply Agreement for Propane Gas' approved by Decrees No. 329/2007 (12 Apr. 2007 [31133] BO 3), 645/2004 (27 May 2004 [30409] BO 1), 809/2002 (14 May 2002 [29897] BO 2), 473/2002 (11 Mar. 2002 [29855] BO 3), 355/2002 (22 Feb. 2002 [29844] BO 2) and 310/2002 (14 Feb. 2002 [29838] BO 3), which even specifically clarified that it benefitted the 'general economic interest'.
141. *See*, e.g., 'El Gobierno presiona a proveedores de insumos para que bajen precios', El Cronista Comercial (6 Apr. 2010) (available at http://www.cronista.com/general/El-Gobierno-presiona-a-proveedores-de-insumos-para-que-bajen-precios-20100406-0062.html).
142. For example, the regulation of pay-TV rates approved by the Secretaríat of Domestic Trade, Resolution No. 50, 4 Mar. 2010 [31856] BO 10.
143. *See*, generally, *Argentina Establishes Import Restrictions on Broad Range of Products*, Hong Kong Trade Development Council (31 Aug. 2007) (available at http://info.hktdc.com/alert/us0718c.htm) and *EU suggests Argentina's import restrictions could delay Mercosur trade talks*, MercoPress (2 Jul. 2010) (available at http://en.mercopress.com/2010/07/02/eu-suggests-argentina-s-import-restrictions-could-delay-mercosur-trade-talks).

Part I, Ch. 5, Consequences of Violations

legal frameworks empowered them to apply competition rules, such as, for example, the electricity and gas regulators.

207. The referred to abrogation does not mean, however, that laws containing provisions inspired on competition grounds were modified. For example, both the electricity and natural gas legal frameworks provide for vertical separation of generation, transmission and distribution, which remain in force.

208. A partial exception to the foregoing can be found in the telecommunication sector, which even when it is not exempt from the application of the Competition Act, includes several references to competition law aspects, which somewhat overlap with the enforcement of the Competition Act.

209. For example, section 40 of Law 27,078 provides that telecom licensees shall be obliged to interconnect in non-discriminatory, transparent conditions based on objective criteria, based on the provisions issued by the enforcement authority, which will foster competition and will be oriented to the progressive reduction of asymmetries among licensees.

210. In the same direction, one of the obligations of licensees is to act under loyal and effective competition conditions (section 62 l).

211. Also, the enforcement authority of Law 27,078 does have among its powers to regulate and promote competition (section 81 a), promote and regulate the access to information and communication technologies and telecommunication services in conditions of effective competition (section 81 g), and identify the existence of market participants with significant market power and impose such measures that may be necessary to prevent competition to be impaired

212. The joint application of competition law principles by the enforcement authorities of both the Competition Act and Law 27,078 creates the possibility of contradictory or overlapping decisions, which however may differ in the type of sanction eventually applied.

IV. Administrative Fines

213. Section 46, paragraph b) provides that anticompetitive practices contemplated in section 1, or the breach of final decisions regarding mergers, are subject to fines ranging from Argentine Peso (ARS) 10,000 to ARS 150 million.[144] Fines – which can be doubled in case of recidivism – will be applied based on the:

(i) losses by the affected party;
(ii) benefits obtained by the infringing parties; and
(iii) value of the assets involved.

---

144. As of the date of this report, the Argentine Peso (ARS) : Euro exchange rate was around 17:1.

214. Section 49 includes additional fining guidelines, providing that the authority shall also consider the seriousness of the infringement, damage caused, any evidence of intention, the position of the infringing party in the relevant market, the size thereof, the length of the practice or concentration and the background or recidivism of the infringing party and its financial strength.

215. The Competition Act improved the regime in force with the Former Competition Act, which just referred to a relatively low range of fines, which could only be increased by reference to the illegal profits (effectively or potentially) generated by the practice. To calculate those profits, however, the CNDC had to estimate the prices that would be in force were the anticompetitive practice not to exist, which was difficult or impossible to achieve.[145] This led to the CNDC to adopt conservative yet speculative approaches, like for example, estimating that the illegal profits represented at least 1% of the total sales of the relevant period.[146]

216. There are few cases imposing significant fines under the Competition Act which allow a clear appreciation of the fining guidelines. The most significant case where the guidelines were used was the Investigation on the Liquid Oxygen Market,[147] where fines in excess ARS 70 million were applied to a cartel (*see* as from paragraph 306 below).

217. Section 46 d) of the Competition Act also contemplates fines of up to ARS 1 million *per day* of delay in: (i) reporting a merger;[148] (ii) breaching a cease-and-desist order; or (iii) breaching a settlement agreed with the authorities.

218. Section 47 of the Competition Act provides that legal entities are liable by the conducts carried out by individuals acting on their behalf, while section 48 makes those persons jointly and severally liable with the company for the payment of the fine. The Regulation provides, however, that a separate summary investigation has to be pursued against those individuals in order to apply the fines.

219. Finally, persons obstructing or impairing the investigation or not fulfilling other requirements of the competition authorities may be subject to daily fines of up to ARS 500 (section 50).

---

145. As stated by the CNDC in the cement cartel case ('Loma Negra Compañía Industrial S.A. y otros', *supra* n. 107, items 435 and 739), 'it should be noted that the reference against which the detriment to the general economic interest must be evaluated is not the market situation including the charged anticompetitive practices, but such situation which would have existed absent those conducts. However, it would be virtually impossible for the CNDC to prove such situation, that is, how quantities and prices would have behaved absent the anticompetitive conducts'.
146. 'Loma Negra Compañía Industrial S.A. y otros', at point 741. In other cases, however, the speculative nature of such reasoning led to the CNDC not recommending the calculation of the fine based on a measure of 'illegal profits'. *See*, i.e., 'Tele Red Imagen S.A. y Televisión Satelital Codificada S.A.', Secretariat of Competition, Deregulation and Consumer Protection, Resolution No. 28 (28 Sep. 2002).
147. 'Oxígeno Líquido', *supra* n. 106.
148. As regards fines for late filing, please refer to para. 659.

Part I, Ch. 5, Consequences of Violations

220. There is still no leniency programme for cartels available under the Competition Act. However, the CNDC has been working on one for the last few years and in 2010 formally approved a draft[149] that was forwarded to the Secretariat for its review and, ultimately, submission to Congress, as its adoption would require an amendment of the Competition Act. The new Administration has expressed its willingness to include a leniency programme in a future amendment to the Competition Act.

221. The draft programme contemplates both immunity from fines to the first applicant (companies and individuals) as well as reductions of fines of up to 50% to subsequent ones.

222. In order to be eligible for immunity, the CNDC must not have had information on the collusive conduct or opened an investigation, and the applicant must not have been the ringleader. The applicant must be the first to apply, furnish evidence that may allow the CNDC to determine the existence of the cartel, immediately cease with the practice unless agreed to the contrary with the CNDC, cooperate fully with the agency throughout the proceedings, and not destroy, falsify or conceal evidence or make public its participation in the programme.

223. Applicants requesting fine reductions must provide additional valuable evidence and comply with requirements similar to those identified above.

224. The programme even contemplates 'leniency plus' provisions, as revealing the participation in another cartel may grant the reporting person of the original cartel under the programme a reduction of one-third of the amount of the fine on top of whatever amount would have been applied by application to the leniency provisions.

V. Administrative Injunctions and Other Restrictive Orders

225. Section 35 of the Competition Act provides that:

> The Tribunal, at any stage of the proceeding, may impose the fulfilment of conditions or order the ceasing or suspension of the infringing conduct. When a serious injury to competition may occur the Tribunal may order measures which under the circumstances may be more relevant to prevent such injury. Likewise, the Tribunal may order, ex officio, or at the request of a party the suspension, amendment or revocation of those measures due to subsequent events that could not be known at the time of adopting the measures.

226. Whether the CNDC or the Secretariat can apply cease-and-desist orders has been subject to debate.

---

149. Comisión Nacional de Defensa de la Competencia (15 Dec. 2010) (available at www.cndc.gov.ar/archivos/anteproyecto_de_ley.pdf).

227. As mentioned in paragraph 187 above, section 58 of the Competition Act allows for the enforcement authorities of the Former Competition Act to apply the Competition Act until the new enforcement agency be formed. Before the enactment of the 2014 Amendment, uncertainty remained as to whether the CNDC or the Secretariat was empowered to issue them.

228. Under the Former Competition Act, neither of the two agencies was empowered to issue injunctions as an interim measure. Only the Secretariat could issue them, but in its final decision.[150] Section 3 of Decree 2284/91,[151] which complemented the Former Competition Act, included similar language than that of section 35 of the Competition Act and stated that those measures were to be applied by the 'enforcement authority' of the Former Competition Act. The few injunctions issued after the passing of Decree 2284/91 followed the standard division of tasks employed by the CNDC and the Secretariat, meaning that the former issued a non-binding recommendation to the latter, which then decided to issue the injunction.

229. Those precedents were clearly not followed under the Competition Act, initially only the CNDC applying section 35, which readily became a remedy of a permanent rather than temporary nature, meaning that, in most cases where injunctions were issued, no final decision was adjudicated or the case was ultimately closed.

230. In contrast with the area of anticompetitive practices, where the CNDC regularly issued injunctions, the CNDC largely failed to apply injunctions in the merger control arena to enforce the suspension of effects contemplated in section 8 of the Competition Act (for further reference in this respect please refer to the considerations made as from paragraph 653 below).

231. Attempts to issue injunctions in the 2007 *Cablevisión–Multicanal* merger[152] were faced with a court order, affirmed by an Appellate Court in re *Multicanal*,[153] ordering the CNDC to refrain from issuing cease-and-desist orders altogether until a final decision as regards the merger under review was issued. The Appellate Court stated that, although section 35 had repeatedly been relied on by the CNDC, such provision actually referred to the Tribunal, and such power might not be temporarily awarded to the CNDC. According to this decision, the issuance of a cease-and-desist order may only be issued provided that a court has previously authorized such measure.[154]

---

150. Former Competition Act, s. 26 para. 2.
151. Decree No. 2284 (1 Nov. 1991) [27254] BO, 9.
152. 'Grupo Clarín S.A., Vistone LLC, Fintech Advisory Inc., Fintech Media LLC, VLG Argentina LLC y Cablevisión S.A. s/ Notificación Art. 8 Ley 25.156 (conc. 596)', Secretaría de Comercio interior, Resolution No. 257 (7 Dec. 2007).
153. 'Multicanal S.A. y otro c/ Conadeco', CNCont. Adm. Fed., Sala III [2009-F] LL, 425.
154. The injunction was issued in the context of a request for a declaratory judgment (*acción declarativa de certeza*) by which plaintiff sought to obtain immunity from injunctions (both from third parties as well as issued by the CNDC) pending the merger review. This possibility was denied by the

Part I, Ch. 5, Consequences of Violations 232–234

232. In 2008 and 2009, however, the CNDC issued several such orders in the *Telecom Italia S.p.A. y Telecom Italia Internacional N.V./ Telefónica de España, Olimpia y Otros* case: (i) prohibiting the exercise of a call option;[155] (ii) prohibiting the *exercise of voting rights* in the target companies;[156] and (iii) undoing the effects of decisions adopted at shareholders meeting of the target companies and initiating legal proceedings against officers appointed by the acquirer/gun-jumper, for infringing the decision suspending the exercise of political rights in the target.[157]

233. Most of those injunctions were examined by the courts.[158] The Courts of Appeals – National Court of Appeals on Economic Crimes and Federal Civil and Commercial Court of the City of Buenos Aires – reversed those measures[159] under the argument that the Former Competition Act did not include such powers,[160] and given the extraordinary delay in the formation of the Tribunal, of which only the government was responsible, the transitory provision of the Competition Act embodied in section 58 could not be deemed to include extraordinary powers such as those to issue injunctions, in particular taking into account that the Competition Act, through the appointment of an independent tribunal, provided for additional due process guarantees than the former Competition Act, where the enforcement authorities were purely political. Following the Appeal Court judgment in *Multicanal*,[161] the courts concluded that until the Tribunal be formed injunctions had to be requested to the courts.[162]

234. In spite of those judicial shortcomings, the CNDC continued to apply interim measures, even in the case of cartel enforcement, in which the scope of the injunctions included not only the prohibition to increase prices, but also to restitute

---

Supreme Court, in re 'Multicanal S.A. y otro c/ Conadeco – dto. 525/05 y otros', 334 Fallos 236 (2011), although the Supreme Court did not refer to the injunction, which was based on different arguments.
155. 'Telecom Italia S.p.A. y Telecom Italia Internacional N.V.', Secretaría de Comercio Interior, Resolution No. 123 (29 Dec. 2008).
156. 'Telefónica de España, Olimpia y Otros', Comisión Nacional de Defensa de la Competencia, Decision No. 44 (6 Apr. 2009).
157. 'Telefónica de España, Olimpia y Otros', Comisión Nacional de Defensa de la Competencia, Decision No. 64 (26 May 2009).
158. 'Telecom Italia S.p.A. y Otro', CNCiv. Com. Fed., Sala II (27 Jul. 2009), 'Telefónica de España, Olimpia y Otros', CNPenal Económico, Sala A (21 Oct. 2009), 'Telecom Italia S.p.A. y Otro s/ recurso de queja por apelación denegada', CNPenalEconómico, Sala A (17 Jun. 2010) and 'Telecom Italia S.p.A. y Otro s/ recurso de queja por recurso directo denegado', CN Penal Económico, Sala A (17 Jun. 2010). For a complete description of the Telefónica/Telecom case, please refer to paras 507 et seq. below. For a general reference of the Judicial System in Argentina, please refer to *§3. The Legal System supra*.
159. For a description of the appeal process, please refer to Ch. 3. *Challenging of the Administrative Decision, infra*.
160. Apparently, the courts did not take into account the language of s. 3 of Decree No. 2284/91.
161. *Supra* n. 154.
162. The judgment of the National Courts Of Appeals on Economic Crimes also implies that the Secretaríat (and not the CNDC) could issue these measures.

the increases attributed to the cartel to the consumer.[163] In some cases, these decisions have also been appealed with the same results mentioned above.[164] With the enactment of the 2014 Amendment, however, it is clear that the CNDC is not empowered to issue cease-and-desist orders, which might now only be applied by the Secretariat, albeit this opinion has yet to be tested by the courts.

VI. Interim Measures

235. As set out in point E. above, most interim measures under the Competition Act have been issued by the CNDC or the Secretariat. However, the increase in litigated cases has led several courts to issue injunctions as well, on matters such as the suspension of: (i) the merger review process,[165] (ii) interim measures dictated by the CNDC,[166] or (iii) the effects of a merger,[167] to (iv) imposing an obligation to deal.[168]

236. Cases where the courts have issued interim measures on competition matters unrelated to an ongoing investigation by the CNDC are relatively rare but on the rise. They are mostly circumscribed to the context of *amparo* proceedings, as will be seen immediately below.

§2. CIVIL ENFORCEMENT

I. Competent Civil Courts

237. The 1994 Reform of the Federal Constitution not only declared that authorities may protect competition, but also included this right within the potential scope of *amparo* proceedings.[169]

---

163. For example, in 'Investigación de oficio de los abonos de la televisión paga', Comisión Nacional de Defensa de la Competencia, Resolutions No. 8 (21 Jan. 2010) and 13 (2 Feb. 2010). Please note that, in other recent cases, interim measures have been applied by the Secretariat, the CNDC adopting an advisory role. *See*, e.g., 'Boldt S.A. y Ciccone Calcográfica s/ notificación art. 8 ley 25.156 (Conc. 847)', *infra* n. 505.
164. 'Cablevisión S.A. s/ medidas cautelares', CNCiv. Com. Fed., Sala II (19 Feb. 2010), 'DirecTV de Argentina S.A. s/ medidas cautelares', CNCiv. Com. Fed., Sala II (25 Feb. 2010), 'SADAIC c/ apelación de resolución de la Comisión Nacional de Defensa de la Competencia', CNCiv. Com. Fed., Sala II (21 Dec. 2010).
165. 'Belmonte Manuel y Asociación Ruralista Gral. Alvear', Juzg. Fed. San Rafael (16 Apr. 2004).
166. 'Cablevisión S.A. s/ medidas cautelares' and 'DirecTV de Argentina S.A. s/ medidas cautelares', *supra* n. 164.
167. For example, in 'Cervecería Argentina S.A. Isenbeck', CNCiv. Com. Fed., Sala III (24 Aug. 2006).
168. 'Medic World Mandatary S.A.', CNCom, Sala D [2002-II] JA, 119. This is an exceptional decision, as the interim measure was issued within a commercial lawsuit involving two private parties.
169. Const. Arg., Arts 42 and 43.

Part I, Ch. 5, Consequences of Violations 238–242

238. The *amparo* proceeding is defined as a type of swift individual or collective action, available in case of lack of an alternative more suitable legal proceeding, aimed at redressing the consequences of any act or omission of public authorities or private parties, which currently or imminently harm, restrict, alter or threaten, with patent arbitrariness or illegality, rights and guarantees recognized in the Federal Constitution, a Treaty or law. It should be noted that this action cannot be used to claim damages.

239. As regards competition cases, any affected individual, the ombudsman and consumer associations have standing to sue. The legal framework of the *amparo* proceedings is complemented by Law 16,986.[170] This Law, inter alia, provides that a first instance judge with jurisdiction over the place where the challenged act or omission had or may have effects (in cases under the Competition Law, a federal first instance judge) will hear the case. Sections 321 and 498 of the CPPN, which provide that *amparo* actions will follow the provisions regulating summary proceedings, also apply.

240. This type of constitutional action has been successfully used in a variety of well-publicized cases, to seek results – sometimes with the aid of interim measures – such as the suspension of a merger review process or a certain acquisition transaction,[171] the inclusion in a professionals network to which plaintiff had been excluded pursuant to an exclusionary abuse of dominance,[172] or the continuation of commercial activities of a company which had been prevented to do so by regulatory action.[173] When addressed to challenge conducts of private persons, it could be regarded as an alternative means of applying the principles of the Competition Law, without the intervention of the administrative authorities.

241. As regards actions for damages, section 51 of the Competition Act provides that:

> Individuals or legal entities injured by the acts prohibited by this law may initiate damage actions under the provisions of ordinary laws, before the competent judge.

242. The Competition Act has apparently facilitated private damages litigation, as it has not conditioned it to the progress of the administrative action before the competition agencies, as was the case of the Former Competition Act, which established in its section 4 that litigation could be initiated *only*:

---

170. Law No. 16,986 (20 Oct. 1966 [21050] BO) applies in the city of Buenos Aires and also in all cases handled by federal judges when the challenged act be issued by a national authority.
171. 'Belmonte Manuel y Asociación Ruralista Gral. Alvear', Juzg. Fed. San Rafael (16 Apr. 2004, 2 Dec. 2004 and 3 Aug. 2005) (interim measures suspending the administrative proceedings and the conclusion of the transaction and decision granting the *amparo*, respectively).
172. 'Berruti, Ricardo A, v. Círculo Odontológico Santafesino', Corte Sup. Just. Santa Fe (12 Dec. 2008), Lexis No. 70051248.
173. 'Unión de Consumidores de Argentina c/Cablevisión – Estado Nacional s/ Medida Cautelar', Juzg. Fed. Salta No. 2 (10 Nov. 2010).

(i) when the competition authority closed the investigation immediately after filing of a third-party complaint, due to failure to express a cause of action;
(ii) upon approval by the competition authority of a settlement with the investigated party to immediately or gradually cease with the investigated conducts;
(iii) upon issuance of the final decision imposing sanctions; or
(iv) upon closing of the investigation at the end of the administrative proceeding.[174]

243. In practice, the simplification of the requirements to file a civil action contained in the Competition Act may not be enough to fully separate the civil action from the result of the administrative proceedings. If the provisions of the CPPN were to come into play (which after the 2014 Amendment is not certain), it would be reasonable to assume that the provisions of the CCC regulating the interplay between civil and criminal actions should apply. In particular, the CCC provides that if a criminal proceeding is initiated before or during a related civil action, there can be no judgment on the civil case before a judgment on a criminal case is passed, with few exceptions that do not apply to competition cases.[175] Applying the foregoing provisions to the competition law framework, it could be argued that: (a) the opening of an investigation before the CNDC on a certain conduct would prevent a civil judge from passing a judgment on a damages claim based on the same antitrust infringement, but not adopting other actions; (b) a civil judge may not challenge a finding of anticompetitive behaviour made by the Secretariat on an earlier decision; (c) a civil judge may not make a finding of anticompetitive behaviour if a prior decision by the Secretariat did not find illegality in the same conduct; and (d) a judgment of a civil judge with res judicata effects (presumably because no administrative proceeding before the CNDC was initiated until its issuance) may not be affected by the holding of a subsequent decision on the same conduct by the Secretariat.

244. It would be possible to initiate the civil action without making a complaint before the CNDC, and a judge could adjudicate the case without a prior decision from the competition agency.[176] This in fact has occurred in at least the *Mar-tra* case,[177] where the Appeal Court ratified the lower court judgment which dismissed the damages claim based on an allegation of abuse of dominance, but due to lack of evidence. In spite of the foregoing, judgments of this type are so far extremely rare, maybe because of the powers expressly granted by the Competition Act to the

---

174. Notwithstanding, s. 4 of the Former Competition Act also provided that private litigation could be initiated after a period of eighteen months as of the commencement of the investigation had elapsed.
175. Sections 1774 to 1780, CCC.
176. On the issue of whether an administrative decision is required to initiate civil proceedings, please refer to Cabanellas de las Cuevas (h), *supra* para. 45, n. 1, at 389–392, and Cassagne, Bernardo, *Derecho Administrativo de la defensa de la competencia: ¿aplicación administrativa o judicial de la ley 25.156? Interrogantes y planteamientos* (EDA ed., 2003) at 281.
177. 'Mar-tra S.A. c. Carrefour Argentina S.A., C. Nac. Com, Sala D (8 Jul. 2009), LLO, AR/JUR/75486/2009.

Part I, Ch. 5, Consequences of Violations 245–248

CNDC and Secretariat for the assessment of anticompetitive actions and the comparative lack of specific skills to examine competition cases of many courts.

245. According to Argentinean law, the courts with jurisdiction to hear damage cases will be the ordinary commercial or civil courts, depending on whether the suit involves a commercial entity or, on the contrary, is between two or more individuals, respectively.[178]

246. Traditionally, only persons that effectively suffered the alleged damage had standing to sue for damages under competition laws. However, after the landmark Supreme Court decision in *Halabi*,[179] it would be reasonable to conclude (although the issue is far from settled) that homogenous individual interests with collective incidence (e.g., the interests of all consumers of a certain product sold at a supra-competitive price as a consequence of a cartel) may be brought to court in a damages action by only one of the persons of such group, or even the ombudsman or consumer associations[180].

247. The requirements to accept these types of class actions (albeit not in a damages context) were summarized in such case by the Supreme Court as follows:

> [B]ecause of the foregoing the Court understands that the formal admissibility of any collective action requires the verification of certain elemental requirements that make it viable, such as the precise identification of the affected group, the aptitude of those who pretend to assume its representation and the existence of an argumentation encompassing, beyond individual issues, matters of fact and law that may be common and homogenous to the entire group. It is also essential that a procedure is set up on each case to guarantee the proper notification of all those persons that may have an interest in the outcome of the litigation, so as to guarantee them the alternative of opting out of the lawsuit as well as appearing in it as party or counterparty. It is also required that adequate publicity measures are implemented in order to avoid the multiplication or juxtaposition of collective proceedings with the same object or purpose, to avoid the risk that different or contradictory judgments over the same matters be issued.

248. The statute of limitations of all actions for violations of the Competition Law is five years (section 54), and according to section 55, said term may be interrupted by the administrative complaint or the commission of another conduct

---

178. Decree No. 1285, 7 Feb. 1958 [18581] BO, 1.
179. 'Halabi, Ernesto c/PEN – ley 25.873, dto. 1563/04- s/Amparo ley 16.986', 332 Fallos 111 (2009).
180. Standing to sue in damage actions for breach of competition laws may be difficult to prove, as portrayed in the Court of First Instance judgment in re 'Asociación Protección Consumidores del Mercado Común del Sur c/ Loma Negra Cía. Industrial Argentina S.A. y otros s/ordinario', Juzg. Nac. de Prim. Inst. en lo Com. No. 24, Sec. No. 47 (23 Feb. 2011) which was however overturned, accepting plaintiff's standing to sue, by the Court of Appeals in 'Asociación Protección Cons del Mercado Común del Sur v. Loma Negra Cía. Industrial Argentina S.A. y otros', CNCom,Sala F (12 Dec. 2011).

prohibited by the Competition Law. Given the principle of *generalibus specialia derogant* (a specific law abrogates a more general one to the extent they conflict) it would seem reasonable that, as regards actions for damages, the referred term prevail over the one set forth under civil law principles, although now the latter is also of five years under section 2560 of the CCC.

249. In addition, the statute of limitations for damage actions should be suspended by virtue of the filing of a complaint based on the same anticompetitive practice before the CNDC (as was the holding of the court in *Auto Gas*,[181] by the opening of an administrative investigation ex officio as well).

250. Pursuant to section 63 of the CPN, the term is to be counted ' ... as from the midnight of the day in which the crime was committed or, should it be continuous, in which it ceased being committed'. The Supreme Court has stated, however, that in case the party affected by the infringement knew about its existence at a later date, such should be the date from which the statute of limitations should be counted.[182] As regards the reference to 'continuous crimes', it is worth noting that case law has recognized that violations included under the Former Competition Act (or the Competition Act, for that matter) are generally considered of such type, thus rarely declaring the expiration of the statute of limitations. This was the case of *Massalin*[183] as regards abuse of dominance conducts, and *Video Cable 6*[184] in connection with cartels.

II. Sanctions

A. Nullity

251. Under Argentinean law, acts that are prohibited by a law, such as the Competition Act, are null and void.[185]

252. From a procedural law perspective, it is common for the Secretariat to issue final decisions not only applying fines in connection with the relevant anticompetitive practice, but also ordering the cessation of the practice. This is probably because the act is to be considered automatically null only once such a decision is final, and the appeal of a cease-and-desist order does not stay its execution.

---

181. *See infra* n. 183.
182. 'Ponce, María Esther c/ Buenos Aires, Provincia de y otros s/ daños y perjuicios', 319 Fallos 1960 (1996); 'Cooper Oil Tool Argentina SAIC c/ Buenos Aires, Provincia de s/ sumario' 320 Fallos 1081 (1997), among others.
183. 'Massalin Particulares S.A. c/ Incidente de prescripción de la acción e incompetencia en autos principales 'SADIC s/ denuncia c/ Massalin Particulares S.A. s/ inf. Ley 22.262 (C. 403)', CNPenal Económico, Sala B (24 Nov. 2011).
184. *Supra* n. 116.
185. CCC, s. 386.

Part I, Ch. 5, Consequences of Violations

B. Damages

253. On 16 September 2009, the decision of the National Court of First Instance on Commercial matters 14, Secretary 27 in *Auto Gas*[186] became the first one known awarding damages caused by anticompetitive practices.

254. This case originated in the ARS 109 million fine imposed in 1999 by the Secretariat of Industry, Commerce and Mining – pursuant to the recommendation of the CNDC – to YPF for abuse of dominant position in the bulk LPG market. Said anticompetitive practice, according to the CNDC, comprised the restriction of domestic LPG supply and resulting price increase, by means of the export of excess LPG with the prohibition of its re-importing to Argentina.

255. The fine was affirmed in 2000 by the National Court of Appeals for Economic Crimes and in 2002 by the Supreme Court. It was in this last year that plaintiff filed the lawsuit.

256. Auto Gas alleged a series of items of damages directly or indirectly related to the anticompetitive practice, to wit: (i) overprice paid to YPF; (ii) lost LPG sales due to the restriction on supply; and (iii) reduction in the value of the company stemming from the above-mentioned restriction.

257. However, the lawsuit included items of damages stemming from abusive practices different from those sanctioned in the administrative proceeding and regarding which no declaration of illegality had been made by the CNDC or any court of law, to wit: (i) price discrimination on sales to plaintiff and its competitors; (ii) interruption of supply of LPG; (iii) price squeeze implemented by YPF and YPF Gas (the latter being plaintiff's competitor) by which the former allegedly increased the sale price of LPG to plaintiff and the latter decreased the retail price of LPG to the end consumer; and (iv) illegal filling of plaintiff's gas bottles by defendants.

258. Based almost exclusively on reports by the court-appointed economic and accounting expert witnesses and even when admitting the difficulty in the determination of the precise damage, the court ruled on the liability of defendants in the following items:

(i) *Overpricing*: the damage was valued at 30% of the claimed amount, expressly recognizing that plaintiff passed most of the overprice to the end consumer (passing on defence).
(ii) *Lost profits*: due to difficulties in determining the type of earnings to be considered, its forecast and the period involved, only 15% of the claimed amount was recognized, and

---

186. 'Auto Gas S.A.', Juzg. Nac. de Prim. Inst. en lo Com. No. 14, Sec. No. 27 (16 Sep. 2009).

(iii) *Discrimination among local bulk LPG retailers*: 50% of the claimed amount was admitted, worth noting given that said conduct was not discussed in the CNDC file.

259. However, the court rejected certain items of damages such as the interruption of supply (it was proved that it stemmed from plaintiff's lack of payment), price squeeze (not proved, a similar complaint had been rejected by the CNDC) and the illegal filling of plaintiff's gas bottles (filling of only an insignificant quantity was allegedly proved).

260. The judge awarded total damages of approximately ARS 13,094,457, plus interest and attorneys' and expert witnesses' fees.

261. The decision was partially reversed on appeal and is being reviewed by the Supreme Court.

C. Interim Measures

262. The principle set forth in the CPCCN is that interim measures may be issued by the tribunal who may decide on the substantive issues of the case.[187] Giving the fact that the Competition Act provides for the jurisdiction of certain courts to hear on appeal, a reasonable interpretation leads to conclude that the relevant Federal Court of Appeals in the provinces and the Federal Civil and Commercial Court of Appeal or National Court of Appeals in Economic Crimes in the City of Buenos Aires would be empowered to issue such measures, as in practice regularly takes place.

263. When the object of interim measures is not related to an act that may be subject to appeal under the Competition Act, like, i.e., to challenge a lack of quorum of the CNDC to issue valid decisions or to impose on such agency a limitation as to its possibility to issue injunctions, in the City of Buenos Aires the courts with jurisdiction on contentious-administrative matters may also have jurisdiction.[188]

264. In addition, the CPCCN allows, under exceptional circumstances, that courts that otherwise would not have jurisdiction on the substance of the case can still issue interim measures, even if they then declare themselves incompetent and hand over the file to the competent court.[189]

265. Interim measures can be requested by any person individually affected and also the enforcement authority of the Competition Act, as provided for in section 18 l) of the Competition Act. As usual, they require the fulfilment of the *fumus bonus*

---

187. CPCCN, s. 196.
188. *See*, e.g., 'Multicanal S.A. y otro', *supra* n. 154, and 'W de Argentina Inversiones S.L. c/ Telecom Italia SpA y otro s/ medida cautelar (autónoma)', CNCont. Adm. Fed., Sala III (6 Nov. 2009).
189. CPCCN, s. 196, para. 2.

Part I, Ch. 5, Consequences of Violations   266–268

juris (the applicant has the right to ask for an interim measure) and *periculum in mora* (if an interim measure is not imposed, it may jeopardize the effectiveness of a future decision) requirements. Courts may require the posting of a bond as guarantee in case the interim measure does not ultimately prevail.

266. In the context of competition law proceedings, interim measures generally adopt the form of restraining orders (*medidas de no innovar*), addressed to suspend the effect of a certain act of the Administration and maintain the *status quo ante* during the pendency of a judicial proceeding on the substance of the case, for the purpose of preventing that the effects of such act of Government may turn the judgment on the substance ineffective.

267. For example, in *Indura*,[190] plaintiff requested the court to order the CNDC to abstain from continuing a cartel investigation until the appeal against the denial to nullify the proceedings was resolved; in *Compañía Industrial Cervecera*,[191] to prevent a divestment which left aside plaintiff as a potential acquirer in the context of a merger proceeding; in *Belmonte*,[192] to suspend a merger proceeding until the Tribunal was formed; in *Isenbeck*,[193] to prevent a final decision on a merger review process until it was decided if plaintiff could be a party to the proceedings; and in *Unión de Consumidores de Argentina*,[194] to abstain from interrupting operations of an ISP.

268. The CPCCN,[195] however, also allows for a broader, 'generic' type of interim measures (*medidas cautelares genéricas*) in case of 'imminent and irreparable danger'. One of the few, and perhaps the most extraordinary of those measures so far was issued in *Supercanal*,[196] where plaintiff, a cable operator of the province of Mendoza, argued that defendant Cablevisión, as a consequence of its challenged merger with Multicanal (please refer to paragraphs 474 et seq.), had committed a number of exclusionary practices that could only be prevented by the application of a structural measure like the separation of the two entities. The court then ordered that, in the term of sixty days, a number of actions be implemented to achieve a full separation of, inter alia, the two companies' networks, clients, accounts, administration and trademarks, and appointed a court official as

---

190. 'Indura S.A. c./ Comisión Nacional de Defensa de la Competencia', CNCiv. Com. Fed., Sala III, Lexis 7005863 (24 Apr. 2002).
191. 'Compañía Industrial Cervecera S.A. c. Estado Nacional -Secretaría de la Competencia, la Desregulación y Defensa del Consumidor- s/ Acción de Amparo -Medida Cautelar', Juzg. Fed. Salta No. 2 (5 Mar. 2003).
192. 'Belmonte Manuel y Asociación Ruralista Gral. Alvear', *supra* n. 165.
193. 'Cervecería Argentina Sociedad Anónima Isenbeck S.A.', CNCiv. Com. Fed., Sala III [7366] LLO (2004).
194. 'Unión de Consumidores de Argentina c/Cablevisión – Estado Nacional s/ Medida Cautelar', *supra* n. 173.
195. Article 232: 'Other than the cases contemplated in the preceding sections, a person having due cause to fear that during the time preceding the judicial recognition of his right the same may suffer an imminent and irreparable danger may request the urgent measures which, according to the circumstances, be more suitable to provisionally guarantee the enforcement of the judgment.'
196. 'Supercanal S.A. c/ Cablevisión S.A. por Amparo', Juzg. Fed. Mendoza No. 1 (16 Dec. 2011).

co-manager of the company for twelve months to achieve the foregoing. The decision seems excessive, particularly considering the lack of substantiation of the allegations of wrongdoing by the court, and appears to confirm that interim measures adopted in the context of *amparo* proceedings may, under certain circumstances, become a 'fast-track' alternative for achieving what would otherwise be more difficult before the CNDC.[197]

§3. CRIMINAL ENFORCEMENT

I. Criminal Sanctions for Antitrust Violations

269. The Competition Act does not contemplate criminal sanctions, as opposed to the Former Competition Act. As anticipated, sections 300, item 1 and 309, item 1 a) of the CPN (Chapter V: Frauds in Commerce and Industry) specifically sanctions cartel activity as follows:

> Section 300, item 1
> Jailing from six months to two years shall be imposed on:
> 1. Any person who causes the price of any good, bonds or securities to raise or drop by means of false news, fictitious negotiations or by connivance or coalition among the principal holders of such good or product, with the purpose of not selling it or not selling it at a specific price.
> Section 309, item 1 a)
> Jailing from one to four years, fine equivalent to the amount of the transaction and disqualification for up to five years shall be imposed to:
> a. Any person who carries out transactions or operations causing the increase, maintenance or decrease of the price of negotiable instruments and other financial securities, by means of false news, fictitious negotiations or by connivance or coalition among the principal holders of such good or product, with the purpose of producing the appearance of higher liquidity or negotiating it at a specific price.

270. It must be noted however, that no individual has been sanctioned under the referred to provision, although in one case individuals have been indicted by a court.[198]

II. Other Application of Criminal Law to Relevant Conducts

271. Section 56 of the Competition Act provides that, in all situations not contemplated in the law and its regulation (the Regulation), the Administrative Proceedings Law No. 19,549 shall apply. This reference was introduced by the 2014 Amendment, as section 57 of the Competition Act provided – and inexplicably still

---

197. This decision was ultimately reversed by the Supreme Court.
198. 'González Correa, Tristán y otros', CNPenal Económico, Sala B (20 Mar. 2006).

Part I, Ch. 5, Consequences of Violations

does – that Law 19,549 *did not* apply, as in its original wording the Competition Act provided for the subsidiary application of the CPN and the CPPN. Given the perception that the changes introduced by the 2014 Amendment will be temporary, and the general lack of case law based on the subsidiary application of Law No. 19,549, we will still refer to judicial precedents which applied the CPN and CPPN.

272. The CPN and CPPN have generally been applied to decide in issues such as venue,[199] jurisdiction,[200] defence, counsel,[201] serving of notice,[202] access to the administrative file,[203] general terms of the legal proceeding, nullifications,[204] evidence,[205] motions to dismiss and appeals. With particular reference to this last point, the courts have expanded the list of decisions subject to appeal in the Competition Act to those that, as provided for in section 449 of the CPPN, also cause irreparable harm.[206]

273. Note should be taken, however, that with the exception of the above-cited provisions of the CPN, which have almost never been applied, all anticompetitive conducts under the Competition Act are considered administrative infractions and not crimes, irrespective of the remittance to the CPN and CPPN, inherited from the Former Competition Act which did provide that concerted practices were to be considered crimes.

III. Role of Prosecutors

274. There are no prosecutors under the Competition Act. The decision to open an investigation rests upon the CNDC (and in the future, the Tribunal).

275. In spite of the foregoing and in a manner that could be deemed unconstitutional, section 26 of the Regulation empowered the Secretariat to:

---

199. 'Cablevisión S.A. s/ solicitud de inhibitoria', CNCiv. Com. Fed., Sala II (9 Aug. 2005), whereby plaintiff requested that the courts of the city of Buenos Aires – where the alleged conduct was in any case decided as was where the headquarters of the company were located – and not those of the province of Santa Fe – where the alleged cartel had had effects – were to assume jurisdiction over the case.
200. *Ibid.*
201. For example, s. 105 of the CPPN provides that the investigated party may not be defended simultaneously by more than two lawyers. This provision has been raised on occasions by the CNDC to allow not more than one lawyer to represent a party in testimonial hearings.
202. 'Repsol YPF S.A. Red XXI', CNCiv. Com. Fed., Sala I (22 Apr. 2004).
203. 'Negri Carlos Alberto s/ recurso de queja s/ resolución de Defensa de la Competencia', CNCiv. Com. Fed., Sala II (5 Feb. 2008).
204. For example, as a consequence of lack of quorum of the CNDC, or the intervention, assistance and representation of the investigated party, to be requested before the CNDC or an Appeal Court.
205. In particular, provisions related to search warrants are only included in the CPPN.
206. 'Cervecería Argentina Sociedad Anónima Isenbeck S.A.', CNCiv. Com. Fed., Sala III [7366] LLO (2004) and 'PSH y otros s/recurso de queja (PSE. Holding LLC)', CNCiv. Com. Fed., Sala III [7/11891] Lexis Nexis (2002), among many others.

(i) make complaints;
 (ii) receive copy of all complaints; ex officio and made by third parties;
 (iii) be a party in the proceedings;
 (iv) carry out market investigations and request information to third parties to such end;
 (v) produce technical evidence over books, documents and remaining items that may be conducive to the investigation, control inventories, verify origin and costs or raw materials or other goods;
 (vi) conduct searches on private premises, with the consent of the resident therein or upon obtaining of a search warrant from a competent judge, which must decide on the request within twenty-four hours;
 (vii) request the issuance of interim measures; and
(viii) offer evidence and file appeals.

276. The aforementioned provisions have in practice still not been applied by the Secretariat, given that they were drafted assuming the formation of the Tribunal as an independent adjudicatory agency. As has been explained above, currently the Secretariat is the adjudicatory authority of the Competition Act, and as such could not have the role of prosecutor.

277. On 20 May 2009, the HR approved a bill incorporating a new section 24*bis* to the Competition Act.[207] This bill, which as of the date of this report has lost parliamentary status, appointed the Under Secretariat of Consumer Defence (which is under the auspices of the Secretariat, and consequently subject to its same contradictions insofar as the latter be the adjudicatory authority of the Competition Act) as prosecutor in all competition matters (investigations and merger control filings), with similar empowerments than those already included in the Regulation for the Secretariat.

IV. Competent Criminal Courts

278. In *Repsol YPF*,[208] the Supreme Court held that the competent court in the City of Buenos Aires to hear on appeals of decisions issued by the antitrust authorities was the National Court of Appeals on Economic Crimes. The Court, following the opinion of the Attorney General, considered that the criminal court was more proficient to deal with the Competition Act and that said choice was coherent with the provisions of former section 56 thereof (which, as was mentioned above, provided for the subsidiary application of the CPN and CPPN).

279. After *Repsol YPF*, however, some chambers of the Federal Civil and Commercial Courts of the City of Buenos Aires continued hearing appeals on decisions under the Competition Act – given that the Supreme Court case failed to refer to the language of section 53 of the Regulation, which expressly granted jurisdiction to

---
207. File 2498-D-2008.
208. 'Repsol YPF GLP envasado en la Ciudad de San Nicolás', 329 Fallos 860 (2006).

Part I, Ch. 5, Consequences of Violations 280–280.1

them – while others declared their lack of jurisdiction. More recently, all such Chambers hear competition cases.[209]

280. In the more recent *Telecom Italia* case,[210] the Attorney General reaffirmed its opinion on *Repsol YPF*, suggesting that section 53 of the Regulation was unconstitutional. The Supreme Court, however, failed to expressly address the potential unconstitutionality of section 53 of the Regulation and decided the case on other grounds, and Justice Petracchi, on his dissenting opinion, pointed out that insofar as section 53 was not declared unconstitutional, *Repsol YPF* erred in attributing jurisdiction to the criminal courts.

280.1. As anticipated in 65.1. above, the 2014 Amendment created the National Court of Appeals in Consumer Protection Matters, with jurisdiction in the City of Buenos Aires, as appeal court on competition matters in replacement of the Federal Civil and Commercial Court of Appeals and the National Court of Appeals on Economic Crimes. This new Court of Appeals should have become operational in a term of 180 days as from the publication of the Amendment, but has not been formed as of the date of this report. Consequently, the discussion above on the competent appeal court remains open.

---

209. Please refer to Ch. 2. *Challenging of the administrative decision, infra.*
210. 'Telecom Italia S.p.A. y otro s/ solicitud de inhibitoria', 333 Fallos 385 (2010).

Part II. The Application of the Prohibitions

Chapter 1. Restrictive Agreements

§1. HORIZONTAL AGREEMENTS

I. Cartels

281. The track record of the antitrust authorities as regards cartels is not very impressive. Finding the reason for this under enforcement is not easy, but some hints can be found on the recurring application of price controls – which sometimes created incentives for competitors to collude, both during the period of price regulation as well as after the controls were lifted – and the lack of good investigative techniques. More recently, as from the passing of the Competition Act in 1999, merger control became a central part of competition policy, downgrading the importance of antitrust investigations. Evidence of the foregoing is that only very few cartel cases have been adjudicated under the Competition Law.[211]

A. *Price-Fixing*

282. The first price-fixing cartel case under the Former Competition Act was decided in 1986 and involved the sand market of the Buenos Aires area,[212] where collusion was found among manufacturers and labour unions commanding the relevant shipping companies. The unions helped in the monitoring of the cartel in exchange for an agreement by the sand companies to maintain a certain employment and salary level.

283. The investigation gathered sufficient evidence to impose fines to both the sand companies and the unions. It is also worth noting that the CNDC followed a sensible economic approach to define the concept of 'general economic interest', by stating that:

---

211. The reader should bear in mind that given that CNDC decisions are not made public until a final decision of the Secretariat is issued, there might be several closed investigations where the CNDC has recommended the application of sanctions that still lack the Secretariat's decision and thus are not considered herein.
212. 'Silos Areneros Buenos Aires S.A. Comercial y empresas y sindicatos obreros', Secretaría de Comercio Interior, Resolution No. 442 (27 Oct. 1986).

[P]rice is an information provided by the market itself in order that offerors and consumers adapt their demands until reaching a situation of equilibrium. Price is no more than the reflection of the transactions effectively carried out in the market, which when operating in freedom may reach its equilibrium. If through a mechanism of market planification the offer is artificially reduced, the achievement of such equilibrium would be difficult and delayed, then being probable that the increase in the price of sand has disincentived demand of such product, which to some extent may have contributed to extend the crisis in the construction sector, and consequently the sand sector, more than necessary. The search of such equilibrium through the market was the objective of the legislator when he specifically included such conducts within the several types of anticompetitive practices.

284. Two years later, two other cartels in the same business were sanctioned.[213] The collusive agreements were even agreed in writing and the participating companies showed an evident lack of understanding of competition laws, given that they justified the agreement by the industry crisis. A common feature of the two decisions mentioned above is that in neither of the two cases the CNDC made a thorough analysis of the effects of the cartel in the relevant market, as the Former Competition Act would have required. Nonetheless, they involved a majority of the producers of sand, and it is unlikely that a technical definition of the relevant market would have led to a different outcome.

285. In 1989, an important decision in the LPG was issued,[214] which was reversed by the National Court of Appeals on Economic Crimes on the basis that it lacked adequate reasoning.[215] The case was remanded to the CNDC, which issued a new decision that was ratified by the Under Secretariat of Industry and Commerce in June 1991.[216] The case involved collusion by LPG producers through the industry trade association, which had been given the role of monitoring agent. The members of the association amounted to 85% of the relevant market. The cartel also allocated clients through a system of distribution of LPG bottles directed by the association. The new decision of the Under Secretariat was for the most part confirmed by the Appellate Court,[217] and the case was ultimately decided by the Supreme Court, which confirmed the Court of Appeals' decision.[218] The Supreme Court's decision remains a landmark case insofar as it clarified that the Former Competition Act – and this principle also applies to the Competition Act – does not require the harm to the 'general economic interest' to be effectively produced, but

---

213. 'Arenera del Litoral S.R.L y otros', Secretaría de Comercio Interior, Resolution No. 361 (26 Aug. 1988).
214. 'A. Gas S. A. y otras c. Agip Argentina S. A. y otras', Secretaría de Comercio Interior, Resolution No. 132 (Dic. 14, 1989).
215. 'A. Gas S.A. y otras c. Agip Argentina S.A. y otras', CNPenal Económico, Sala II (6 Apr. 1990).
216. 'A. Gas S.A. y otras c. Agip Argentina S.A. y otras', Subsecretaría de Industria y Comercio, Resolution No. 175 (21 Jun. 1991).
217. 'A. Gas S.A., Agip Argentina S.A.', CNPenal Económico, Sala II, JA-1993-II, 251.
218. 'A. Gas S.A. y otros c. AGIP Argentina S. A.', 316 Fallos 2561 (1993).

Part II, Ch. 1, Restrictive Agreements

only that the anticompetitive conduct *may have* the potentiality to produce it.[219] The decision was instrumental in releasing the antitrust authorities in future cases from the burden of proving the actual effects of anticompetitive conducts.

286. In 1996, a group of port operators were investigated as a consequence of their application, through their trade association, of an overcharge per container.[220] Evidence of the cartel was clear, and the defendants tried to justify their conduct by the increasing labour costs stemming from a union conflict. Fines imposed varied depending on the benefits obtained by each cartel member (i.e., parties which applied the overcharge more times received increased fines).[221]

287. The sand business was subject to a new investigation which ended up in fines being applied in 2003.[222] The investigation was prompted by a complaint by the Argentinean Construction Chamber, which alleged that a regional trade association was again used for collusive purposes, and that as of the creation of the association, which acted as middleman for its members, prices of sand had increased in a range of between 10% and 70%. The investigation led to the findings that the association: (i) had sent letters to the construction companies of the area indicating the new prices under which sand would be sold and informing that future purchases of sand had to be made through the association; (ii) kept detailed registries of the commercial operations of its members; (iii) would, in most of the cases, do the invoicing. A number on each invoice indicated which company had made the sale; and (iv) held regular meetings in which different aspects of the cartel were agreed.

288. The case is also interesting on two other grounds. First, the complainants and the investigated companies reached a private agreement which was presented with the CNDC and rejected by it, as competition matters, and in particular collusive conducts, cannot be disposed of by private agreement.

289. In addition, it is worth noting that at some advanced stage of the investigation the parties tried to settle the case through the commitment to a series of self-undertakings, which included the ultimate dissolution of the trade association. The CNDC was of the view that the assessment could not be accepted given the nature of the infringement and that the damage to the general economic interest had effectively occurred, thus the settlement could not lead to the investigated companies remaining unscathed after they had clearly profited from the legal conduct.

290. The fine that was applied to the companies was graded upon the volume of sand sold through the association and the difference between the price imposed by

---

219. The Supreme Court clarified though that the harm which may be produced should be specific and reasonably identifiable for each particular case.
220. 'Administración General de Puertos Sociedad del Estado c/ Centro Coordinador de Actividades Portuarias' Secretaría de Industria, Comercio y Minería, Resolution No. 382 (3 Dec. 1996).
221. Germán Coloma, Defensa De La Competencia (Ciudad Argentina ed., 2009) at 164.
222. 'Cooperativa Entrerriana de Productores Mineros Ltda. s/ infracción Ley 22.262', Secretaría de Coordinación Técnica, Resolution No. 46 (16 Sep. 2003).

it and the average price in force before its creation (intended as a rough estimate of the *supra* competitive margin applied by the cartel).

291. In 2003, the Secretariat of Technical Coordination imposed fines to several LPG companies acting in the city of Bariloche, province of Río Negro.[223] The fines in themselves were immaterial, unless it is considered that the cartel in question lasted only one month. The background of the case refers to a regional LPG retailer of the neighbouring city of El Bolsón, heavily subsidized, which entered into a price war with its competitors, subsidiaries of international companies. The month of the alleged collusion the price of LPG of said local retailer jumped by 50%, at the level of its competitors. A month later, however, the Governor of the Province of Río Negro extended the subsidies to the city of Bariloche, thus re-establishing the competitive level-playing field.

292. The case is surprising as regards the scarce evidence under which the antitrust authorities adjudicated the case: proof of parallel conduct and the testimony of a manager and distributor of one of the competitors. The administrative decision was reversed by the Federal Court of General Roca, province of Río Negro in 2004[224] but was affirmed by the Supreme Court.[225] The High Court decided that the Courts of Appeals' decision was both arbitrary – as it had omitted to consider relevant evidence as regards at least one of the parties – as well as incorrect in its interpretation of the Former Competition Act. In this last connection, it is interesting to note that the Court of Appeals had accepted the arguments of one of the parties in that the 'general economic interest' could not have been affected because none of the presumed members of the cartel had had any gains in the relevant period. This argument stemmed from a superficial interpretation of the parties of the 1997 Report, which defined 'total welfare' as the sum of 'consumer welfare' and 'producers' welfare'.[226]

293. In spite of the case described in the preceding paragraph where the CNDC, rightfully or not, believed that there was enough evidence to determine the existence of a cartel, the holding that parallel conduct in itself does not suffice to find a cartel seems to be well established in other decisions.[227]

---

223. 'Comerciantes de la Ciudad de San Carlos de Bariloche s/ infracción Ley 22.262', *supra* n. 105.
224. 'Repsol YPF Gas S.A. – Cooperativa de Obras y Servicios Publicos, Sociales y Viviendas El Bolson Ltda. (Coopetel Ltda.) – Totalgaz Argentina S.A. – Shell Gas S.A. s/infracción a la Ley 22.262', CF Gral. Roca [327] JA, 3723 (2004).
225. 'Repsol Yacimientos Petrolíferos Fiscales Gas S.A. y otros', 330 Fallos 2192 (2007).
226. Subsequent to the Supreme Court decision, however, the Court of Appeals handed down a new judgment revoking the administrative decision which imposed the fines due to the expiration of the statute of limitations, and the Supreme Court rejected the extraordinary appeal filed by the Government. *See* 'Repsol YPF Gas SA – Cooperativa de Obras y Servicios Públicos Sociales y Viviendas El Bolsón Ltda (Coopetel LEDS) – Totalgas Argentina SA – Shell Gas SA s/ infracción Ley 22.262', CSJN, file R 884 XLIV (26 Jun. 2012).
227. 'YPF Sociedad Anónima, Esso Sociedad Anónima Petrolera Argentina, Shell Compañía Argentina de Petróleo Sociedad Anónima', Secretaría de Comercio e Inversiones, Resolution No. 99 (11 Apr. 1994); 'Defensor del Pueblo de Posadas y otros', Secretaría de Industria, Comercio y Minería,

Part II, Ch. 1, Restrictive Agreements 293.1–295

293.1. On 12 December 2014 the Secretariat imposed surprisingly heavy fines (in excess of ARS1 billion, approximately EUR 95.7 million) on several major automobile manufacturers (Fiat, Ford, GM, Honda, Peugeot-Citroën, Renault and VW) for alleged concerted practices in the sale of automobiles, for their resale in the southernmost province of Tierra del Fuego.[228] The decision states that the companies implemented a series of actions aimed at artificially maintaining the price of vehicles sold in such province (which is subject to a special tax regime whereby transactions carried out therein are exempt from federal taxes) as high as in the rest of the country. Those practices included the decision to nationalize the vehicles outside Tierra del Fuego prior to their resale to the dealers network, and mostly failing to import from Tierra del Fuego non-Mercosur vehicles at a 0% customs rate, which would have allegedly fostered competition with Mercosur-made models, as automobiles made in the Mercosur – the South American free trade bloc – are exempt from customs taxes as well. The decision was reversed on appeal,[229] as the court was not convinced of the evidentiary value and cohesiveness of the 'facilitating practices' identified by the CNDC and the Secretariat in support of their decision.

294. In recent years, some price-fixing cartel investigations have been opened with possible political considerations in mind. An example of the foregoing can be found in the pay-TV market,[230] where an injunction was issued by the CNDC to prevent a future price increase presumably derived from a price-fixing cartel. Shortly after the parties obtained from the courts an interim measure suspending the effects of that of the CNDC, the Secretariat issued a regulation fixing maximum prices for the entire industry,[231] which made evident that the CNDC investigation was motivated on non-competition concerns. This case along with a similar one in the retail sector[232] are two of very few cases where the CNDC has issued injunctions to prevent allegedly collusive conducts.

B. *Market/Client Allocation*

295. As stated in section A above, several price-fixing cases also include some sort of market or client allocation, since obviously the latter is a way to achieve the former. For illustrative purposes, we will refer to only three cases, two of which represent the most important cartel decisions issued as of the date of this report.

Resolution No. 366 (31 May 1999); 'Dirección General de Comercio Interior y Defensa del Consumidor de la Provincia de Entre Ríos', Secretaría de la Competencia, la Desregulación y la Defensa del Consumidor, Resolution No. 107 (7 Sep. 2001); and mainly, 'Asociación de Agencias de Viaje de Buenos Aires (AVIABUE)', *supra* n. 103.
228. 'Hugo Atilio Riello Gasperini y José Luis Catalán Magni s/ solicitud de intervención de la CNDC', Secretariat of Trade, Resolution No. 271 (12 Dec. 2014).
229. C. Fed. Com. Riv., 'Honda Motors Argentina S.A. y otros c/ Estado Nacional – Secretaría de Comercio s/ Recurso directo Ley 25.156' (13 Aug. 2015).
230. 'Investigación de oficio de los abonos de la televisión paga', *supra* n. 163.
231. Resolution No. 50/2010 of the Secretaríat of Domestic Trade, *supra* n. 142.
232. Comisión Nacional de Defensa de la Competencia, Resolution No. 131/2009 (19 Nov. 2009).

296. The *Cement Cartel* case[233] initiated at the end of August 1999 after a publication of a magazine article which referred to the existence of a nationwide cartel in the cement industry which included market allocation, boycott, price-fixing, information exchange practices and bid rigging, among other collusive practices. The publication was based on the statements of an informant, a former employee of one of the cement companies, which on appearance had written a book describing allegedly collusive practices in the cement industry during a period of over ten years. Even though the alleged informant never appeared before the CNDC, the journalist who wrote the article did, and furnished all the documents on which he based his publication. Fines of over ARS 309 million were applied, the highest ever as of the date of this report.[234]

297. The decision was confirmed by the Court of Appeals[235] and ultimately by the Supreme Court[236] and so far stands out as a notable victory in cartel enforcement for the antitrust agencies.

298. Not surprisingly, it raised a number of procedural as well as substantive issues worth considering, such as the following:

299. Applicable law. The case was pending at the time of enactment of the Competition Act, and as provided for in section 58 of said law, was decided under the Former Competition Act. An argument was made as to which of the two laws had to be considered as more lenient to the accused under the principle of retroactive leniency, it being decided in favour of the Former Competition Act.

300. The statute of limitations that applied to the issuance of the final administrative decision that imposed the fine: the Former Competition Act did not specifically provide for such a term, although it did contemplate the term of six years for the commencement of the 'criminal action'.

301. In the Supreme Court ruling in the *YPF* case,[237] it was decided that such six-year term applied to the commencement of the judicial action by the Secretary of State before the courts in the case of concerted conducts, which under the Former Competition Act could receive criminal sanctions in addition to the ones imposed by the Secretary of State as a consequence of the prior administrative proceeding. In the case no criminal action was filed and only an administrative investigation was

---

233. *Supra* n. 107.
234. Loma Negra S.A. received a fine of ARS 138,7 M; Minetti S.A., ARS 100,1 M; Cementos Avellaneda S.A., ARS 34,6 M; Cemento San Martín S.A., ARS 28,5 M; Petroquímica Comodoro Rivadavia S.A., ARS 7,3 M and the Cement Trade Association (*Asociación de Fabricantes de Cemento Portland*), ARS 529,289. It is worth noting, however, that the ARS 109 M fine imposed to YPF S.A. in 1999 was applied at a time where the parity between the Argentine Peso and the US Dollar was 1:1.
235. 'Loma Negra Compañía Industrial S.A. y otros', n. 102.
236. 'Recurso de Hecho deducido por Loma Negra S.A. y Cemento San Martín S.A. en la causa Loma Negra Compañía Industrial S.A. y otros s/ Ley 22.262', CSJN, L. 154. XLV (7 May 2013), among others.
237. *Supra* n. 91.

Part II, Ch. 1, Restrictive Agreements

pursued, however, the Supreme Court had decided that section 62 item 5 of the CPN applied, which contemplates a statute of limitation of just two years.

302. The Court of Appeals in the *Cement Cartel* case departed from this opinion since it understood that, inter alia, considering that the criminal action under the Former Competition Act could be initiated once the administrative proceeding that resulted in an imposition of an administrative sanction was finalized, it was unreasonable to conclude that the former action had a statute of limitation of six years, while the latter one of just two years. It then held that the six-year statute of limitations contemplated in section 35 of the Former Competition Act applied to both the administrative as well as the criminal proceedings under the Former Competition Act. It is worth noting that the Court of Appeals' decision was ultimately accepted for review by the National Criminal Court of Cassation,[238] which issued a decision on 9 September 2011 reversing the judgment due to its departure from the holding of *YPF* as regards the applicable statute of limitations.[239] However, little over three months later, the same Court of Cassation, with a different composition, annulled the prior decision at the request of the Government due to the fact that the latter had not been given participation in the appeal.[240]

303. Treatment of cartels as single or continuous conduct. Whether cartels had to be considered as a sum of several single collusive conducts, each with its own statute of limitations, or, on the contrary, as a single, continuous conduct which statute of limitations would be counted as from the ceasing of the same. The latter was the view adopted by the CNDC and confirmed by the Court of Appeals, which allowed for an investigation of the activity of the cartel during a term of eighteen years.

304. Evidence. The evidential value of the 'book' prepared by a presumed former employee of one of the investigated companies, given that said person did not provide testimony before the CNDC, although the journalist who contributed said material to the CNDC confirmed that he had received it from such employee.

305. Information exchange. The confirmation of the illegality of the exchange of confidential commercial information between competitors.

306. Concurrently with the passing of the resolution on the *Cement Cartel* case, the CNDC and Secretariat decided another important cartel case, in the liquid oxygen market.[241] This was the first cartel case decided under the Competition Act.

307. The *Liquid Oxygen* case bears little resemblance with the particularities of the *Cement Cartel* case. It was investigated and sanctioned under the Competition

---

238. *See supra* n. 104.
239. 'Cementos San Martín S.A. y Loma Negra S.A. s/ recurso de casación', CNCP, Sala IV (9 Sep. 2011).
240. 'Cementos San Martín S.A. y Loma Negra S.A. s/ nulidad', CNCP, Sala IV (12 Dec. 2011).
241. 'Oxígeno Liquido', *supra* n. 106.

Act, and consequently lacked most of the procedural issues raised in the other case as a consequence of the passing of the new legislation. It is also a rather pure market allocation case, and there was no trade association involved.

308. The probe was initiated ex officio due to the suspicion of the existence of a cartel in the companies providing medicinal oxygen to public and private hospitals. A search was conducted in the companies' premises, which led to the finding of numerous memorandums, e-mails and other documents with specific reference to a market allocation and bid rigging cartel. In addition, the CNDC collected several testimonies to the same effect from hospitals staff in charge of procurement.

309. This case is interesting in at least two respects.

310. On one hand, it is the single conduct case to date where an economic concentration – in the instant case, the acquisition of Messer by competitor Air Liquide – was considered an anticompetitive practice in itself and ancillary to the cartel behaviour which prompted the investigation. This is particularly relevant when considered that such acquisition did not require a mandatory filing. The CNDC argued that Messer was one of the few companies showing a willingness to compete – even though it apparently was also part of the cartel – and considered Air Liquide's acquisition as restricting competition, even though, as alleged by the defendant, the acquisition had been made at a worldwide level and consequently it was most probably not made with the *intention* to affect the Argentine market. It is worth noting that proof of intent is not required under the Competition Act, as a consequence of which the decision of the CNDC seems a reasonable one.

311. On the other hand, the CNDC applied for the first time the fining guidelines contained in the Competition Act, and thus took into account:

(i) the scope of the cartel: (a) formed by companies concentrating almost the entire offer of liquid oxygen; (b) with participation of high-level employees; (c) its nationwide reach; and (d) its length (five years);
(ii) the fact that several of the companies involved in the cartel had been exposed to fines for similar conducts in other countries; and
(iii) the assets and turnover of the parties.

312. As a consequence of the foregoing, total fines in excess of ARS 70 million were imposed. The decision was confirmed by the Federal Court of Appeals on Civil and Commercial Matters of the City of Buenos Aires[242], and is being heard by the Supreme Court.

313. In 2006, the Secretariat decided a case related to the alleged allocation of distributors between two LPG producers in the Province of Misiones.[243]

---

242. 'Air Liquide Argentina y otros s. apelación resolución de la Comisión Nacional de Defensa dela Competencia', CNCiv. Com. Fed., Sala III (10 Aug. 2012), elDial.com, AA7E65.
243. 'Ref. Eleva Denuncia', Secretaría de Comercio Interior, Resolution No. 32 (20 Oct. 2006).

Part II, Ch. 1, Restrictive Agreements 314–318

314. The administrative decision was reversed by the Federal Court of Appeals of the City of Posadas less than two years later,[244] mostly due to the fact that the CNDC did not adequately prove the charges. Most interestingly, the Court also pointed out that the CNDC had failed to define the relevant market, and thus could not reasonably prove that the alleged cartel members had the required market power to infringe section 1 of the Competition Act (as stated above, all conducts prohibited under the Competition Act require a rule of reason approach). This court decision is final, since the Supreme Court declined to hear the case on extraordinary appeal.[245]

315. The latest market allocation cases as of the date of this publication are *Multicanal*[246] and *Video Cable 6*.[247] The cases date back to the joint acquisition in 1997 by Multicanal S.A. and Cablevisión S.A. of the only two cable companies which at such dates had operations in the cities of Santa Fe and Paraná, Videocable Comunicación S.A. (VCC, in the city of Paraná acting as its subsidiary Video Cable 6 S.A.) and C.V. Inversiones S.A. (known by the trade name Cablevideo). Cablevideo was the main operator, while VCC had recently entered those markets.

316. The joint purchase was made prior to the implementation of merger review under the Competition Act, and thus did not require government approval.

317. Subsequent to the acquisition, Cablevisión and Multicanal spun-off the assets of VCC and Cablevideo at a national level. Claiming technical and economic reasons, they divided the assets in Santa Fe and Paraná in two areas of similar sizes and characteristics. Such situation, coupled with the fact that during some months the programming offer of the new operators was reduced, prompted a complaint by a consumers association and the opening of a probe by the CNDC.

318. Due to the fact that none of the two companies had extended its network to the area of its competitor even several years after the spin-off had occurred, the investigation was mainly directed to determining if such conduct concealed a collusive agreement, as clearly stems of the accusation made by the CNDC in 2004, which considered that the companies had divided the Santa Fe and Paraná markets 'as from the spin-off of VCC'. For this reason, it is remarkable that the final decision considered the spin-off as an anticompetitive conduct in itself.

---

244. 'Shell Gas S.A. – Totalgaz Argentina S.A.', CFed. Posadas (30 May 2008).
245. 'Shell Gas S.A. y Totalgaz Argentina S.A.', *supra* n. 88.
246. 'Multicanal y otro s/ inf. Art. 1 Ley 22.262', Secretaría de Comercio Interior, Resolution No. 219 (17 Jun. 2010). The Court of Appeals of Rosario denied the motion for expiration of the applicable statute of limitations as it considered the collusive conduct discussed in the case of a continuous type. 'Cablevisión S.A. s/ ley 22.262 – Incidente de prescripción – (Expte 1333P)', C. Fed. Rosario (22 Jul. 2011).
247. 'Video Cable 6 S.A. y otras s/inf. art. 1 Ley 22.262', Secretaría de Comercio Interior, Resolution No. 19 (10 Feb. 2011). This decision was confirmed by the Court of Appeals of Paraná in re 'Video Cable 6 S.A. y otros s/ infracción Art. 1 ley 22.262', *supra* n. 116, and eventually by the Supreme Court in re 'Video Cable 6 S.A. y otros s/ infracción Art. 1 ley 22.262', CSJN, L. 548. XLVII (22 Aug. 2012).

319. Furthermore, for its most part the decision dedicated to challenge the evidence on the supposed non-viability or inconvenience by the companies to deploy new networks in the area of its competitor.

320. The decision is curious in several respects. On the one hand it seems clear that, faced with the absence of concrete evidence on the existence of the market-division agreement, the CNDC decided to consider the spin-off as the externalization of such conduct. The emphasis given by the agency to circumstances that should have prompted Cablevisión and Multicanal to overlap their networks and compete seems to illustrate that the burden of proof was shifted, by requiring the companies to justify why they did not compete instead of the CNDC proving that they did not do it due to anticompetitive reasons.

321. Given that the spin-off was related to the earlier joint acquisition of VCC and Cablevideo, in a way the decision can be regarded as a substitute remedy for an undesirable economic concentration which occurred at a time when merger review was not contemplated in the law. It is debatable, however, whether the competitive outcome of a situation where each of Cablevisión and Multicanal acquired VCC and Cablevideo in their then current status (Cablevideo being a highly dominant player), which the decision suggests as the desired choice, would have been better than the 'spin-off of equals' that actually took place, assuming subsequent competition between the companies. If the latter would have been the preferred choice, it follows that the spin-off in itself could not have been found in violation of competition laws, and the finding of additional proof of an anticompetitive agreement would have been unavoidable.

C. Production/Innovation Limitation

322. Several of the cartel cases mentioned under items (i) and (ii) above involved production limitations, given that rarely do the parties involved agree on a single anticompetitive dimension.

323. The economic crisis experienced by Argentina in 2002, with a sharp devaluation of the local currency, created supply shortages in several areas of the economy. This was understood by the CNDC, which closed investigations in the retail gas sector by stating that the restriction was based on difficulties in the importation of fuel more than in actions of the local refiners.[248]

324. The increased incentive for the exportation of gas due to the attractiveness of international prices led the Government to foster the adoption in 2002 of Supply Stability Agreements with the relevant producing and refining companies. Those agreements, to achieve its purpose of guaranteeing the supply of diesel for local use, established supply quotas which restricted competition by providing little incentive

---

248. *See*, e.g., 'Empresas Petroleras s/ infracción Ley 25.156', Secretaría de la Competencia, la Desregulación y la Defensa del Consumidor, Resolution No. 69 (20 May 2003).

Part II, Ch. 1, Restrictive Agreements 325–328

to price competition. In addition, integrated refiners used most such oil in their own gas stations, to the detriment of non-integrated retailers. The CNDC and Secretariat, however, were of the view that such agreements had been approved by a regulatory act and thus were outside of the reach of competition laws.[249]

325. It is worth noting that domestic oil shortages continued in the following years, the Government applying other direct regulation measures such as export tariffs and the much criticized Supply Law of 1974,[250] which empowers the Government to, inter alia, order companies to maintain production in order to satisfy public demand in a broad range of activities. The Supply Law was enforced repeatedly against an oil company in 2006, where fines in excess of ARS 50 million were applied.[251]

326. Innovation limitation cartels are clearly illegal under the Competition Act, which also includes specific references to such conduct in section 2, by prohibiting:

(e) agreements to limit or control technical development or investments destined to the production or commercialization of goods or services.
[…]
(h) the regulation of markets of goods or services, through agreements to limit or control research and technical development, production of goods or services, or to difficult investments destined to the production of goods or services or its distribution.

327. In fact, as anticipated even Cooperation Joint Ventures, mentioned in paragraph 174 above may be considered economic concentrations subject to approval. One case that might fit into this cartel category is *Siderar*,[252] where a major flat- and long-steel company was accused by a competitor of, inter alia, agreeing with a long-steel manufacturer to interrupt production in its long-steel blast furnace so as to eliminate competition between them through the specialization in only one type of steel.

328. The CNDC dismissed the complaint, due to the lack of relevant evidence and because it understood the presumed agreement lacked consideration on the side of the benefited long-steel producer, given that it did not have flat-steel capabilities.

---

249. 'Petronor S.R.L. s/ solicitud de intervención CNDC', Secretaría de Coordinación Técnica, Resolution No. 128 (27 Jul. 2005).
250. Law No. 20,680, 25 Jun. 1974 [22939] BO, 2.
251. *See,* generally, 'Moreno anunció que aplicará la ley de abastecimiento', Clarín (22 Apr. 2008) (available at http://edant.clarin.com/diario/2008/04/22/elpais/p-00401.htm). The Supply Law was also applied in 2010 against pay-TV companies, by the application of maximum prices. *See*, generally, para. 294 *supra*.
252. 'Siderar S.A. s/ *Infracción Ley 22.262*', Secretaría de Coordinación Técnica, Resolution No. 30 (15 Mar. 2004).

D. Group Boycott

329. The word 'boycott' is largely absent from the Competition Act and case law; it being replaced by the more general and inclusive term 'exclusionary practices', included in the non-exhaustive list of section 2 as follows:

> (f) To impede, difficult or obstruct the entry or stay of third parties in a market or exclude them from the same.

330. Concerted exclusionary practices have by and large been considered in the context of professional associations. However, they have been examined as a type of exclusionary abuse of dominant position by the association, as an entity following commercial objectives of its own, different from its members. This idea has been strengthened by the fact that, precisely, many complaints involved members challenging statutory provisions that prevented them from dealing with competing associations.

331. Should we consider the practice as the result of an agreement by a group of professionals commanding the association against a competing network (following the example, the actual exclusionary action being the restrictions imposed to members to provide services outside the association), the existence of a group boycott would be more clearly seen.

332. In any case, as explained above the end result under the Competition Act would be the same: insofar as the infringer or group of infringers bear substantial market power, the exclusionary conduct will be considered in violation of the Competition Act.

333. The important number of cases considered by the CNDC in the health care sector led to the issuance of the 1997 Health Care Guidelines referred to in paragraph 554 below, the only ones so far that include thresholds indicating when market power is to be considered to be held. A number of those cases will be mentioned below.

334. In *Circulo Médico Alto Paraná*,[253] for example, a physician association that had entered into agreements with most health care associations in the relevant market provided services exclusively through physicians included in a 'Providers' list', excluding professionals from said registry in case they decided to avoid the association and render services directly, through affiliations with hospitals or other health care associations. The same institution was subject to another investigation in 2000 for similar reasons, which concluded with an injunction and application of a fine. By then the 1997 Health Care Guidelines[254] were in force and the CNDC

---

253. 'Circulo Medico Alto Paraná', Secretaría de Industria y Comercio, Resolution No. 309 (4 Sep. 1992).
254. 'Asociación de Ayuda Mutua El Dorado c/ Circulo Medico Alto Paraná' Comisión Nacional de Defensa de la Competencia, Resolution No. 330 (12 Jul. 2000).

Part II, Ch. 1, Restrictive Agreements 335–336

applied Guideline No. 6, which forbids the establishment by an association comprising more than 50% of the providers in a given market of clauses impeding the affiliation of providers fulfilling the requirements of aptitude.

335. The same situation was examined in re *Dirección de Bienestar de la Armada*,[255] where the two associations included similar exclusionary provisions in its statutes preventing dentists from providing services to plaintiff directly, as happened before the creation of the associations. Pursuant to the CNDC, said provisions were the core of the restricting practices under review, since:

> [M]embers are put in the option of foregoing the clientele they would receive through the defendants, or foregoing the possibility of entering into agreements with other health care organizations. In that connection it must be noted that it has been proven in this proceedings that the largest income of the professionals stems from the rendering of services to affiliates of the health care organizations, as a consequence of which the restriction imposed by defendants turns out to be highly detrimental to them and to those health care organizations that have not entered into agreements with defendants, which thus experience a restriction in their possibility of obtaining professionals for the rendering of services to their affiliates, given that the majority thereof (being part of the Providers' Lists of defendants because such entities concentrate the largest number of agreements with the main health care organizations) are prevented from entering into contracts with them. This argument also dismisses that other that is made by defendants on the free choice or freedom of association of the professionals, because given that being defendants, as already stated and proved in these proceedings, who concentrate the largest number of agreements with the main health care organizations, they turn out to be the safest ways for dentists to obtain clientele.[256]

336. In *Federación Argentina de Asociaciones de Anestesia, Analgesia y Reanimación*,[257] the dispute arose between anaesthesiologists, who decided to unionize and deal directly with hospitals and not through physician associations, the latter then deciding to threat hospitals to halt the rendering of services of its affiliates if the 'entire medical team' was not affiliated with defendant. Defendant was involved in similar exclusionary conducts involving physicians who decided to render services directly to a hospital which had not reached a commercial agreement with the association.[258]

---

255. 'Dirección de Bienestar de la Armada' (complaint against *Agremiación Odontológica de La Plata, Berisso y Ensenada y Sociedad Odontológica de La Plata*), Secretaría de Industria, Comercio y Minería, Resolution No. 1138 (29 Oct. 1997). *See also* 'Colegio Médico de Corrientes', Secretaría de Industria, Comercio y Minería, Resolution No. 819 (30 Nov. 1998).
256. 'Dirección de Bienestar de la Armada', at 8 and 9.
257. 'Federación Argentina de Asociaciones de Anestesia, Analgesia y Reanimación' (complaint against Asociación Médica de Bahía Blanca), Secretaría de Defensa de la Competencia y del Consumidor, Resolution No. 180 (11 Sep. 2000).
258. The same defendant was sanctioned for exclusionary conducts against physicians in 'Asociación Médica de Bahía Blanca (caso DIBA/C. 687) s/ infracción Ley 25.156', Secretaría de Comercio

337. A typical boycott case is found in *Coordinadora de Salud*,[259] where a health care association and seventeen of its hospital members comprising around 70% of the relevant market agreed at an association meeting not to provide services to patients affiliated with health insurance organizations that had entered into contracts with plaintiff. Here the CNDC and Secretariat did regard the conduct as a cartel, and applied fines both to the association and its members.

338. It is worth noting that the reasonableness of the Health Care Guidelines has been ratified by the Supreme Court in re *Círculo Odontológico Regional de Venado Tuerto*,[260] in which the restriction of competition caused by the exclusionary practices of another dentists association were considered as subject to greater constitutional protection than rights such as that of work and free association.

339. Exclusionary practices by bar associations have also been under scrutiny in their opposition to prepaid legal services. In one case, *Cámara Argentina de Empresa de Servicios Jurídicos Prepagos*,[261] the sending by the association of certified letters to the legal service company requesting general information on the specific lawyers providing the services and the financial arrangements with them was deemed as not imposing undue restrictions to the activity of the company, while a more aggressive approach, involving publications of newspaper advertisements warning the public of the illegality of those services was regarded as outside the scope of the association's purpose and thus illegal in another complaint filed by the same plaintiff.[262]

340. The interplay of competition with other constitutional right, to petition to the authorities, was also reviewed in re *Multicanal S.A. y Cablevision S.A. (Gigacable)*,[263] where identical but separate presentations by defendants before a local municipality directed to the revocation of a cable-TV license to plaintiff were upheld given that the restriction, if existent, would have originated in State rather than private action. As stated by the CNDC:

Interior, Resolution No. 136 (4 Oct. 2011) and 'Asociación Médica de Bahía Blanca s/ infracción Ley N° 25.156', Secretariat of Domestic Trade, Resolution No. 45 (7 Jun. 2012). It is worth noting that, on appeal, Resolutions No. 136/2011 and 45/2012 of the Secretariat of Domestic Trade were revoked due to the expiration of the statute of limitations. See 'Asociación Médica de Bahía Blanca y Círculo Médico de Punta Alta s/ apel. Res. 136/11 Sec. Com. Int. – Mrio. Econ. y Fin. Púb. Nac. (ley 25.156: 53)', CFed. de Bahía Blanca (23 Nov. 2012).

259. 'Coordinadora de Salud S.R.L.' (complaint against Asociación de Clínicas y Sanatorios de Tucumán), Secretaría de Defensa de la Competencia y del Consumidor, Resolution No. 235 (17 Oct. 2000).
260. 'Círculo Odontológico Regional de Venado Tuerto', 328 Fallos 1063 (2005).
261. 'Cámara Argentina de Empresa de Servicios Jurídicos Prepagos' (complaint against Colegio de Abogados de San Isidro), Secretaría de Industria, Comercio y Minería, Resolution No. 587 (9 Sep. 1998).
262. 'Cámara Argentina de Empresa de Servicios Jurídicos Prepagos' (complaint against Colegio de Abogados de San Nicolás), Secretaría de Industria, Comercio y Minería, Resolution No. 589 (9 Sep. 1998). This restriction was also portrayed as a type of 'limitation to the innovation' presented by the prepaid services.
263. 'Multicanal S.A. y Cablevision S.A. (Gigacable) s/ infracción Ley 25.156', Secretaría de Coordinación Técnica, Resolution No. 84 (30 May 2005).

Part II, Ch. 1, Restrictive Agreements

Competition law does not comprise the review and enforcement of acts or facts of public entities issued within public empowerments of administration, regulation or control of a certain economic activity. These acts must be submitted to the administrative or judicial review specifically contemplated in the legal system in force.[264]

E. Collusion on Other Objects

341. Bidding processes, both public and private, are part of daily business in Argentina. Actually, some of the largest companies, formerly State-owned, were sold through such processes. It is then remarkable that there is little case law on bid rigging.[265]

342. Earlier cases seem to suggest that lack of proper investigative tools seemed to have played an important role in defining the scope of the investigations.

343. For example, in the *Secretario de Seguridad de la Provincia de Buenos Aires*[266] case, defendant's initial bids, while similar between themselves, were lowered by more than 80% when the buyer – in the case, Police Department of the Province of Buenos Aires – called for submissions of new bids. The CNDC admitted that one of the reasons for such conduct could have been the existence of collusion, but instead of proceeding with the investigation seemed satisfied with the fact that, eventually, the buyer prevented possible overpricing by mandating the new bid.

344. A similar situation occurred in re *Melenzane*,[267] where plaintiff's bid – around 50% lower than those of defendants – was disqualified due to certain formalities, and in the second call for bids one of the defendants won, at a much lower price than originally bid.

345. The *Liquid Oxygen* cartel case may have represented a pivotal point in the enforcement of bid rigging. The difference stems in that it is one of the few publicized cases where searches were conducted in company premises, with favourable results. According to the final decision, the CNDC proved, inter alia, that:

(i) 65% of the hospitals had not changed supplier;
(ii) the average number of bidders was just two; and
(iii) the investigated companies simulated competition, evidence pointing to the fact that they purposely avoided presenting certain bids, or filed them with

---

264. *Ibid.*, at 40.
265. Statutorily, bid rigging is mentioned in s. 2 (d) of the Competition Act.
266. 'Secretario de Seguridad de la Provincia de Buenos Aires'(complaint against Contartese S.R.L. and Torello Hermanos S.A.), Secretaría de Comercio e Inversiones, Resolution No. 16 (1 Apr. 1996).
267. 'Melenzane S.A. s/ solicitud de intervención CNDC (c. 1002)', Secretaría de Coordinación Técnica, Resolution No. 7 (10 May 2006).

formal mistakes, or at prices that were substantially higher than those of the incumbents.[268]

345.1. In the same line of investigation, including the use of dawn raids that resulted in the gathering of incriminating evidence, more recently four pharmaceutical companies were fined ARS 10 million each for allegedly participating in a bid rigging scheme involving gelatin sales.[269]

II. Information Exchange Practices

346. The *Cement Cartel*[270] is the premier case as regards information exchange as an anticompetitive conduct.

347. The CNDC proved the existence of a very detailed exchange of statistical information, organized by the industry trade association (*Asociación de Fabricantes de Cemento Portland*). The information was exchanged on a monthly and weekly basis, and included data on:

(i) production and inventory of each of the companies, per month and YTD;
(ii) cement sales per customer (public sector, private sector and exports) per plant;
(iii) cement sales divided by means of transportation (railway, track, boats, etc.);
(iv) cement sales divided by type of container used (plastic bags or wholesale); and
(v) cement sales divided by province and city.

348. The information was audited by third parties, and was provided by high-level executives in the sales and/or commercial areas of each of the companies. It was also proved that the association effectively had an active monitoring role in the follow-up of requests made to the member companies.

349. In addition, some of the documents collected at the association's premises pointed out to the fact that the information exchanged was expressly recognized as confidential and was not part of the statistical information publicly disclosed by the association.

350. It is worth noting that, even when the CNDC considered the exchange of confidential information illegal both due to its use as a way to monitor the cartel and as an anticompetitive practice in itself, the Court of Appeals did not refer to this last possibility, although ultimately confirmed the administrative decision in full (with the sole exception that it slightly reduced the fine applied to one of the companies).

---

268. 'Oxígeno Líquido', *supra* n. 106.
269. 'Oficina Anticorrupción s/ solicitud de intervención CNDC (c. 1142)', Secretaría de Comercio, Resolution No. 705 (4 Dec. 2015).
270. 'Loma Negra Compañía Industrial S.A. y otros', *supra* n. 107.

III. Cooperation Agreements

351. A cooperation agreement can be analysed under the provisions of the Competition Act dealing with mergers or anticompetitive practices, depending on the scope of the joint venture. In order to be considered an economic concentration, the parties must contribute assets from which an independent turnover can be attributed, and at least one of the parties must acquire control or substantial influence over the assets (in the case, an activity with independent economic existence in the market) of the other. If such control or influence is acquired over assets or processes which do not have an independent projection on the market, like R&D, buying or selling, the agreement would then be examined under the standard of section 1 of the Competition Act. No guidelines for cooperation agreements have been issued to date, so in all cases the rule of reason analysis will be the same: whether the agreement, in itself or as a consequence of the some facilitating factor – i.e., information exchanges – may have the ability to substantially restrict competition, and what its pro-competitive aspects are.

A. Research and Development

352. While R&D agreements have occasionally been considered as economic concentrations, the author is not aware of case law in which their competitive effects were examined. As anticipated under paragraph 174 above, these agreements, generally of an extended duration, may take the form of a 'Cooperation Joint Venture' (ACE). Under the CCC, the purpose of an ACE is to set up a common organization with the aim of facilitating or developing certain stages of the commercial activity of its members or to perfect or increase the result of said activities. Thus, by definition an ACE is not an independent market agent.

353. Agreements creating ACEs must be registered with the Public Registry of Commerce. The parties to the joint venture must make contributions to the activity of the ACE, which must have its own accounting. The foregoing, of course, does not grant the JV members any right in engaging in anticompetitive activities, as illustrated by the Court of Appeals in re *Altamirano*.[271]

354. As seen above, even when section 1455 of the CCC provides that a copy of the ACE agreement must be forwarded to the CNDC for information purposes, since the enactment of the Competition Act a merger filing will be made only if required. This was the case of the *Cargill–Buyatti ACE*, not a typical R&D JV since it allowed Cargill to increase its soybean, sunflower and cotton-processing facilities through the control and use of the assets of Buyatti, while the latter only derived a financial benefit from it.[272]

---

271. 'Altamirano Miguel s/ denuncia Empresas Areneras' CFed. Rosario, Sala A [1993-A] LL, 132.
272. 'Cargill S.A.C.I. y Buyatti S.A.I.C.A. (c. 374)', *supra* n. 120.

B. Specialization

355. As mentioned in paragraph 327 above, a specialization agreement was examined in *Siderar*,[273] the CNDC concluding that there was no evidence of the existence of the agreement given that only one of the parties participated in both areas before it decided to cease activity in one of them, and thus the agreement would have lacked consideration.

C. Standardization

356. The author is not aware of the existence to date of standard-setting cases worth commenting on.

D. Joint Production/Purchasing/Selling

357. Competition issues surrounding joint production/purchasing/selling agreements have so far not been subject to significant debate.

358. As anticipated, those practices will generally be considered acceptable if made for efficiency purposes, even if they stem from an improvement of the parties' bargaining position vis-à-vis a concentrated market upstream or downstream, up to the limit where the resulting market power is too great.[274]

359. It is common for small producers to associate in the form of cooperatives,[275] civil associations or even commercial companies.[276] Given the generally irrelevant market power of each individual associate, as has been seen above in the area of health care the CNDC will mostly regard them as a single entity for purpose of the Competition Act when they are formed by numerous associates.

---

273. *Supra* n. 253.
274. *See*, e.g., 'RTS Holding Argentina S.R.L.', Secretaría de Defensa de la Competencia y del Consumidor, Resolution No. 221 (11 Oct. 2000) at 26.
275. Under the Former Competition Act some courts were of the view that cooperatives were outside of the scope of its provisions, given that they lacked a profit purpose and their acts were not formally considered as acts of commerce. This view has changed under the Competition Act, which under s. 3 includes ' … *all individuals or entities, public or private, for profit or not carrying out economic activities in all or part of Argentina,* … , *insofar as their acts, activities or agreements may produce effects in the national market*'.
276. For example, in the pay-TV market Red Intercable S.A. was a corporation comprised by over 200 regional cable companies, which for the most part was regarded as a single entity with a combined market share of around 6%. *See* 'Nofal Sports Holding S.A., DLJ Offshore Partners C.V., DirecTV Latin America LLC, DirecTV Argentina S.A. y otros s/ notificación art. 8 Ley 25.156 (Conc. No. 709)', Secretaría de Comercio Interior, Resolution No. 168 (28 Sep. 2008) at 126.

Part II, Ch. 1, Restrictive Agreements

360. The foregoing is exposed in re *Federación Argentina de Entidades de Servicios Fúnebres y Afines.*[277] Defendants were associations of funeral services companies. The investigation focused on agreements among those entities and an insurance company, which provided for a fixed price for the services.

361. The CNDC concluded that the agreements did not violate the Former Competition Act, due to the fact that defendants' clients acted at a national level, and thus the 'single shop' approach was more efficient. Once a single agreement was signed with each client, a uniform price for the services had to be applied.

362. The agency also pointed out that the agreements – which covered a minor portion of the total funeral services market – covered only basic funeral services, additional services to be arranged with the specific provider.

363. In *Pafundi*[278] defendants, a cooperative and corporations, decided to become shareholders of one of the defendant's corporations, Fadespo, to jointly distribute their products. Due to a market recession and for efficiency considerations, it was also decided that each of the members specialized in one or reduced types of machinery. The CNDC justified the validity of the agreement on the market decline and the decline of the joint venture itself in the market vis-à-vis its competitors.

364. Quite on the contrary, in *Sánchez Gas*[279] a similar conduct, but carried out by all competitors, concluded with a fine. The opinion of the CNDC on joint distribution agreements (presumably by parties with substantial market power) was clear:

> It cannot be ignored that through shared distribution systems the basis for concerted practices and other collusive activities is laid out. The unified commercial representation that is subject to reproach herein, carries out an infringement in the mechanisms of competition in the market, and implies an obstacle for the operation of the genuine incentives that form part of the central core of market dynamics.[280]

---

277. 'Federación Argentina de Entidades de Servicios Fúnebres y Afines (FADESFYA), Federación Argentina de Asociaciones Funerarias (FADAF) e Instituto Cooperativo de Seguros', Secretaría de Comercio e Inversiones, Resolution No. 282 (4 Dec. 1995).
278. 'Pafundi, Alfredo Leopoldo' (complaint against COFAMHYA Cooperativa de Trabajo Ltda., FADESPO S.A., Biper S.A.C.I.F. and WDW S.A.I.C.), Secretaría de Comercio Interior, Resolution No. 470 (18 Nov. 1988).
279. 'Sánchez Gas S.A., Gas Arrecifes S.A., Gas Brill S.A. y Sánchez Gas Las Armas S.R.L. (complaint against Vaspia S.A.I.C., Forargen S.A., Establecimiento Metalúrgico Tidar S.R.L. Metalúrgica Errepol S.R.L., Metalúrgica V.C. S.A.I.C. and Axle S.A.), Secretaría de Industria, Comercio y Minería, Resolution No. 730 (5 Aug. 1997).
280. *Ibid.*, at VIII, para. 4.

§2. Vertical Agreements

I. Distribution

A. Exclusive Distributorship

365. The first case decided by the CNDC was in re *Igarreta and Acfor*.[281] Defendants were the only two Ford dealers handling sales to the public sector nationwide. The investigation commenced as a consequence of a complaint of a provincial authority, which noticed that no other Ford retailer participated in bidding processes. Acfor used to be the exclusive Ford distributor for the entire public sector from 1956 to 1979, when due to the increase in demand produced by the exit of General Motors from the Argentine market Igarreta, a former GM distributor, became the second exclusive distributor of the brand. Acfor was granted the distribution of cars of most national, provincial and local State agencies located in the city and province of Buenos Aires, while Igarreta had the exclusive right to distribute commercial vehicles in the same area granted to Acfor, and all types of vehicles in the rest of the country.

366. Defendants argued that there were several competitors to Ford vehicles, and that Ford's distribution network did not differ from that of its competitors (moreover, Igarreta had been included as a new distributor a few years ago). They also claimed that public sector sales required from the retailer specific characteristics – such as financial strength or logistical capabilities – which were not easily found. Finally, they claimed that should the fact that other Ford dealers were excluded from such sales be contrary to competition laws, the responsibility should be attributed to the manufacturer and not the dealers.

367. The CNDC first examined the reasons which according to the retailers advised the selection of few, selected retailers, concluding that the structure of retailers specialized in public sector sales did not differ from their private sector counterparts, which on the contrary in some cases were used to handle larger orders.

368. A critical issue in the analysis was the fact that about 80% of all purchases of vehicles from the public sector were handled by the two defendants, which suggested weak interbrand competition.

369. The CNDC explained that the agreements violated the Former Competition Act as follows:

> On one hand, it is obvious that the State, as purchaser of vehicles, has been excluded from the possibility of accessing to real competitive options existing in the relevant market and at the disposal of other consumers; on the other it is equally obvious that a significant number of offerors have also been prevented from reaching an important demand such as the aforementioned, being

---

281. 'Igarreta S.A. y Acfor S.A.', Secretaría de Comercio, Resolution No. 368 (10 Oct. 1983).

Part II, Ch. 1, Restrictive Agreements 370–374

restricted to the private sector. The foregoing means that the principle of equal treatment and opportunity is doubly affected in this case, because neither the State has the same possibilities of dealing than the private businessmen, nor the regular brand retailers have the same possibilities of dealing than the exclusive ones.[282]

370. Even when a comparison between prices paid by the public and private sector was non-conclusive, the CNDC was of the view that should additional competition be introduced, public purchasers would benefit from certain discounts granted by the manufacturers to the retailers, or otherwise obtain lower prices as a consequence of the more reduced profit margins of the retailers.

371. The Secretariat ultimately imposed a fine to each of the two defendants, for the 'setting up of an exclusivity system in sales to the State' and ordered them to cease making use of their exclusivity rights.

372. However, the Court of Appeals in Economic Crimes ultimately reversed the decision,[283] on the basis that the freedom of election of each consumer was exercised mainly through its choice for a specific brand and not determining the distribution structure elected by the manufacturer.

373. Even when the CNDC incorrectly considered the conduct as one of a horizontal nature, the restriction in interbrand competition seemed clear. The court however focused more on whether barriers of entry to other competitors existed rather than the effects of Ford's distribution structure on competition. The issue did not rest on whether retailers had achieved its relevant market position through illicit means, because clearly the public sector customers preferred Ford vehicles by use of independent choice. Also, the fact that the investigation was not prompted by a change in Ford's distribution network but through an observation of the existing one may have weighed in the court decision.

374. In re *Soda Fernández*,[284] a forty-eight building housing cooperative selected an exclusive mineral water, sparkling water, juices and sodas distributor for a period of twenty years, albeit through a bidding process. The losing bidder, which was the existing sparkling water supplier until the new agreement was signed, filed a complaint against the cooperative and distributor for the alleged exclusionary anti-competitive effects of the distribution agreement. The case was closed with a formal commitment on the side of defendants to allow entry to plaintiff to the housing complex in specific dates and terminate the agreement. The decision failed to define the relevant market, in particular its geographic scope. This would have been important to determine whether consumers living in the housing complex were able to

---

282. *Ibid.*, at 814.
283. 'Igarreta S.A. y Acfor S.A.', CNPenal Económico, Sala I (27 Dec. 1983).
284. 'Soda Fernández y Cía.' (complaint against Bootz y Cía.), Secretaría de Comercio Interior, Resolution No. 381 (2 Nov. 1994).

purchase competing products outside of it – as stated by the cooperative – in reasonable volumes, thus evidencing the existence of sufficient interbrand competition.

375. More recently, in re *Sociedad Argentina de Distribuidores Independientes de Tabaco*,[285] a group of cigarette sub-distributors complained of a change in the distribution systems of defendants, the largest tobacco manufacturers (Phillip Morris and BAT subsidiaries), which basically restricted distribution of those products to a fewer number of exclusive distributors.

376. A particular feature of the tobacco business was the fact that the manufacturer was imposed sales taxes based on the consumer price of the product, as a consequence of which competition among intrabrand retailers had no impact on the final price.

377. The foregoing, coupled with the fact that in spite of the reorganization of the distribution network the products of both defendants continued reaching the final points of sale, led the CNDC to conclude that no violation of competition laws had taken place.

378. The Court of Appeals remanded the decision to determine whether Massalin had abused of a presumed dominant position in the amendment of its distribution system.[286] The CNDC and Secretariat ultimately ratified its prior decision, indicating that even when Massalin had around 60% of the relevant market, the remaining 40% was in the hands of Nobleza Piccardo, which aggressiveness as competitor led to the conclusion that Massalin could not act independently and thus was not dominant.[287]

379. Massalin is however subject to a new complaint by the same sub-distributors association, seeking a holding that the exclusive distribution system adopted by the company in 1997 (as opposed to the *change* from the older to the newer scheme) would entail an abuse of dominant position.[288]

---

285. 'Sociedad Argentina de Distribuidores Independientes de Tabaco' (complaint against Massalin Particulares S.A.), Secretaría de Industria, Comercio y Minería, Resolution No. 942 (18 Sep. 1997).
286. 'S.A.D.I.T. c/ Massalin Particulares S.A.', CNPenal Económico, Sala B, [1999 – A] LL 294.). The other defendant, Nobleza Piccardo, had raised this argument even when it quickly adopted a similar distribution system.
287. 'Sociedad Argentina de Distribuidores Independientes de Tabaco', *supra* n. 61. Lack of market power was also the decisive factor in dismissing the claim in 'Autolatina Argentina S.A., Autolatina Argentina de Ahorro para Fines Determinados and Ford Argentina' Comisión Nacional de Defensa de la Competencia, Resolution No. 422 (8 Jul. 2003), where plaintiff, a Ford retailer, complained of a series of changes in the manufacturer's distribution network stemming from Ford's local merger with Volkswagen and subsequent spin-off that ultimately drove it out of business. This decision also confirmed a holding previously expressed in Massalin in the sense that antitrust laws protect competition, and not individual competitors.
288. Please refer to 'Massalin Particulares S.A. c/ Incidente de prescripción de la acción e incompetencia en autos principales "SADIC s/ denuncia c/ Massalin Particulares S.A. s/ inf. Ley 22.262 (C. 403)"', CNPenal Económico, Sala B (24 Nov. 2011), where the Appeal Court ratified a decision of the CNDC which rejected the motion to dismiss filed by Massalin.

Part II, Ch. 1, Restrictive Agreements 380–383

380. The test to be followed to examine the effect of exclusive distribution contracts was clearly defined in *DirecTV*,[289] where HBO, a pay-TV programming company, agreed with DirecTV for the exclusive distribution of certain movie channels for the term of one year:

> From the standpoint of competition law, exclusive distribution contracts may be sanctioned when certain specific circumstances are met. Firstly, the product or service sold under exclusivity must not have current or potential close substitutes. Moreover, the product must be an essential input for those competing in the buyer market, this meaning that the impossibility of having it will turn the competitors' business non-viable. Lastly, it is worth pointing out that the period under which said exclusivity is granted is an important factor to be made in order to conclude if the exclusivity is or not in violation of Law No. 25,156.
> Moreover, it is also relevant to examine the benefits that may be obtained by a seller through the exclusive contracting of a distributor as opposed to its unrestricted offering, as this would allow to obtain evidence that could be helpful to understand the underlying rationale in each case.

B. Exclusive Dealing

381. The policy of the CNDC as regards exclusive dealing was briefly summarized in *Cámara de Empresas de Asistencia Farmacéutica*:[290]

> Exclusivity clauses bear a restriction which is censurable and punishable under a competition law perspective *when those who apply it bear a dominant position* in a market, that is, when they concentrate most of the offer in a market without the demand have similar alternatives and when the application of the same effectively or potentially affect the general economic interest.[291]

382. This principle has been consistently applied, as the above and below cases demonstrate. As in the case of group boycotts, most of them relate to the health services market.

383. For example, in *Farmia and Okane*,[292] the CNDC objected to the abuse of dominance of a professional association which represented 92% of all pharmacy

---

289. 'Formula denuncia c/ la empresa de televisión abierta al hogar mediante satélite DirecTV', Secretaría de Coordinación Técnica, Resolution No. 68 (16 Oct. 2003).
290. 'Cámara de Empresas de Asistencia Farmacéutica' (complaint against Colegio de Farmacéuticos de la Provincia de Buenos Aires), Secretaría de Industria, Comercio y Minería, Resolution No. 752 (8 Oct. 1999).
291. *Ibid.*, at para. 84.
292. 'Farmia S.A. and Okane S.A.' (complaint against Colegio de Farmacéuticos de la Provincia de Santa Fe, Asociación Profesional Farmacéutica de la ciudad de Rosario, Sistema de Prestaciones Farmacéuticas a Obras Sociales de Rosario and Sistema Abierto Solidario de la ciudad de Santa Fe), Secretaría de Comercio Interior, Resolution No. 51 (29 Aug. 1989).

stores of the province of Santa Fe in its dealing with health care providers. The abuse was implemented through the expulsion of non-conforming pharmacies from the system, which prevented them from receiving affiliates of the health care providers. The restrictions of competition were clearly put by the CNDC:

> [T]he conduct of COLEGIO DE FARMACEUTICOS DE LA PROVINCIA DE SANTA FE has negative effects on the market; because it prevents the free interplay of offer and demand, and in addition through its prohibitions erects entry barriers to other agents, as plaintiffs; over pharmacists, because they cannot freely contract with the system of network of their choice, without losing purchasers linked to health care providers with agreements with the professional association; over health care providers, because due to the sanctions or exclusions by the professional association see their list of pharmacies reduced; over affiliates or users, because they have to withstand the limitations imposed by the trade association.[293]

384. In *Asociación Mutual Personal Sancor*,[294] the exclusivity was imposed by the dominant health care services provided – which was vertically integrated with the main town employer – over its affiliates, who were directed to satisfy all their medical supplies needs through only one of the six pharmacies of the city of Sunchales, province of Santa Fe, which was also partially integrated with the provider.

385. Remedies applied in the cases mentioned above included fines and cease-and-desist orders.

C. *Selective Distribution*

386. No specific cases to comment on. *See*, generally, item A (*Exclusive Distributorship*) above.

D. *Franchising*

387. The author is not aware of franchising agreements being the core of a case under the CNDC. It seems unlikely that the homogeneity in processes and policies – including pricing policies – derived from those agreements could be regarded as anticompetitive, given that such aspects are central to the idea of franchising. A customer expects to receive the same service or good, at the same price, in each point of sale. This opinion would be supported by the principle stemming from *Ifrisa*,[295] given that even when the franchisor is totally controlling the business decisions of

---

293. *Ibid.*, at 134.
294. 'Asociación Mutual Personal Sancor (Farmacia de Sunchales/C. 715)', Comisión Nacional de Defensa de la Competencia, Resolution No. 462 (17 Sep. 2004).
295. 'Ifrisa S.R.L.', *supra* n. 58.

Part II, Ch. 1, Restrictive Agreements   388–391

the franchisee, it does so with respect to its own product and for the purpose of extending to the fullest degree possible its way of doing business.

388. However, it is unclear whether the acquisition of a franchisee by the franchisor would require a merger filing. On the one hand, franchisee would be a separate business entity with obviously a separate turnover, and thus, at least formally, its acquisition would be an economic concentration under the Competition Act. Another question is whether the acquisition would entail a transfer of control or not. Insofar as franchisees were to exclusively render services under the franchise, and not own its assets, the answer could be a negative one. On the contrary, were franchisees to own assets that could be readily used for other commercial or industrial activity, a filing could be required.

II. Technology Licensing

A. *Patent Licensing*

389. Given the lack of antitrust cases involving patent licensing under competition laws, the paragraphs below will refer to the issue of compulsory licensing under patent legislation.

390. Patents and utility models are regulated under Law 24,481 and amendments thereof, and is consolidated by Decree 260/1996 of 20 March 1996 (hereinafter 'Patent Law').[296]

391. Under certain circumstances discussed below, antitrust-related or other concerns may give rise to compulsory licensing:

(i) *Refusal to deal*: Under Article 42 of the Patent Law, the National Institute of Industrial Property (hereinafter 'INPI') may authorize the use of a patent without a license if the potential user has unsuccessfully attempted for 150 consecutive days to obtain a license from its owner under reasonable commercial terms.[297] The INPI must notify the situation to the CNDC. It is debated whether this disposition applies only in where the refusal constitutes an abuse by the patent owner, or anytime the latter refuses to deal.[298] Even when a literal interpretation of the Article would suggest the last alternative, legal

---

296. Decree No. 260, 20 Mar. 1996, [LVI-B] ADLA 1764. Also, Argentina acceded to the Paris Convention on 27 Dec. 1966. Argentina has also ratified the TRIPS Agreement, but it has not subscribed to the Patent Convention Treaty.
297. Patent Law, Art. 42.
298. Guillermo Cabanellas De Las Cuevas. Derecho De Las Patentes De Invención, Tomo 2 (Heliasta ed., 2004) at 430 to 449.

scholars support the former option, as it is the one in accordance with Trade-Related Aspects of Intellectual Property Rights (TRIPS) and the Competition Law.[299]

(ii) *Inactivity*: Additionally, where, in the absence of force majeure, three years have elapsed from the grant of a patent or four years have elapsed from the patent application, and the invention has not been exploited, no serious and real steps have been taken to exploit it, or the exploitation of the invention is discontinued for more than one year, any person may ask the INPI to use the invention without the owner's authorization.[300] The INPI is required to set a reasonable royalty for such a license, taking into account the circumstances of each case, the economic value of the authorization, and the average royalties paid in the specific market area.[301] The INPI is required to decide on such applications within ninety working days. Its decision can be appealed before the Federal Civil and Commercial courts. The appeal does not stay the decision.[302]

(iii) *National security or health emergency*: Furthermore, the Patent Law authorizes the Executive Power to provide for the exploitation of certain patents by granting exploitation rights in cases of health emergency or national security.[303]

(iv) *Patent dependency*: The Patent Law also allows the INPI to grant authorization for the use of a patent without the owner's authorization to permit exploitation of a second, dependent patent, insofar as: (i) the invention claimed under the second patent provides for a significant technical advancement of considerable economic importance as regards the original patent; (ii) the owner of the first patent is granted the right to a cross-license under reasonable conditions to exploit the second patent; and (iii) the authorized use of the first patent may not be transferred without the transfer of the second patent.[304] All such authorizations and royalty determinations by the INPI are subject to judicial review.[305] Anyone requesting such authorization must prove that he or she has the economic capacity to efficiently exploit the patentable invention and an establishment authorized to do so.[306] To date, the INPI has never granted such an authorization.

(v) *Antitrust concerns*: Consistent with Article 40(1) and (2) of the TRIPS Agreement, the Patent Law provides that licensing agreements may not contain restrictive commercial clauses affecting production, commercialization, or the technological development of the licensee; restricting competition; requiring

---

299. Competition Act, Art. 2 (f) and (h) and TRIPS Agreement, Art. 31(b).
300. Patent Law, Art. 46, para. 1.
301. Patent Law, Art. 44.
302. Patent Law, Art. 43.
303. Patent Law, Art. 45.
304. Patent Law, Art. 46.
305. Patent Law, Art. 48.
306. Patent Law, Art. 50.

Part II, Ch. 1, Restrictive Agreements

exclusive grant-back conditions or mandatory joint licensing; prohibiting challenges to the validity of the license or any other conduct contemplated under the Competition Law.[307]

392. Following the principle laid out in Article 40 of the TRIPS Agreement, the Patent Law provides for the possibility of granting compulsory licenses on antitrust grounds,[308] considering as specific anticompetitive practices the following:

(a) Imposition of prices which are excessive when compared to the average market price or discriminatory of the patented products; in particular when there exist in the market supply offers at prices that are considerably lower than those offered by the patent holder for the same product.
(b) Refusal to supply the local market under reasonable commercial conditions.
(c) Obstruction of commercial or productive activities.
(d) Any other act that may be considered as in violation of Law 22,262 or such other legislation that may replace it.

393. As can be appreciated, the foregoing violations of the Patent Law are not necessarily violations of the Competition Law.

394. As noted earlier, the Competition Act employs a rule of reason approach in all cases, i.e., it does not deem any conduct as per se illegal.[309] Thus, market power in a relevant market must be demonstrated.[310] A patent in and of itself does not necessarily create market power because substitutes for the patented product may well exist.[311] It is thus highly unlikely that the CNDC would declare the acts mentioned in the Patent Law per se illegal under the Competition Act. It must be noted that neither the CNDC nor the INPI have definitively resolved this question and thus uncertainty in this area remains.[312] Moreover, the acts mentioned in the Patent Law could be considered unconstitutional for being contrary to Article 17 of the Argentine Constitution as well as Article 28 of the TRIPS Agreement.

---

307. Patent Law, Art. 38 (referencing the Former Competition Act).
308. Patent Law, Art. 47.
309. Competition Act, Art. 1 and Otamendi, Jorge, *supra* n. 86.
310. Competition Act, Art. 5 and Cabanellas (h), *supra* n. 19, at 247 to 268.
311. *Ibid.*, and Art. 5.
312. The CNDC or INPI could possibly take a different view. On the one hand, Art. 44 could be interpreted as requiring its application *jointly with* the Competition Law and its principles. On the other, since the Competition Law has been passed more recently, than the Patent Law, and could be deemed more specific as to the treatment of anticompetitive practices, the legal principles of *lex posteriori priori derogat* (a more recent law abrogates a prior law on the same subject) or *generalibus specialia derogant* (a specific law abrogates a more general one to the extent they conflict) may be applicable. Moreover, Art. 59 of the Competition Act abrogates any jurisdiction of agencies other than antitrust agencies to deal with antitrust issues. However, from a study of the parliamentary discussions held in connection with this Article, it appears that Congress may have intended to consider the range of conduct identified in subss (a), (b) and (c) of Art. 44 as different types of anticompetitive acts not demanding the general requirements of the Competition Act.

395. Where the adjudicatory agency of the Competition Act determines that the patentee has engaged in anticompetitive practices,[313] it informs the INPI, who then publishes a notice in the Official Gazette (*Boletín Oficial*), informing third parties that they can make offers for a license.[314] The INPI will then consider the offers and decide whether or not to grant compulsory license.

B. Trademark Licensing, Know-How and Trade Secret Licensing

396. Indirect reference to cases involving trademark licensing (in the tying context) will be outlined in paragraphs 433–437 below. The author is not aware of the licensing of such assets having been examined by the CNDC or Secretariat. As explained in paragraphs 687 et seq. below, however, transfers of know-how are considered in merger review to determine the length of the non-compete obligation, of five years of know-how if they were part of the transaction and two years if they were not.

---

313. Patent Law, Art. 44.
314. Patent Law, Art. 32.

Chapter 2. Dominant Undertakings' Prohibited Practices

§1. EXPLOITATIVE PRACTICES

I. Excessive/Unfair Pricing

397. Excessive pricing is not expressly mentioned in the Competition Act, but can be found in the interplay of section 1 (which prohibits abuses of dominance in general) and items (a) and (g) of section 2, which list as examples of anticompetitive conducts:

> (a) Directly or indirectly fixing, concerting or manipulating the sale or purchase price of goods or services offered or demanded in the market, as well as exchanging information with the same object or effect.
> (g) Directly or indirectly and by any means fixing, imposing or implementing, in agreement with competitors or individually, purchase or sale prices and conditions, of goods, services or production.

398. The rationale for sanctioning this conduct is clear. If there is consensus in finding exclusionary abuses of dominant position – incurred for the purpose of allowing the unfettered exercise of market power – as illegal, there should be no doubt that the direct application of excessive – meaning supracompetitive – prices by a dominant undertaking, if determined to be the result of an abuse of such conduct, should receive a similar legal consideration.

The foregoing theory has been difficult to apply in practice, not only due to the difficulties in determining when a certain price will become 'excessive' or 'unfair' – which at a minimum would require an assessment of what the 'normal', 'fair' or 'competitive' prices should be, but also because rarely in Argentina's recent economic history an extended period has passed without inflation or market distortions been experienced, and thus potential abusive pricing conducts could have become mingled with external factors justifying price increases to a certain extent.

399. In addition, in periods of economic instability the Government has regularly resorted to direct market intervention, in the form of price stability agreements, export restrictions, price freeze measures and the like, in the understanding that they provide a direct – albeit distortive – relief that could not be provided in a timely fashion by the application of competition laws.

400. Case law development in this area thus should be examined under the foregoing limitations.

401. Probably, *S.A. Industrias Welbers Ltda.*[315] was the first case to deal directly with this matter, and the only one in which this conduct was sanctioned in its purest form.

---

315. *Supra* n. 56.

402. Defendant, a sugar manufacturer, forced sugarcane producers to grant it financing in very favourable terms to guarantee them the purchase of the crop. Key to the decision was the fact that said payment terms were apparently contrary to sectorial regulations protecting producers. In any case, defendant was found dominant given its share in the processing of sugar in the relevant area. Plaintiff was fined and appealed. The Court of Appeals confirmed the administrative decision in full, expressly ratifying the illegality of abusive pricing as follows:

> It must be considered as duly proved that the pricing conditions under which S.A. Industrias Welbers Ltda. acquired the crop are not those mandated by Article 35 of the Sugar Law, and are solely the result of a dominant position in the area that was abusively used by imposing purchase price conditions; that a detriment to the general economic interest occurred, by diverting from the terms under which the Sugar Law protects the interests of the producer. Defendant's arguments that there was neither an abuse of dominant position nor a detriment to the general economic interest cannot prevail.[316]

403. Most post–*Industrias Welbers* investigations did not conclude with a sanction. For example, in *Federación Argentina de la Industria del Caucho*[317] defendants' extended payment terms were mainly justified by the effects of an industry crisis, in *Resinfor*[318] by a lack of dominant position and in *UCR Lobos*[319] by the effects of the 2002 currency devaluation on imports. But in *SADAIC* a hotel association obtained an injunction against a musical performing rights organization which conditioned the way the latter charged fees as they were found prima facie exploitative. The injunction, however, was reversed by the Court of Appeals based on lack of empowerments of the CNDC to issue the injunction.[320]

404. In spite of the foregoing, it is interesting to note that the most important abuse of dominance case to date can be characterized as an abusive pricing case.

405. In re *YPF*, mentioned earlier in this work (in paragraph 167, among others) the fine amounted to 20% of the total price surcharge applied by defendant. Said differential could be calculated, pursuant to the CNDC, by the comparison between lower export LPG prices – which resale in Argentina was contractually prohibited – and higher domestic LPG prices. YPF's exports and the conditions imposed on them were regarded by the CNDC not as an exercise of defendant's right to structure its overseas sales as it deemed fit for its business, but rather as a manoeuvre to artificially increase the price of the product in Argentina.

---

316. *Ibid.*, at 461.
317. 'Federación Argentina de la Industria del Caucho' (complaint against Sevel Argentina S.A. and Renault Argentina S.A.), Secretaría de Industria y Comercio, Resolution No. 26 (5 Feb. 1992).
318. 'Resinfor S.A.' (complaint against Compañía Casco S.A.I.C.), Secretaría de Comercio e Inversiones, Resolution No. 14 (11 Jan. 1996).
319. 'UCR Lobos s/ solicitud de intervención de la CNDC (c. 828)', Secretaría de Comercio Interior, Resolution No. 74 (13 Oct. 2005).
320. 'SADAIC c/ apelación de resolución de la Comisión Nacional de Defensa de la Competencia', *supra* n. 165.

II. Discrimination

406. Case law presents a collection of primary-line and secondary-line cases. It must be noted, though, that the Competition Act does not require an actual restriction of competition, since unjustified discrimination is examined as a type of exploitative abuse of dominance which may directly impact on consumer welfare. In spite of the foregoing, the authorities have been open to consider all types of business justifications.

407. It is well settled that a variety of commercial considerations can justify price discrimination. For example, in *FECRA*[321] defendant, an oil company, decided to sell its products at lower prices to a retail station operated by a major supermarket, which was built in said retail store's parking lot. Issues such as higher volume sold, marketing considerations and the financial strength of the supermarket could explain the price differential.

408. Discrimination was also accepted as a means to enforce a maximum resale price maintenance scheme by YPF, whereby the price of gas to retailers was increased insofar as they did not agree to limit their consumer prices to the values suggested by the oil company.[322] Even when the CNDC recognized the restriction of competition stemming from the practice, it appreciated the fact that its purpose was to guarantee that YPF gas would be sold at a lower price than its competitors, and validated the practice.

409. Meeting the lower price of a competitor only in the areas where such competition existed, even if it implied an abrupt reduction in the regular price of the product (i.e., 50%) was accepted as a defence in re *Cablevisión*[323] has also been accepted. However, concerns have been raised in cases of competition between new entrants in markets with important sunken costs, as allowing the incumbent to lower the price only in the area in which entry was produced could prevent entry to occur altogether.[324]

---

321. 'Federación de Empresarios de Combustibles de la República Argentina (FECRA)' (complaint against EG3 S.A.), Secretaría de Defensa de la Competencia y el Consumidor, Resolution No. 59 (6 Mar. 2001).
322. 'Dirección General de Comercio Interior y Defensa del Consumidor de la Pcia. de Entre Ríos' (complaint against Repsol Gas S.A., Totalgaz Argentina S.A., YPF Gas S.A. and Rosa Gas S.A.), Secretaría de la Competencia, la Desregulación y la Defensa del Consumidor, Resolution No. 107 (7 Sep. 2001).
323. 'Cablevisión S.A. (Río Cuarto) s/ infracción Ley 25.156', Secretaría de la Competencia, la Desregulación y la Defensa del Consumidor, Resolution No. 78 (28 Dec. 2002).
324. This was the situation in 'Multicanal S.A. y Cablevisión S.A.', CFed. Paraná (14 Sep. 2005), where a Federal Appeal Court confirmed an injunction that was issued by the CNDC ordering defendants – cable-TV companies – to apply the reduced price in the entire city and not the more reduced area where plaintiff was entering the market.

410. One of the older precedents is *Fiscalía Nacional de Investigaciones Administrativas*,[325] where the legality of a first refusal provision inserted in a coke supply agreement was examined. The clause granted defendant the right to purchase coke destined to exports at the price of the lowest bidder.

411. The fact that the coke over which one of the defendants had a priority was not the one reserved to satisfy domestic demand was decisive in the outcome of the case, given that whatever restriction or disincentive in price competition could occur, the same would not have effects in Argentina.

412. In addition, the decision was justified by a broad decision of the term 'general economic interest' which would not be accepted at present, covering not only consumer or total welfare in the relevant market, but also the welfare of society as a whole. This was influenced by the fact that Great Lakes Carbon had built the first coke processing plant in Argentina for YPF. As stated by the CNDC:

> From an economic analysis perspective, the general economic interest can be assimilated as the benefit received by society from the conduct under review. And evidently referring to foreign exchange benefits and other benefits such as the use of local workforce, supply of raw materials, etc. without neglecting the supply of traditional local consumers, through a contract that allowed YPF the sale of an important volume of coke to the domestic market, with excess reserves for exportation, … means that we are talking about a benefit received by society and not a detriment to the general economic interest.[326]

§2. EXCLUSIONARY PRACTICES

I. Predation

413. Up-to-date the author is not aware of a decision condemning predatory pricing. There are, however, several decisions that have defined with some level of certainty the structure of reasoning to be followed by the enforcer.

414. In the oldest case, *Eolo*,[327] the CNDC anticipated that it would use internationally accepted theories to pursue the investigation of predatory pricing. In particular, the agency cited a then recent work by Joskow and Klevorich[328] that would guide most investigations ever since. It was then decided that a two-step test would be applied, requiring that:

---

325. 'Fiscalía Nacional de Investigaciones Administrativas' (complaint against Yacimientos Petrolíferos Fiscales, Great Lakes Carbon Corporation and Copetro S.A.), Secretaría de Industria y Comercio, Resolution No. 135 (29 Apr. 1992).
326. *Ibid.*, at point VI para. 7.
327. 'Eolo S.A.' (complaint against La Platense S.A.), Ministerio de Comercio e Intereses Marítimos, Resolution No. 574 (24 Nov. 1981).
328. Paul L. Joskow & Alvin Klevorich, *A Framework for Analyzing Predatory Pricing Policy*, 89 Yale L.J. (1979).

Part II, Ch. 2, Dominant Undertakings' Prohibited Practices 415–419

(i) the sale price be below production cost; and
(ii) as a consequence thereof, defendant increase its market share.

415. No relevant cases were examined until 1997, where the CNDC decided three: *Roberto José Díaz*,[329] *Cámara Argentina de Papelerías, Librerías y Afines*[330] and *Odipa*.[331]

416. *Cámara Argentina de Papelerías, Librerías y Afines* required the simultaneous existence of three conditions for predation to exist: (i) possession by the predator of market power or dominance; (ii) intent to exclude competitors; and (iii) existence of barriers of entry to future competitors. It then adopted the procedure suggested by the OECD, which consisted in focusing on whether barriers of entry were high or not and, only if they were, determining whether the sale had been made below the average variable cost (AVC) or, even if made above the AVC, whether defendant significantly increased prices in the following two years without an objective justification (this last part of the test never left aside though).

417. *Cliba*[332] considered the issue of predatory pricing in the context of public bidding processes, rejecting its existence entirely:

> The possibility of predatory pricing policies aimed at excluding competitors in the bidding process to obtain monopoly gains during the contract period must be discarded, because, by definition, the presumed predatory price must coincide with that to be applied during the rendering of the service.

418. It must be noted that while *Cliba* refers that the practice must have the potential to exclude competitors, other cases including *Makro* and the more recent *Cablevisión* mentioned below still inquire into a proof of intent, although not defining whether this last requisite would replace the former were intent to be found.

419. In *Cablevisión*,[333] the CNDC appeared to have found a model case, as it was faced with a defendant with an apparent dominant position in a market (at the time of the complaint, defined by the CNDC as cable-TV), an extremely low price and even some indication of intent.

---

329. 'Roberto José Díaz' (complaint against Cooperativa de Energía Eléctrica Colonia San Bartolomé Ltda., José Mana and Héctor Mana), Secretaría de Industria, Comercio y Minería, Resolution No. 524 (6 Jun. 1997).
330. 'Cámara Argentina de Papelerías, Librerías y Afines' (complaint against Supermercados Mayoristas Makro S.A.), Secretaría de Industria, Comercio y Minería, Resolution No. 810 (22 Aug. 1997).
331. 'Odipa S.R.L.' (complaint against Control y Seguridad S.A.), Secretaría de Industria, Comercio y Minería, Resolution No. 919 (12 Sep. 1997).
332. 'Cliba Ingeniería Ambiental S.A. and Ormas Ambiental S.A.' (complaint against Urbaser S.A., Urbaser Argentina S.A. and Dycasa S.A.), Secretaría de la Competencia, la Desregulación y la Defensa del Consumidor, Resolution No. 112 (7 Sep. 2001).
333. 'Cablevisión S.A., Santa Clara de Asís S.A. y Enlace S.A. (Salta) s/ infracción Ley 25.156', Secretaría de Comercio Interior, Resolution No. 188 (22 Oct. 2008).

420. Proof was presented rebutting the presumption of intent, and in the seven years that lasted the investigation the definition of relevant market was broadened to include satellite-TV, defendant's market position at the time of adjudication then being diluted as a consequence thereof. Before then, however, the case had been decided by a detailed analysis of the costs involved in rendering the cable service, which concluded that programming costs, which represented the majority of the total costs, were mostly fixed and not variable, as a consequence of minimum guaranteed payment obligations included in the relevant agreements.[334]

II. Tying

421. Even when section 2(i) of the Competition Law has explicitly prohibited tying the sale of a good or service to the acquisition or use of another good or service, all relevant cases were decided under the Former Competition Act.

422. Case law on this matter dates back to 1982, in the *Ifrisa* case,[335] in which YPF, a State-owned oil and gas company, was charged of abuse of dominance when it instructed third parties operating gas stations under the YPF brand to change the provider of packed ice (a product normally available in such points of sale in Argentina) from plaintiff Ifrisa to competitor Ecsal, under a contract that guaranteed YPF a percentage of all ice sales.

423. YPF was empowered to impose the sale of the products manufactured by Ecsal by virtue of a clause in the agreement entered into with the gas retailers, in which the latter agreed to sell any product (other than gas) 'sponsored' by YPF, presumably exposing themselves to the termination of the contract with YPF in case they refused.

424. The CNDC did not accept the idea of the retailer losing control over side businesses such as that of packed ice in favour of YPF, characterizing such activity as an abuse of dominance. In the agency's words:

> The sale of packed ice lacks a relation of complementariness with the products manufactured by YPF; it is an activity which forms part of such secondary area under the exclusive decision of the retailer and alien to the influence of the supplier. Ice is neither a product neither used by drivers nor related to the service a driver expects for his or her vehicle. It is sold in gas stations for the

---

334. It is interesting to note that in another predatory pricing claim between the same parties which was adjudicated less than two years later, 'Cablevisión S.A., Santa Clara de Asís S.A. y Enlace S.A. (Salta) s/ infracción Ley 25.156 (c. 1026)', Secretaría de Comercio Interior, Resolution No. 166 (14 May 2010), the CNDC changed the measure of cost to that of long-run average incremental cost.
335. *Supra* n. 58.

Part II, Ch. 2, Dominant Undertakings' Prohibited Practices 425–428

aforementioned reasons, linked to the distinctive features of ice as a commercial product and unrelated to the needs of the driver as such.[336]

[…]

A restriction in the degree of competition in the packed ice market is also observed. Such restriction is a consequence of the preference granted to Ecsal by YPF, its significance in the overall scenario stemming from the significant superiority of its gas stations over those of other brands, … that could translate in the exclusion of other competitors, who see their sale structures limited. And given that the operation of a market is benefitted with the presence of a larger number of persons, obviously the same is restricted with the setting up of an exclusionary system as in the instant case.[337]

When YPF abuses its dominance assuming the power to decide over third-party commercial structures as if they were its own, it transfers its lead in the oil business to one competitor in a different market, and so exerts influence to create a dependent market and restrict its degree of competition.[338]

[…]

425. The final decision imposed fines to both defendants, enjoining the distribution agreement.[339]

426. YPF was subject to a similar investigation in re *Tidem*,[340] which was ultimately closed due to the lack of facts supporting plaintiff's exclusionary allegations.

427. In *Asociacion de Empresas de Servicios Fúnebres y Afines de Villa Maria*,[341] plaintiff, an association of funeral services companies, complained of the abuse of dominance of several cooperatives of the area that, outside the scope of their services, provided funerary services insurance by a reduced additional payment, excluding independent providers.

428. At the heart of the problem was a decision of the cooperatives regulator, which created incentives for the establishment of funeral services run by the cooperatives themselves. Such services could be paid separately, but also through the implementation of a collective financing system contributed pro rata by all applying members. In most cases, payment of the insurance was included in the same electricity bill.

---

336. *Ibid.*, at VII, para. 2.
337. *Ibid.*, at VIII, para. 4.
338. *Ibid.*, at VIII, para. 5.
339. The Supreme Court remanded the judgment, and the Court of Appeals issued a new decision on 12 Sep. 1985 confirming the earlier ruling.
340. 'Tidem S.A.' (complaint against Fram Argentina S.A. and Yacimientos Petrolíferos Fiscales), Secretaría de Comercio, Resolution No. 1184 (13 Dec. 1984).
341. 'Asociacion de Empresas de Servicios Fúnebres y Afines de Villa Maria', CNDC, Resolution dated 24 Aug. 1982.

429. The CNDC understood that:

> The procedure used to carry out the collective financing regulating funeral services entails validating the enforcement of a clause tying such service with that of electricity supply. And through said tying an abuse of dominance is committed, given that the beneficiary of funeral services can be forced to fulfil under the threat of serious consequences that are not those ordinarily contemplated in the law. Through the foregoing a parallel abuse of dominance in the subordinated market is achieved, given that competitors in like services not under similar preferences will not be in the same conditions.[342]

430. As a result, the cooperatives were fined and ordered to separate the sale, invoicing and accounting of funeral services from those of the monopolistic service.[343]

431. Shortly after this decision, however, the cooperatives lobbied the Secretariat and achieved a specific decision authorizing the former to render the services as originally provided, and in a case similar than the one described above a Court of Appeals reversed the Secretariat's decision.[344] Both actions were mostly based in section 5 of the Former Competition Act, which – until its abrogation by Law 24,481 in 1996 – exempted conducts by private parties justified by State action, through general regulations or specific administrative decisions, and thus should not be taken into account for purposes of the Competition Act, which lacks said exemption.

432. In another case involving a cooperative, *Carlos Basilio Vassolo*,[345] defendant acknowledged that it had tied the sale of two herbicides. However, in this opportunity it was evidenced that it lacked market power, and technical reports were of the view that both herbicides were commonly used together, the CNDC then concluding that the joint sale was reasonable.

433. There have been a number of cases concerning broadcasting rights to specific soccer matches that were sold only together with other soccer matches or sports events.

---

342. *Ibid.*, at VI, para. 3.
343. A similar reasoning was followed in 'Asociación de Empresas de Servicios Fúnebres y Afines del Interior de la Provincia de Córdoba' (complaint against Cooperativa de Provisión de Obras y Servicios Públicos y Sociales de Oliva Limitada), Secretaría de Comercio, Resolution No. 132 (24 Feb. 1984), although this case did not conclude with a sanction since defendant had been prevented from selling funeral services by a court order.
344. 'Cooperativas de Electricidad de la Provincia de Córdoba', CNCiv. Com y ContAdm. R. C. [853] LLC 130 (2002).
345. 'Carlos Basilio Vassolo' (complaint against Cooperativa Agraria de Tres Arroyos), Secretaría de Comercio, Resolution No. 315 (22 Sep. 1983).

Part II, Ch. 2, Dominant Undertakings' Prohibited Practices 434–437

434. In *Servicios de Radio y Televisión de la Universidad Nacional de Córdoba*,[346] defendant was the exclusive licensee of TV rights for pre-World Cup soccer matches. The complaint alleged that defendant was charging excessive prices for those events to an open-air channel, and that it tied them to the sale of different matches, since it would sell them only in a package format. The CNDC analysed three issues: (i) whether the general economic interest was compromised; (ii) whether there was an abuse of a dominant position; and (iii) whether the situation could be remedied through the application of antitrust rules.[347]

435. The CNDC concluded that the licensor had a dominant position, as substitutability of rights to such soccer events was quite low.[348] Nevertheless, the CNDC approved the packaged licenses, concluding that, even if the defendant were a monopolist, its prices could not be considered excessive, given that it had to pay substantial sums to purchase the rights from the sports leagues.[349] The CNDC concluded that the defendant could make a reasonable return on its investment only by licensing the events to cable companies, which were willing to buy the entire package and at a price much higher than that offered by open-air systems.[350] Thus, the CNDC held that the defendant's refusal to license individual matches to the complainant was reasonable.

436. In *M.S.O. Supercanal*,[351] the National Commercial Appeal Court confirmed an interim measure granted by a trial court against the two defendants. Both companies owned broadcasting rights of various sporting events that they sold in bundles. Plaintiff, a cable company, sought to buy only the soccer events, claiming a lack of demand for the other events, and the programmers predictably refused. The trial court concluded that the programmers held a dominant position in local soccer programming, and that they abused their dominant position by tying the unwanted events to soccer events.[352] The Court of Appeals confirmed the lower court's decision, ordering the unbundling of the programmes and requiring the license fee to be set based on the soccer events alone.[353]

437. Likewise, in *Fox Sports Latin America*,[354] plaintiff obtained an injunction aimed at suspending for ninety days the termination of the contract for the supply of a high-definition sports channel – which presumably had been tied with another new, unwanted channel – to allow the parties to reach a negotiated result.

---

346. 'Servicios de Radio y Televisión de la Universidad Nacional de Córdoba S.A.' (complaint against Durford Commercial Corporation), Secretaría de Industria, Comercio y Minería, Resolution No.1136 (29 Oct. 1997).
347. *Ibid.*, at 5.1.
348. *Ibid.*, at 5.2.
349. *Ibid.*, at 5.3.
350. *Ibid.*, at 6.3.
351. 'M.S.O. Supercanal', CNCom, [2003-III] JA 502 (2002).
352. *Ibid.*, at 1. 1.b).
353. *Ibid.*, at 4.
354. 'Fox Sports Latin America S.A. s/ infracción ley N° 25.156' Secretaría de Comercio Interior, Resolución No. 122 (18 Aug. 2011).

III. Rebates

438. By and large discounts and rebates are accepted as standard practices of commerce. However, when they foreclose a significant part of the relevant market, they are generally regarded as a form of exclusive dealing.

439. Such foreclosure, as the cases below illustrate, were generally produced when the discount or rebate was not specifically based on the specific volume of commerce between the party applying it and its client, but to such volume vis-à-vis the volume of commerce between the client and competitors of the discounting party.

440. One of the most significant cases to date is *Editorial Amfin*.[355] Defendant's newspaper, with 60% of the total sales in the relevant market, applied a 15% discount to advertisements on condition of exclusivity. Such scheme applied to 25% of the total advertising income of the newspaper.

441. The CNDC understood that the exclusivity could not be justified by efficiency considerations, and that its effects were twofold: (i) reduced the information available to final consumers (customers of competing newspapers); and (ii) affected competition in the newspaper advertising business. A minority opinion of the CNDC, however, understood that the practice was common business usage, and that the short term of duration of the offer did not have the potential to affect entry.

442. The Court of Appeals reversed the decision.[356] As regards the reduction of information to consumers, the Court stated that, by and large, consumers did not purchase plaintiffs or defendant's newspapers due to its advertisements and that, in any event, they could buy a second newspaper to that effect. In connection with the claim that the competition in newspaper advertising was restricted it mentioned that, generally, only 30% of the total income of newspapers derived from advertising sales, and that plaintiff had not proved that its finances had been affected as a consequence of plaintiff's discounts. It therefore reversed the administrative decision.

443. The judgment seems unconvincing. On the one hand, the statement that advertisements played no role in the sale of defendant's newspaper seemed unfounded and, in any case, the fact that a consumer could purchase a second newspaper to read advertisements that were not in the first newspaper due to plaintiff's discounts would imply a direct hit on consumer welfare, which is precisely what competition laws try to prevent. As regards the market for newspaper advertising, where the exclusionary conduct clearly took place, the court seemed confused by the evidence proving that plaintiff's finances had apparently not been affected. Plaintiff had a double source of income, derived from two distinct activities and relevant markets – newspaper sales and advertising – and consequently a potential

---

[355]. 'Editorial Amfin S.A.', Secretaría de Industria, Comercio y Minería, Resolution No. 336 (18 May 1998).
[356]. 'Editorial Amfin S.A.', CNPenal Económico, Sala B (19 Nov. 1998), LL 1999-D, 342.

Part II, Ch. 2, Dominant Undertakings' Prohibited Practices 444–446

exclusion from one of those markets – advertising – should not necessarily mean that its financial viability would be at risk.[357]

444. A similar situation was presented in *Asociación Argentina de Agencias de Viajes de Turismo*,[358] where the main domestic airline applied fidelity discounts to travel agencies that increased pro rata to the increase in the percentage of tickets sold by the agencies from their total ticket sales. The case was closed with the undertaking offered by defendants of not applying those incentives in the future.

445. The practice of bundled discounts was examined in *Telecom Argentina Stet – France Telecom and Telecom Personal*,[359] where a dominant fixed-line telephone company that also was an important competitor in the mobile phone market offered 50% discounts in certain fixed-to-mobile, mobile-to-fixed and mobile-to-mobile calls to customers contracting both types of services to defendant. The decision, inspired in the Third Circuit's decision in *Le Page's Inc. v. 3M*,[360] was dismissed mainly due to the facts that: (i) defendant's prices were not predatory; (ii) plaintiff's inability to compete was not proved; and (iii) the parties' and their competitors' market shares had not shifted towards a more concentrated market.

445.1. On the contrary, in *Clorox* defendant was fined for allegedly conditioning its rebates to resellers maintaining a price gap between defendant's and its main competitor's products.[361]

IV. Refusal to Deal

446. The Former Competition Act only specifically contemplated this practice if carried out collusively, i.e., as in a group boycott case.[362] The Competition Act, however, enunciates it in section 2 in the following terms:

> Unjustifiably refusing to satisfy specific requests, for the purchase or sale of goods or services, made under the prevailing conditions in the respective market.[363]

---

357. For a critical view on the Court of Appeals' judgment, *see* Bogo, Jorge, *El caso AMFIN (Ambito Financiero) Vs. ARGEA (Clarín). Discrepancias en la instancia administrativa y en la judicial*, Boletín Latinoamericano de Competencia, No. 7, Part 1, July 1999 (available at http://ec.europa.eu/competition/publications/blc/boletin_7_1_es.pdf).
358. 'Asociación Argentina de Agencias de Viajes de Turismo (AAAVYT)' (complaint against Junta de Representantes de Compañías Aéreas, Aerolíneas Argentinas S.A. and Austral Líneas Aéreas (Cielos del Sur S.A.), Secretaría de Industria, Comercio y Minería, Resolution No. 755 (9 Oct. 1999).
359. 'Telecom Argentina Stet – France Telecom y Telecom Personal S.A. s/ Infracción Ley 25.156', Secretaría de Coordinación Técnica, Resolution No. 93 (8 Jun. 2005).
360. *Le Page's Inc. v. 3M*, 277 F.3d 365 (3d Cir. 2002), *Ibid.*, at 80–81.
361. 'Clorox Argentina S.A. s/ Infracción Ley 25.156', Secretaría de Comercio, Resolution No. 65 (17 Apr. 2015).
362. Section 41 para. 7.
363. Even when, as anticipated, practices listed under s. 2 require the concurrence of the requirements of s. 1 (restriction of competition or abuse of dominance, potential injury to the 'general economic interest') to be considered in violation of the Competition Act.

447. This is one area in which the CNDC practice clearly departs from its otherwise current consistent policy that all conducts must infringe – at least potentially – the general economic interest, and that this requirement entails the exercise of substantial market power likely to harm consumers, not competitors.

448. Case law on the matter, however, does not focus on the status of competition downstream as a consequence of the refusal, or on the effect on consumers. Implicit in this observation seems to be the understanding that, for the authorities, a competitor, regardless of its importance (or even, particularly in case of new entrants), deserves to compete on equal footing to all others.

449. The foregoing leads to the conclusion that, under the Competition Act, a dominant person has a positive duty to deal with parties downstream insofar as its product or service is necessary to compete in such market.

450. Care should be noted in that case law has *not* required that the refused party be a competitor of the refusing party, although such circumstance is taken into account in a finding of illegality.

451. Something similar occurs with commercial justifications, or the fact that the plaintiff had a course of dealing with defendant: they are taken into account, but it is not clear whether they would be sufficient to dismiss a complaint if the refusing person is dominant.

452. One of the first cases was *Antonio Humberto Savant*,[364] a slaughterhouse which refused to sell to only one of the thirty-one butchers with stores in the city on the basis that it did not have enough installed capacity to deal with plaintiff's requests. It appears though that defendant supplied meat as well as slaughterhouse services to all butchers but the plaintiff, and consequently could have been regarded as its competitor.

453. More contemporary cases have not differed much in their approach. In *Horacio Ignacio Campos*,[365] defendant, a motion picture distributor, was held not guilty due to the fact he was ' … *exposed to substantial competition and acts in a contestable scenario, and thus its refusal to supply motion pictures to a new agent hardly can affect competition or the functioning of the market*'.[366] Subsidiarily, the CNDC noted that defendant's commercial justifications were reasonable, namely, that plaintiff: (i) lacked a business background; (ii) had shown aggressiveness in its dealings with defendant, taking a notary with him to record the results of the negotiations; and (iii) readily sent threatening letters.[367]

---

364. 'Antonio Humberto Savant' (complaint filed against Matadero Vera S.R.L.), Secretaría de Comercio, Resolution No. 78 (11 Mar. 1982).
365. '*Horacio Ignacio Campos v. Buena Vista Columbia Tristar Films of Argentina S.A.*', Secretaría de Defensa de la Competencia y del Consumidor, Resolution No. 15 (20 Jan. 1999).
366. *Ibid.*, at 5.5.
367. *Ibid.* (n. 358), at 5.8. and 5.9.

Part II, Ch. 2, Dominant Undertakings' Prohibited Practices 453.1–457

453.1. In a much more recent case, defendant, a Ford Motor subsidiary and exclusive importer of Volvo spare parts, was held guilty of this conduct for refusing to sell parts to a dealer not belonging to its network, based on its alleged intention to improve official dealers' profitability.[368]

454. In several cases, prospective buyers have argued that the requested price was so high as to amount to a refusal to deal. This occurred, for example, *in M.S.O. Supercanal S.A. and Supercanal Holding*.[369] Defendant was the holder of exclusive broadcasting rights to soccer matches played by the Argentinean soccer team during the qualifying stage of the 2002 Korea–Japan World Cup. The plaintiff, a broadcasting company, filed a claim with the CNDC against the defendant arguing that it had refused to accept the plaintiff's offer for the purchase of a non-exclusive broadcasting license for the match between the Argentinean and Brazilian national teams. Additionally, the plaintiff requested injunctive relief that would have required the defendant to permit the broadcasting, at market prices, of that match as well as subsequent ones in which the Argentinean team participated.

455. In a preliminary determination, the CNDC ordered the rights holder to license on 'non-discriminatory terms'.[370] This order was insufficient from the plaintiff's perspective because the parties could not reach an agreement on price. No sanction was ultimately imposed because the court found that the refusal was based on the existence of unpaid debt of the cable company to the programmer rather than any abuse of dominance.

456. In *Torneos y Competencias*,[371] plaintiff, a small satellite-TV operator, accused defendants (affiliated companies) of trying to conceal an unjustified refusal to license certain non-exclusive broadcasting rights over sports channels by overpricing a package of such channels, which included the most sought-after events. Claimant highlighted the importance of soccer as a competitive tool and asserted that the purpose of such denial was to benefit one of its direct competitors, in whose local operations defendants had an indirect shareholding interest.

457. Defendants argued that they had a single commercial policy, which calculated the price of the license based on the demographics and potential service penetration of each market, rather than the number of subscribers of the pay-TV system. The CNDC verified that such a policy was adopted in the agreement with another satellite-TV client and dismissed the claim without considering the potentially exclusionary effects of the practice (which, e.g., might prevent any new entrants from carrying such channels).

---

368. 'Ford Argentina S.A., Volvo Sudamericana S.A. y otras s/ infracción a la ley 25.156', Secretaría de Comercio Interior, Resolution No. 69 (28 May 2014).
369. 'M.S.O. Supercanal S.A. and Supercanal Holding' (complaint filed against Dayco Holdings Ltd.), Secretaría de Coordinación Técnica, Resolution No. 112 (24 Aug. 2004).
370. Comisión Nacional de Defensa de la Competencia, interim decision (31 Aug. 2001).
371. 'Torneos y Competencias S.A y otros S.A y otros s/ Infracción a la Ley 25.156', Secretaría de la Competencia, la Desregulación y la Defensa del Consumidor, Resolution No. 67 (16 May 2003).

458. In a similar case involving the same defendants,[372] a cable operator alleged the existence of a refusal to license broadcasting rights for certain channels that included different matches of the main Argentine Soccer League; it challenged the abusively high price charged for the channels. As in the previous case, claimant asserted that the purpose of the denial was to benefit its direct competitor, a company that indirectly had common shareholders with the accused firms. Once again, defendants successfully defended the validity of their commercial policy, allegedly applied on non-discriminatory terms.[373]

459. The CNDC concluded that the dispute was a purely commercial one, since during the negotiation licensors had in fact licensed other rights to plaintiff (thus demonstrating that they had no specific intention to exclude this company).[374] Indeed, the parties ultimately reached an agreement. Also, it was shown that, during the dispute, the claimant's market position increased.[375] The file was subsequently closed.

V. Price Squeeze

460. There are very few cases on the area of price squeezes. The latest have all been decided following the principles of *United States v. Aluminium Co. of America*,[376] which according to the decision are basically four: (i) that the firm have monopoly power over a product; (ii) that the price charged for the product be higher than a certain 'fair price'; (iii) that the product be required to compete in a second market where the monopolist competes; and (iv) that the price applied by the monopolist in the second market be so low that its competitors cannot compete in such market if they meet such price.

461. The only case where a sanction was imposed was, precisely, the older one.

462. In *Alianza Gas*[377] defendant, an LPG bottling company, was fined when it changed the financing conditions to its distributor and, when it started buying to alternative suppliers, tried to win the distributor's customers through direct sales at wholesale or even lower prices. Note that even items (iii) and (iv) of the preceding paragraph could be deemed as having been met, and that the change in financing

---

372. 'Tele Red Imagen S.A. y Televisión Satelital Codificada S.A. s/ Infracción Ley 25.156', Secretaría de la Competencia, la Desregulación y la Defensa del Consumidor, Resolution No. 66 (16 May 2003) and Secretaría de Comercio Interior, Resolution No. 174 (14 Oct. 2008) (this last resolution issued after Resolution No. 66 was remanded by the Federal Appeals Court of the province of Salta).
373. *Ibid.*, at 87–92.
374. *Ibid.*, at 97.
375. *Ibid.*, at 98–104.
376. *United States v. Aluminium Co. of America*, USSC 377 U.S. 271 (1964).
377. 'Alianza Gas' (complaint filed against Atlante Gas S.A.C.I., Secretaría de Comercio, Resolution No. 475 (7 Dec. 1983).

Part II, Ch. 2, Dominant Undertakings' Prohibited Practices 463–464

conditions could be regarding as 'unfair', clearly defendant was not dominant, as the fact that plaintiff could easily replace its sales demonstrates.

463. In a more recent case in the same market, *Autogas*,[378] defendants, an integrated LPG producer and bottler, respectively, were charged of price squeezing by a distributor. Plaintiff's market power and abusive price upstream were proved, given that the period in which such practices had allegedly been committed was the same in which the abusive pricing practices of YPF referred in paragraph 405 above had taken place. The complaint was dismissed however since no evidence of predatory pricing was found.

464. On the contrary, in *Siderar*,[379] the CNDC concluded that neither defendant's wholesale price was unfair, nor the retail prices predatory. As regards the former, the agency applied the 'billing' and, to a lesser extent, 'transfer' tests employed by the Alcoa court.

---

378. 'Autogas S.A.I.C.' (complaint against YPF S.A. and YPF Gas S.A.), Secretaría de Defensa de la Competencia y del Consumidor, Resolution dated 27 Jan. 1999.
379. *Supra* n. 253.

Chapter 3. Concentrations

§1. Horizontal Mergers

465. Horizontal mergers are by and large examined according to the Guidelines.

466. There is no clear-cut rule as to what level of concentration would be acceptable, but it could be argued that so far the CNDC has adopted a favourable view towards horizontal mergers, not relying excessively in market shares and having competition dynamics matters into account, in particular in technology markets.

467. Sometimes the election of the appropriate undertaking by the CNDC has become difficult, due to an incorrect judgment of the market. This may have been due to the difficulty in performing economic analysis in the relatively small, yet rapidly changing, Argentinean economy. For example, divestments have taken too long to implement, with no suitable alternative purchaser found. Or the remedy initially chosen has been too ambitious, its failure of course having a negative effect on economic welfare. A good example of the foregoing is found in the *Quilmes* merger mentioned in paragraph 485 below, where the CNDC aspired that a new entrant would purchase the assets, instead of allowing the much smaller incumbent competitors of Quilmes to do it, which eventually took place but many years later.

468. The role of efficiencies is yet relatively uncertain, because, as anticipated in paragraph 137, the Guidelines require that they be at least partially transferred to the consumer, particularly in the form of lower prices. With the notable exception of the *Grupo Clarín* case mentioned below, their recognition has not substantially influenced the outcome of merger review.

469. Up to the date of this publication, five horizontal or horizontal/vertical mergers have been prohibited. In addition, it is not uncommon for a horizontal merger to have been subject to some kind of undertaking, of which the most common are two: behavioural, including the amendment of non-compete clauses, non-discrimination and reporting obligations; and divestment obligations. A brief summary will be provided below.

470. In *International Mail Corporation and Sideco Americana*,[380] the CNDC advised the Secretariat to stop the planned merger between the concessionaire of the Argentine Post Office, Correo Argentino S.A., and OCA, the leading private postal operator. The notifying parties abandoned the concentration before the Competition Secretariat could issue its resolution on the matter. The CNDC found that the merger would have created excessive levels of concentration (over 7,500 points under the Herfindahl-Hirschman Index) in at least six of the ten relevant markets identified in the investigation. Other factors which influenced the CNDC's decision were: (i) the existence of relatively high economic rather than regulatory barriers of entry; (ii) the

---

380. 'International Mail Corporation and Sideco Americana S.A. (Correo Argentino S.A.)', Secretaría de Defensa de la Competencia y del Consumidor, Resolution No. 64 (8 Mar. 2001).

Part II, Ch. 3, Concentrations 471–476

inapplicability to Correo Argentino of the 'failing company' defence; and (iii) the failure of the parties to identify valid efficiency gains.

471. In *LAPA*,[381] the vertical merger whereas a major airport operator purchased the then second-largest domestic airline was prohibited due to the inherent discrimination risks to other airlines, in spite of the existence of specific prohibitions in that respect by sectorial regulation, which were nonetheless deemed insufficient by the CNDC.

472. In *Esmeralda Televisión*,[382] T.V. Interactiva, a cable company controlled by an investment fund, outbid another interested party and obtained court authorization to acquire the assets belonging to its sole competitor, who had previously filed for bankruptcy. The competition authorities however denied clearance, on the grounds that granting the assets to T.V. Interactiva would lead to a monopoly, and that the bankrupted company's cable network and market position was a 'competitive asset', meaning that it could hardly be replicated by a new entrant.

473. In November 2006, the CNDC issued its opinion on the acquisition by oil and gas company YPF of a going concern consisting of a single CNG filling station.[383] Surprisingly, the CNDC concluded that the transaction infringed section 7 of the Act and therefore recommended the Secretariat to deny approval, to which the Secretariat agreed. Key to the decision was a particularly narrow definition of the relevant geographic market and the belief of the existence of high barriers of entry in the short term.

474. On 7 December 2007, the CNDC issued Recommendation 637, through which it recommended the approval of the economic concentration resulting in Grupo Clarín controlling Cablevisión S.A. and Teledigital S.A.[384]

475. At the date of the decision, Grupo Clarín was the largest media conglomerate in Argentina, engaged in the financial, telecommunications, broadcasting, graphics and editorial businesses, among others. Prior to the transaction Clarín already controlled Multicanal, the second biggest multiple system operator (MSO) in the country, with more than a million subscribers.

476. While Cablevisión was the leading MSO with then over 1,500,000 subscribers, Teledigital, with approximately 175,000, had a strong presence in certain Argentinean provinces.

---

381. 'LAPA, Fexis S.A., Elenor S.A., Eduardo Eurnekian y Otros (conc. No. 335) s/ notificación art. 8 Ley No. 25.156', Secretaría de la Competencia, la Desregulación y la Defensa del Consumidor, Resolution No. 29 (27 Sep. 2002).
382. 'Esmeralda Televisión S.A., 14; Venado Tuerto T.V. S.A. and 14;T.V. Interactiva S.A', Secretaría de la Competencia, la Desregulación y la Defensa del Consumidor, Resolution No. 32 (14 Mar. 2003).
383. 'YPF S.A. y Destilería Argentina de Petróleo S.A. s/ Notificación Art. 8 Ley 25.156', Secretaría de Comercio Interior, Resolution No. 4 (22 Jan. 2007).
384. *Supra* n. 153.

477. Prior to this merger, the CNDC had had the chance to issue an opinion on the acquisition of approximately 20% of Cablevisión by Grupo Clarín. In such instance, by a 3–2 vote, the CNDC decided that such a deal did not result in Grupo Clarín controlling or acquiring substantial influence over Cablevisión, thus the transaction was not deemed as reportable.[385] As a result thereof, Grupo Clarín appointed two out of ten directors of Cablevisión.

478. Recommendation 637 is debatable in many respects, which are dealt with as follows.

479. Broader definition of the relevant market. For the first time, the CNDC broadened the definition of the relevant market to include satellite-TV companies – in particular, DirecTV – as MSO's competitors.

480. Until the issuance of Recommendation 637, even though the CNDC had considered that in the near future satellite television could be a competitor to cable television, the former had never been included in the same market, due to the significant price gap between those services (according to the Recommendation, this gap was of approximately 25% as of the date thereof). This fact, together with the evident similarity of both services from the consumer standpoint, had led the CNDC to conclude in its then most recent precedent[386] that competition between both services was 'one sided', meaning that companies offering cable-TV services competed with those offering satellite-TV services, but not the other way around.

481. As a result of said change of interpretation, the CNDC included in the Recommendation the company DirecTV as a competitor of Cablevisión and Multicanal, therefore diluting their shares in the relevant market. The CNDC was of the opinion that the merged companies had a 55% stake nationwide, and participations ranging from 77% to 94% in at least eighteen regional markets, including the city of Buenos Aires and the capitals of the main Argentinean provinces.

482. Brief analysis of existing vertical relationships. The creation of a dominant company in a considerable number of markets mandated the examination of the effects of existing vertical relationships in connection with the pay-TV television services rendered by the merged companies and the supply of programming content controlled, totally or partially, by the same corporate group.

483. The Recommendation did not provide a thorough examination of the matter in spite of the acknowledgement of the existence of market power on the part of the merged companies in several programming markets, maybe due to the fact that

---

385. 'Grupo Clarín S.A. and Vistone Trust', Comisión Nacional de Defensa de la Competencia, Advisory Opinion No. 219 (21 May 2006).
386. Approval of the purchase of a stake in DirecTV by The News Corporation Limited, 'The News Corporation Limited, Hughes Electronics Corporation y General Motors Corporation s/ Notificación Artículo 8 Ley 25.156 (Conc. N° 0438)', Secretaría de Coordinación Técnica, Resolution No. 49 (11 Apr. 2005).

Part II, Ch. 3, Concentrations

those concerns were being separately examined by the CNDC in different proceedings (a fact that, however, should not be confused with the *ex ante* analysis of the merger control regime).

484. Efficiency gains. As anticipated, the Guidelines admitted on exceptional basis efficiency gains as a justification for a merger producing or strengthening market power. More precisely, it is required that a transaction causing such a fall in the marginal cost of the merged companies that the pre-merger competitive price turns to be higher than the post-merger supracompetitive price.

485. The CNDC never expressly justified an economic concentration on the basis of efficiency gains that might be possibly derived from it. However, in a few instances it took this variable into account, for example approving subject to undertakings certain transactions that would have otherwise been prohibited. The conditional approval of the purchase of Quilmes by AmBev in 2003[387] is an illustrative case, where the CNDC adopted a critical position with respect to the economic studies submitted by the parties.

486. In Recommendation 637, the CNDC only listed the efficiency gains alleged by the parties (savings arising from the reorganization of call centres, reduction of advertising expenses and inefficiencies originated in network duplication, etc.), without giving an opinion on them.

487. Considering that the CNDC did not recommend the imposition of divestment undertakings, it may be concluded that the above-mentioned efficiencies – in addition to the considerations stated in the section below – determined the approval of the merger without other undertakings than those proposed by the parties.

488. Barriers of entry and 'triple play'. The Recommendation expressly identified the existence of high barriers of entry to the relevant market, both from a legal and a financial (i.e., necessary investments) perspective. From the legal viewpoint, the CNDC highlighted the restrictions imposed on telecom companies by the Government Decree issued on occasion of the privatization of the former State-owned company and the former Federal Broadcasting Act 22,285, which prohibited such companies to render broadcasting services like those offered by Cablevisión and Multicanal. Besides, it was acknowledged that no new competitors had entered the market at issue during the previous years.

489. Notwithstanding these considerations, the CNDC afforded paramount importance to the possibility of new telecom companies competing through the use of 'triple play' technologies, which enable a company to offer television, Internet and telephone services under a single platform. The Recommendation reproduced the testimony given by officers of the main telecom operators, Telecom and

---

387. 'CCBA S.A. y Cervecería y Maltería Quilmes S.A. (C. 276) s/ Notificación Art. 8 Ley 25.156', Secretaría de la Competencia, la Desregulación y la Defensa del Consumidor, Resolution No. 5 (13 Jan. 2003).

Telefónica, on the actual legal feasibility for these companies to render 'triple play' services. While the Telecom representative stated that these were not broadcasting but telecommunications services (and therefore falling within the scope of the license granted to said company), the Telefónica representative recognized that the company could not render broadcasting services – as opposed to offering pay video contents through the Internet – and advocated for the reform of telecom regulations so as to adapt them to technological changes.

490. The testimony referred to above, in addition to others that accounted for the material investments made by telecommunications companies in apparent anticipation to those new kinds of services, persuaded the CNDC that those companies were likely to become actual competitors of pay-TV companies in the short term.

491. What is surprising about this conclusion is that it does not follow from the Recommendation that the CNDC requested the opinion of the telecom regulator on the matter, as would have been expected given the degree of controversy arising from the matter under consideration. Instead, the opinion of the CNDC rested upon that of market participants, in contradiction with the position adopted in similar cases, where it mostly gave evidentiary value to the opinions of specialized public officials and, in any case, the existing regulatory framework.[388] Additionally, as stems from the Recommendation, the aforementioned testimonies were obtained two days before the issuance of the Recommendation, an evidently brief term to examine the issue in detail.

492. *The undertaking submitted by the parties.* The Recommendation concluded by accepting a compromise proposal submitted by the notifying parties one day prior to its issuance.

493. The CNDC concluded – in a rather vague manner – that competition issues could be identified in three areas:

(i) Vertical restrictions that MSOs and non-integrated programming providers could face in accessing the signals owned by the parties.
(ii) Strengthening of post-merger market power in some pay-TV markets, sufficient to cause a restriction in the offer and increase the price of the service.
(iii) Transfer of efficiency gains.

494. The CNDC understood that the obligations assumed by the parties satisfactorily solved the three issues listed above. We will refer to each of these solutions and briefly comment on them.

---

388. In fact, s. 25 item (d) of the new Broadcasting Law (Audiovisual Communication Services Act 26,522, 10 Oct. 2009, [31756] BO 1), did not allow at the time of the decision telecommunications companies to render pay-TV services.

Part II, Ch. 3, Concentrations

495. Vertical Restrictions:

(i) Guaranteeing the free availability of television signals exclusively owned or distributed by the merging companies, under non-discriminating conditions, to every pay-TV operator who may so request them, irrespective of whether such operators be competitors of Cablevisión, Teledigital and/or Multicanal.
(ii) Ensuring a place in the programming grid of Cablevisión, Teledigital and Multicanal to every programming provider, competitor of the parties or not.
(iii) Guaranteeing pluralism, freedom of information and entertainment, ensuring that the programming offered by Cablevisión, Teledigital and Multicanal reasonably provide users with a wide range of information, sports and entertainment signals.

496. Through the first obligation, the companies simply undertook to comply with the national antitrust law, which, following European law, contemplates more burdensome commercial dealing obligations for dominant companies. The second obligation seems inappropriate in case it is interpreted literally (i.e., stating that companies are not afforded the right to freely determine their programming content).

497. The last obligation seems alien to competition law, the CNDC not being qualified to control its fulfilment.

498. Increasing horizontal market power:

(i) Ensuring, during the term of the undertaking [note: two years], that in certain urban areas with overlapping networks of the merged entities and no alternative cable-TV provider, the 'representative basic service rate' does not exceed the one in force in the Buenos Aires Metropolitan Area.

499. The CNDC should not take the role of a price regulator. Moreover, even acknowledging that competition in the city of Buenos Aires is greater than that in other areas of Argentina, considering that the merged entities have substantial market power in most relevant geographic market, the referred to cap does not seem useful.

500. Efficiency Gains:

(i) Guaranteeing:
  (a) the extension of the geographic reach of pay-TV services and Internet access within the scope and under the terms included in an investment plan submitted by the parties; and
  (b) that an ever increasing number of cable-TV users gradually receive digital services with the following benefits: image and sound quality improvement, wider programming offer and the opportunity of incorporating new services.

501. It is unusual for a competition authority to accept investment undertakings in lieu of divestment undertakings, since the former will be very hard to control, especially due to the ambiguity with which they have been formulated. Neither does the opinion state that investments could only be made in case the merger is approved, as provided by the regulations in force.

502. Miscellaneous:

(i) Securing, during the term of the undertaking, the implementation of an optional digital pay-TV service at a reduced price with a minimum of ten channels in addition to open-TV signals. This service shall be available for a certain number of homes within the city of Buenos Aires Metropolitan Area. The companies undertake to perform the necessary technical studies in order to examine the possibility of expanding this social service to other areas.
(ii) Providing basic pay-TV services at no cost to hospitals and public health centres, schools, police stations, firemen headquarters and public residences for elderly people fulfilling certain criteria.

503. The antitrust authority exceeded the purpose and scope of the antitrust law by accepting certain limited social benefits to make up for potential price increases applied to a much larger number of people, the consumers of pay-TV services, who should be the recipients of the protection of the State.

504. In sum, this decision could be characterized by:

(i) The marked departure of the agency from its earlier position on the involved market. For instance, the *Esmeralda Televisión* case, which had almost no significance when compared with this merger, was prohibited based on the fact that the competitor's cable network was a 'competitive capital' to be preserved.
(ii) The reduced analysis of the effects of potential vertical restrictions.
(iii) The decisive role attributed to new technologies as substitute services, in spite of the existence of reasonable doubts about the legal viability of their actual use in the short or medium term.

505. Shortly after receiving clearance, the merging companies' relationship with the authorities quickly deteriorated, and the CNDC opened an investigation to verify the compliance with the undertakings, which ultimately concluded that none of them were fully complied with and led to a December 2009 decision of the Secretariat withdrawing the authorization granted by the same agency in December 2007.[389]

---

389. 'Grupo Clarín S.A., Vistone LLC, Fintech Advisory Inc., Fintech Media LLC, VLG Argentina LLC y Cablevisión S.A. s/ Notificación Art. 8 Ley 25.156 (Conc. 596)', Secretaría de Comercio Interior, Resolution No. 1011 (14 Dec. 2009).

Part II, Ch. 3, Concentrations 506–510

506. The parties challenged most decisions with the courts and achieved the suspension of the effects of the December 2009 decision of the Secretariat[390] and the separation of the Secretariat from the case,[391] only to be notified of an almost similar decision in March 2010 issued by the Ministry of Economy and Public Finance, which was ultimately reversed by the courts.[392]

507. The *Pirelli & C* merger, mentioned elsewhere herein,[393] originated on 29 April 2007, when the media reported the sale by Pirelli of Olimpia, a company which in turn owned 18% of Telecom Italia S.p.A. (TI). The sale was the conclusion of a series of negotiations in which the Italian Government was not absent, as it purportedly wanted to avert the possibility of the company not being owned by Italian – or at least European – investors.[394]

508. The acquisition was implemented through a corporate vehicle named Telco, whose shareholders were Telefónica (42.3%), the insurance company Assicurazioni Generali (28.1%), the banks Intesa San Paolo and Mediobanca (10.7% each) and Benetton (8.2%) (hereinafter the 'Telco Transaction').

509. The Telco Transaction enabled Telefónica to enter into TI's board of directors with two of the then nineteen members, and obtain veto rights in certain decisions related to share ownership changes, dividend policy and divestitures. However, it was foreseen that both companies were to be managed separately and independently, and that both Telefónica and the directors appointed by it would abstain from participating and voting in meetings of the relevant corporate bodies whose purpose would be to consider business decisions related to countries in which both companies had a presence.[395]

510. The concentration was conditioned upon the approval of the European Commission and any relevant EU national authority. Accordingly, it was submitted to the review of the European Commission, where the Director-General for Competition concluded on 12 June 2007 that it did not entail an acquisition of control, given that none of the parties had acquired sole control over TI, and neither did all

---

390. 'Grupo Clarín SA c/ Secretaría de Comercio Interior y otros s/ medidas cautelares', CNCiv. Com. Fed., Sala II (18 Dec. 2009).
391. 'Grupo Clarín S.A., Vistone LLC, Fintech Advisory Inc., Fintech Media LLC, VLG Argentina LLC y Cablevisión S.A. s/ Notificación Art. 8 Ley 25.156 s/ Medida Cautelar – Expte. 0373486/2006 (Conc. N° 595 s/ Recurso de Apelación Contra Res. 969/09', CNPenal Económico, Sala A (26 Feb. 2010).
392. Ministerio de Economía y Finanzas Públicas, Resolution No. 113 (3 Mar. 2010). Reversed by 'AMI Cable Holding Ltd y otros s/apelación Resolución Comisión Nacional de Defensa de la Competencia', CNCiv. Com. Fed., Sala II (17 Sep. 2015).
393. The reader should note that the CNDC opened several files regarding the transaction by means of which Telefónica S.A. acquired an indirect stake in Telecom Argentina S.A., whose names refer to Pirelli, Telefónica and/or Telecom Italia, depending on the case.
394. www.elmundo.es/mundodinero/2007/04/28/economia/1177795730.html.
395. www.telefonica.com/en/shareholders_investors/pdf/hr070429.pdf.

or a group of them.³⁹⁶ The Telco Transaction was also reported in Germany, where it did not receive objections.³⁹⁷

511. Outside Europe, the deal was notified in Brazil, where the authorities generally have had a far-reaching view as regards what transactions require a merger notification.³⁹⁸ On 31 October 2007 and 7 July 2009 Anatel, the telecommunications watchdog, approved the Telco Transaction subject to a series of behavioural undertakings aimed at keeping Telefónica's and TI's mobile operations (Vivo and Tim Brasil, respectively) fully independent.³⁹⁹ The decision was confirmed and expanded by CADE on 28 April 2010.⁴⁰⁰

512. The Telco Transaction was not initially notified in Argentina, as the parties understood that no reportable change of control occurred. On 3 May 2007, shortly after the initial deal announcement, the CNDC initiated an ex officio investigation to enquire on the reasons for the lack of filing.⁴⁰¹

513. The opening of such investigations is a standard practice in Argentina, at least for cases raising competition concerns. Such worries appeared to be warranted here, as TI jointly controlled Telecom Argentina, while Telefónica held exclusive control over Telefónica de Argentina, both the largest telecommunication companies in the country, originally awarded a monopoly over, respectively, Northern and Southern Argentina as a consequence of the privatization of the telephone service in the 1990s.

514. The scenario in which the transaction unfolded in Argentina included issues in addition to those of competition law: TI was amidst a fierce corporate dispute with its local, minority partner in Telecom Argentina, allegedly as regards the price of a call in favour of TI on the shares of a company controlling Telecom Argentina.⁴⁰²

515. TI's local partner, who also occupied significant executive positions in Telecom Argentina, then became the major advocate against the Telco Transaction.

---

396. Comisión Nacional de Defensa de la Competencia, Resolution No. 835 (12 Oct. 2010), points 964 and 1210, attached to Resolution No. 148/2010, Secretaría de Política Económica. [32012] B.O., 34.
397. www.mediobanca.it/it/stampa-comunicazione/news/comunicato-congiunto-generali-intesa-sanpaolo-mediobanca-sin-2.html.
398. José Regazzini & Marcelo Calliari. *Getting the Deal through – Merger Control 2010*, at 66 (L. Bus. Research (2009).
399. Agência Nacional de Comunicações, Ato do Conselho Diretor No. 68,276 (31 Oct. 2007) and 3804 (7 Jul. 2009), cited in CADE's Termo de Compromisso de Desempenho, *supra* n. 9, whereas, item (iv).
400. Conselho Administrativo da Defesa Econômica, Acordo (28 Apr. 2010) (available at www.cade.gov.br/temp/D_D000000522411420.pdf); and Termo de Compromisso de Desempenho (available at www.cade.gov.br/temp/D_D000000546881169.pdf).
401. Comisión Nacional de Defensa de la Competencia, Resolution No. 4 (9 Jan. 2009), Whereas 1.
402. 'Werthein no quiere vender sus acciones en Telecom Argentina', La Nación (14 Mar. 2008) (available at www.lanacion.com.ar/nota.asp?nota_id=995461).

Part II, Ch. 3, Concentrations   516–518

The battle was fought over several board of directors meetings of Telecom Argentina, where each of the sides would present the other opposing arguments in support of their view. Those arguments were also shared with the CNDC, which clearly took sides early on the proceedings, deciding on 16 October 2007 to appoint overseers '... *for the purpose of reporting any fact or act they may be aware of that may affect public interest ...* '.[403] In the CNDC's view:

> Evidently, from the evidence stemming from the investigation it can be inferred that in this transaction provisions have been incorporated in the corporate agreements which would self-limit Telefónica (Spain) from taking part in the decisions of its competitor Telecom Argentina S.A., [provisions] which would be prima facie irrelevant at the time of exercising the pre-eminence that would correspond [to Telefónica] in the adoption of decisions.[404]

516. On 20 February 2008, a lengthy internal report of the overseers was leaked to the press.[405] The report concluded that Telefónica had substantial influence over Telco and thus indirectly over TI and Telecom Argentina, with the additional risk of acquisition by Telefónica of sensitive and strategic information from its major competitor. It was not until 30 December 2008, however, that the CNDC adopted its first decision, issuing an injunction that prevented TI to exercise its call over the shares of its minority partner.[406]

517. Early in January 2009, the CNDC issued a very lengthy decision with the conclusions of the investigation conducted so far.[407] Not surprisingly, it confirmed the arguments of the overseers' report and ordered the parties to notify the transaction, which by then had closed several months ago. The same decision suspended the parties' voting rights in Telecom Argentina and its related companies, which basically left the minority shareholder – which was not restricted by the decisions – with the sole control of the companies. Subsequent interim decisions were issued in this direction in April[408] and May 2009.[409] Some of those decisions were later reversed by the courts, as will be seen below.

518. On 25 August 2009, the Secretariat ordered the full divestiture of TI's holdings in Argentina,[410] which under guidelines subsequently approved by the CNDC[411] had to be completed in the initial term of one year. As they did with all other decisions issued by the CNDC and SCI, the parties vigorously challenged the SCI decision, which on 1 February 2010 was reversed by the courts on due process

---

403. Comisión Nacional de Defensa de la Competencia, Resolution No. 78 (16 Oct. 2007).
404. *Ibid.*, at para. 18.
405. www.enciclomedios.com/files/u1/Informe_VeedoresTeleom.pdf.
406. Comisión Nacional de Defensa de la Competencia, Resolution No. 123 (29 Dec. 2008). The decision was adopted one day before the date on which TI was legally entitled to exercise the call.
407. Comisión Nacional de Defensa de la Competencia, Resolution No. 4 (9 Jan. 2009).
408. Comisión Nacional de Defensa de la Competencia, Resolution No. 44 (3 Apr. 2009).
409. Comisión Nacional de Defensa de la Competencia, Resolution No. 64 (26 May 2009).
410. Secretaría de Comercio Interior, Resolution No. 483 (25 Aug. 2009).
411. Comisión Nacional de Defensa de la Competencia, Resolution No. 1 (6 Jan. 2010).

considerations.[412] The courts instructed the Government to appoint a public official different from the Secretary of Domestic Trade to issue a new decision. Shortly before this last reversal, though, the SCI imposed the parties' aggregate fines in the shocking amount of ARS 235,977,000 for late filing.[413]

519. By this time, the transaction made front page headlines in the local media and prompted high-level political meetings, as the Government was also warning that it could nationalize Telecom Argentina.[414] The TI was, on the one hand, conducting a bidding process to reportedly sell its Argentine holdings and, on the other, still forcefully challenging decisions by the CNDC and other governmental agencies.

520. The solution, it seems, came with the commercial agreement reached between TI and its local shareholder, which was publicly informed on 5 August 2010.[415] Absent the aggravated shareholder, the CNDC's attitude towards the deal changed, and was inclined to accept a stricter, Government-controlled version of the behavioural undertakings that were originally part of the deal. This position ultimately concluded in the issuance of decisions approving the transaction subject to those undertakings,[416] and even an increase in the original TI's stake,[417] similar to the case in Brazil.

521. As regards other less controversial transactions, the following are among the most significant cases where some sort of undertaking was imposed:

522. EDF/Endesa:[418] after acquiring control of the Chilean company of the same name, the Spanish group Endesa ended up controlling the only two electricity distribution companies of the Buenos Aires region, Edenor and Edesur. The Secretariat and the electricity regulator ordered Endesa to sell one of the two distribution companies, which Endesa did about seven months later to the French group EDF.

---

412. 'Incidente de Apelación S.A. y Otros contra Resolución SCI No. 483/09 (en autos principles: 'Pirelli & C S.p.A. y otros s/notificación Art. 8 Ley 25.156)', Cámara Nacional de Apelaciones en lo Penal Económico, Sala A (1 Feb. 2010).
413. Secretaría de Comercio Interior, Resolution No. 2/2010 [31816] B.O., 47. An Appeal Court reduced the fine applied to Telefónica to slightly more than half and eliminated the fine applied to the rest of the parties (*see* 'Recurso de apelación en la causa Pirelli & C.S.p.A y otros s/ notificación art. 8 ley 25.156 – Incidente de apelación en la Resolución SCI No.2/10 en Concentración 741', CNCiv. Com. Fed. (1 Feb. 2011)) but such decision was reversed by the Supreme Court, which confirmed the original sanctions ('Pirelli y C.S.P.A. y otros s/ notificación art. 8 Ley 25.156 incidente de apelación de la Resolución SCI N°2/10 en Concentración 741' CSJN, P. 208. XLVIII (10 Mar. 2015).
414. 'Telecom Italia moviliza a Berlusconi para evitar la nacionalización en Argentina', Cinco Días (30 Jan. 2010), www.cincodias.com/articulo/empresas/Telecom-Italia-moviliza-Berlusconi-evitar-nacionalizacion-Argentina/20100130cdscdiemp_7/.
415. Letter sent by Telecom Argentina to Argentina's Comisión Nacional de Valores (available at www.cnv.gob.ar).
416. Resolution No. 148/2010, Secretaría de Política Económica [32012] B.O., 34.
417. Comisión Nacional de Defensa de la Competencia, Resolution No. 836 (12 Oct. 2010).
418. 'Edenor; EDFI; YPF; Endesa y EASA (concentración No. 325) s/ notificación Art. 8 Ley 25.156', Secretaría de la Competencia, la Desregulación y la Defensa del Consumidor, Resolution No. 70 (16 Jul. 2001).

Part II, Ch. 3, Concentrations 523–526

523. Bayer/Aventis: The economic concentration in which Bayer AG acquired 100% of the shares of Aventis Cropsciense Holding S.A. was approved subject to the divestment of assets (related to the exploitation of a number of active ingredients) owned by the multinational pharmaceutical company Aventis.[419] This transaction had been conditioned upon certain other actions in Europe and the United States prior to the CNDC decision. In Argentina, the parties were also ordered to execute supply agreements with the acquiring parties at their request and to transfer all related intellectual property rights.

524. Ambev/Quilmes:[420] The Competition Secretariat approved the Ambev/Quilmes merger, subject to the compliance with several divestment undertakings, including the transfer – only to a new entrant – of several beer brands and production plants. The divestiture process was suspended by interim measures obtained from two existing competitors, which as such were left outside of the divestiture process. The assets were ultimately sold to a new entrant with no experience in the beer industry, only to be sold shortly thereafter to one of the incumbents that were prevented to purchase them in the first place.

525. Pecom Energía/Alto Paraná:[421] Pecom Energia sold its forestry division to Alto Paraná, a competitor in eight relevant markets. The transaction was ultimately approved subject to the following conditions: (i) Alto Paraná would have to supply the same wood volume historically offered by target Pecom Forestal. Likewise, Alto Paraná undertook to (ii) maintain the effectiveness of the technology cooperation and assistance agreements in force with the Misiones National University; and (iii) share, jointly with research and other entities, the genetic forestry materials that previously belonged to Pecom Energía.

526. PSH/ Fox/Liberty:[422] The joint venture submitted to approval would result in the creation of a company, Fox Pan American Sports LLC, in which three companies would participate and to which a fourth company (Torneos y Competencias) would be contractually related. The CNDC found that the transaction had the potential of infringing the merger control regulations, since it would result in the joint operation by some of the involved companies of the only two television signals existing in the relevant market, which had been defined as the market for broadcasting live soccer games played by first division Argentine teams. The parties submitted undertakings consisting, inter alia, in a shares swap with the purpose of achieving total independence between the shareholders of the new joint venture and Torneos y Competencias, the other sports signal.

---

419. 'Bayer AG y Aventis Cropscience Holdings S.A. (c. 352) s/ notificación art. 8 de la Ley N° 25.156', Secretaría de la Competencia, la Desregulación y la Defensa del Consumidor, Resolution No. 45 (1 Nov. 2002).
420. *Supra* n. 388.
421. 'Pecom Energía S.A. y Alto Paraná S.A. s/ notificación art. 8 Ley 25.156', Secretaría de Coordinación Técnica, Resolution No. 110 (16 Dec. 2003).
422. 'PSH, Fox y Liberty (C. 378) s/ notificación art. 8 Ley 25.156', Secretaría de Coordinación Técnica, Resolution No. 134 (29 Sep. 2004).

527. *Bimbo/Fargo*:[423] This transaction entailed the acquisition of control by Grupo Bimbo by México of local bread company Fargo. Given that target and acquirer were the main competitors in the bread products market, the parties submitted a divestment commitment whereby they undertook to transfer a business unit (under the 'Lactal' trademark) to an independent third party and, consequently, ensure an appropriate distribution system. The commitment contemplated a second phase involving an independent 'Selling Agent' who would implement the divestment. Although not formally accepting the 'failing company' defence, the CNDC accepted this proposal in view of the reorganization proceedings Fargo was going through.[424] The commitment included the condition that Grupo Bimbo could not exercise its purchase option before the closing of the sale of the business unit to be divested. Only then the CNDC would recommend approval to the adjudicatory authority.

528. The divestment was effectively made in 2010,[425] and until such date the merging companies had to operate independently. Given that the original divestments could not be completed in full, the Secretariat issued a new decision approving the proposed new acquirer of the divested assets and including a new set of undertakings, to wit: (i) limiting any price gap among small retail stores and supermarkets to a maximum of 10%; and, for a term of three years in all cases; (ii) limiting advertising expenses; (iii) prohibiting the parties from displaying their products in endcaps; (iv) not exceeding certain market shares; (v) increasing investments in physical capital; and (vi) provide to the authorities information on certain key competitive indicators of their activity.

529. *Telefónica/Bellsouth*:[426] The transaction consisted in the purchase by one of the companies of the Telefónica Group (Telefónica Móviles) of the assets of Bellsouth Corporation in Latin America. In particular, the CNDC found that the transaction would result in the concentration of the radio-electric spectrum for mobile calls in excess of the statutory limit, and thus subjected the same to the divestment by Telefónica of the excess spectrum within a deadline to be agreed upon with the telecommunications regulatory agency.

530. *Pernod Ricard/Allied Domecq*:[427] The CNDC recommended the approval of the acquisition of Allied Domecq by Pernod Ricard subject to several disinvestment undertakings. The CNDC held that the transaction raised competition

---

423. 'Grupo Bimbo S.A.C.V. y Compañía de Alimentos Fargo S.A. s/ notificación art. 8 Ley 25.156', Secretaría de Coordinación Técnica, Resolution No. 131 (23 Sep. 2004).
424. In fact, the CNDC expressly recognized that this fact was decisive in approving the transaction subject to undertakings, as absent it would have recommended its prohibition. *See* Comisión Nacional de Defensa de la Competencia, Report No. 395/2004 (10 Sep. 2004), point 246 (attached to the decision of the Secretariat referred to in n. 417 *supra*).
425. 'Grupo Bimbo S.A.C.V. y Compañía de Alimentos Fargo S.A. s/ incidente de desinversión', Secretaría de Coordinación Técnica, Resolution No. 545 (29 Dec. 2010).
426. 'Telefónica Móviles S.A. y Telefónica Comunicaciones Personales S.A. s/ notificación art. 8 Ley 25.156 (Conc. 448)', Secretaría de Coordinación Técnica, Resolution No. 196 (27 Dec. 2004).
427. 'P.R. Argentina S.A., Goal Acquisitions Limited y Allied Domecq PLC s/ Notificación Art. 8 Ley 25.156 (Conc. 512)', Secretaría de Coordinación Técnica, Resolution No. 181 (21 Oct. 2005).

Part II, Ch. 3, Concentrations 531–532.1

concerns in the market segment for whisky, gin, vodka and liquors. Accordingly, it suggested the Secretariat to impose the following undertakings: (i) Pernod Ricard would transfer to a third party certain whisky businesses, (ii) one of its gin business would be transferred to a company independent from the parties, and (iii) the parties would refrain from launching new brands in the Argentine gin, vodka and liquor markets, and to discontinue certain brands in the same for a term of two years.

531. Arcor/Benvenuto:[428] In examining the acquisition of food company Benvenuto by its much larger rival Arcor, the CNDC concluded that the transaction violated the Act and recommended approval subject to a number of conditions. Regarding the marmalades and jellies markets, the CNDC found that the transaction would substantially increase the degree of concentration and that, even when entrance was likely in the short term, any such competitors would not dispute the merging parties' market power. In spite of the findings described above, the CNDC finally accepted relatively mild undertakings. Arcor offered to refrain from creating new marmalade or jelly brands for a term of three years and making investments in television advertising for a term of two years. In addition, the acquirer offered to submit a quarterly report on the average price per kilo of marmalades and jellies manufactured by Arcor and Benvenuto, for a term of two years. Finally, the CNDC required that the five-year non-compete term included in the purchase agreement be reduced to two years, given that in, the agency's view, the agreement did not include the transfer of know-how.

532. Saint Gobain/Abrasivos Argentinos – Dancan:[429] The transaction was approved subject to divestment undertakings in 2007, ahead of the closing. However, the parties could only sign the relevant agreement in 2011. Section 13 of the Decree provides that mergers have to be implemented no later than one year from the issuance of the final decision or when the transaction is deemed tacitly approved, if appropriate. Consequently, the Secretariat declared the lapsing of the proceedings, and the parties had to refile the transaction with the CNDC. As expected, the deal was approved in a shorter period of time and under similar conditions than the earlier decision.

532.1. Bridas/ExxonMobil:[430] The Secretariat approved the acquisition by Bridas Corporation (jointly owned by China National Offshore Oil Corp. and the Bulgheroni family) of Exxon's oil and gas assets in Argentina. Even when the decision did not point out to any significant restrictions of competition directly stemming from the transaction, it referred to the bottleneck caused by lack of refining capacity in Argentina as a major structural problem. In that connection, the self-undertaking offered by Bridas to increase capacity in target's refinery through a

---

428. 'Arcor S.A.I.C. y Benvenuto S.A.C.I. s/ Notificación art. 8 Ley 25.156 (conc. 554)', Secretaría de Comercio Interior. Resolution No. 11 (29 Aug. 2006).
429. 'Saint Gobain Performance Plastics Europe, Abrasivos Argentinos S.A. y Dancan S.A. s/ notificación art. 8 de la ley 25.156 (Conc. 909)', Secretariat of Domestic Trade, Resolution No. 140 (26 Oct. 2011).
430. 'ExxonMobil International Holding Inc. y Bridas Corporation s/ notificación artículo 8 Ley N°25.156 (Conc. 887)', Secretariat of Domestic Trade, Resolution No. 82 (30 Aug. 2012).

USD 800 million investment was regarded by the authorities as a means to improve the conditions of competition from those *ex ante*, thus taking into account both industrial policy and competition considerations.

532.2. Cinemark/Hoyts: following the line of cases represented by *Arcor/Benvenuto*, the acquisition by theatre chain Cinemark of rival Hoyts was approved subject to a detailed set of undertakings, mainly addressed at not increasing the number of theatres (in some cases subject to the evolution of its market share) and not increasing prices in areas where the merger created higher concentration levels above those increases in force in areas subject to more competition.[431]

§2. VERTICAL MERGERS

533. According to point VII of the Guidelines:

> Vertical concentrations are those in which the Involved Companies act in vertically related markets. The general comments made in these Guidelines apply to vertical concentrations. However, certain aspects will need to be taken into account. A vertical concentration may be prejudicial in those cases in which the elimination of a supplier upstream or distributor downstream significantly increase barriers of entry of new competitors. The foregoing will especially occur if a potential purchaser wishing to enter in any of the involved stages be forced to enter in both stages simultaneously, with the subsequent increase in sunken costs associated to it.
>
> Notwithstanding, the foregoing condition will not per se mean a violation of Section 7 of the Act; each case shall be examined according to its specific characteristics and the impact it may cause in the general economic interest.

534. The above-mentioned principle has been consistently applied, ordering – as will be mentioned below – remedies ranging from 'behavioural warnings' (i.e., parties shall not discriminate upstream or downstream – to the prohibition of the acquisition, as in the *LAPA* case.[432] Also, as regards the concerns raised by vertical mergers, please refer to the CNDC report on pay-TV television mentioned under paragraph 564 below.

535. Note should be taken that in several of the mergers mentioned under point 1 above – i.e., Esmeralda,[433] YPF,[434] Grupo Clarín,[435] Ambev,[436] Endesa,[437] Bridas[438] – one or more vertical relationships were reviewed.

---

431. 'Hoyts General Cinema South America Inc. y Cinemark Argentina Holdings Inc. s/ notificación art. 8 de la Ley 25.156 (Conc. 938)', Secretariat of Trade, Resolution No. 88 (6 Mar. 2015).
432. *Supra* n. 382.
433. *Supra* n. 383.
434. *Supra* n. 59.
435. *Supra* n. 153.
436. *Supra* n. 388.
437. *Supra* n. 419.
438. *Supra* n. 431.

Part II, Ch. 3, Concentrations

§3. MARKET/PRODUCT EXTENSION MERGERS

536. Product and market extension considerations have been examined in certain horizontal and conglomerate mergers.

537. For example, in *Adecco and Olsten*,[439] merger between two temporary staffing companies, the CNDC observed that there were geographic areas where only one of the companies was active, but was not concerned due to the existence of very low barriers of entry.

538. In *Quilmes/Elaboradora Argentina de Cereales*,[440] the concern was related to the fact that Quilmes' varied beverage offering could lead to tying practices, but the company self-compromised to avoid such practices. In *Atanor*,[441] however, no similar undertakings were necessary due to the lack of market power of the merging parties.

§4. PURE CONGLOMERATE MERGERS

539. Section VIII of the Guidelines state that:

> Conglomerate mergers are those in which the Involved Companies neither operate in the same relevant market nor in vertically related markets. In principle, said mergers will not be objected and will only be considered that they are potentially restrictive in those cases in which it is proved that, absent the concentration, one of the Involved Companies would have entered as a competitor in the relevant market in which the other Involved Companies operate. In those circumstances, the merger will be evaluated on the basis of the general considerations contained in these guidelines.

540. Formally, conglomerate mergers have so far been approved without undertakings. However, a more in depth view yields different results.

541. In the last few years, an increasing number of relevant (total or partial) conglomerate cases, such as *Petrobras/Pérez Companc, Petrobras/Eton Park or Gaz de France/Suez* have raised, explicitly or not, national interest or plain political issues, as will be seen below.

---

439. 'Adecco Argentina S.A. y Olsten Ready Office Sociedad Anónima de Servicios Empresarios s/ notificación Art. 8 Ley 25.156', Secretaría de Defensa de la Competencia y del Consumidor, Resolution No. 164 (29 Aug. 2000).
440. 'Cervecería y Maltería Quilmes S.A.I.C.A. y Elaboradora Argentina de Cereales S.A. (Productos Gatorade – c. 364) s/ notificación art. 8 Ley 25.156', Secretaría de la Competencia, la Desregulación y la Defensa del Consumidor, Resolution No. 3 (11 Mar. 2002).
441. 'Atanor S.A. s/ notificación art. 8 Ley No. 25.156 (Conc. 521)', Secretaría de Coordinación Técnica, Resolution No. 167 (3 Oct. 2005).

542. Petrobras/Pérez Companc[442] consisted in the acquisition by Petrobras of a majority stake in the local companies Pérez Companc and Petrolera Pérez Companc, which resulted in a horizontal concentration in the gas, petroleum and liquid fuel markets as well as conglomerate relations in other markets. In particular, this transaction resulted in the indirect transfer of the exclusive control exercised by Pérez Companc in Transener and other local concessionaires of electricity transportation services, in which Petrobras was for the most part neither horizontally nor vertically related. As a consequence of the intervention of other areas of the Government, Pecom Energia, one of the target companies, submitted a unilateral irrevocable commitment to sell its participation in Citelec (company which controlled the aforementioned company Transener).

543. As a consequence of the foregoing transaction, Petrobras was requested to divest its stake (50%) in Transener. The Brazilian company had agreed to sell the interest when Transener's financials improved, and eventually reached a deal with US investment fund Eton Park in 2006.[443]

544. The transaction did not possibly raise competition concerns (Eton Park had no investments in Argentina, at least in the energy sector) but nevertheless was strongly opposed by the Government, which rejected the sale in early 2007 through the energy regulator, *Ente Nacional Regulador de la Electricidad* or ENRE. The approval of this agency was required as part of Petrobras' 'self-undertaking' in the 2003 Pérez Companc deal. The ENRE opposed the incorporation of Eton Park in Transener based on the argument that the fund lacked technical expertise and long-term commitment,[444] in spite of the fact that, in 2004, the Government approved the purchase by another investment fund, but this time of Argentine origin, of the remaining 50% in Transener held by National Grid.[445] The CNDC just referred to the fact that ENRE's approval was required in this case as a consequence of the language of the divestment undertaking, and closed the case due to ENRE's rejection to the merger.[446] Eton Park lost on appeal.[447]

---

442. 'Fundación Pérez Companc, Goyaike y Otros y Petróleo Brasileiro s/ notificación art. 8 Ley 25.156', Secretaría de la Competencia, la Desregulación y la Defensa del Consumidor, Resolution No. 62 (12 May 2003).
443. Petrobras Energia Participaciones S.A., 6-K for 21 Feb. 2006 (available at www.secinfo.com/d11HEa.v3.htm).
444. 'Rechazan formalmente la venta de Transener al fondo Eton Park', Clarín (10 Feb. 2007) (available at www.clarin.com/diario/2007/02/10/elpais/p-00401.htm).
445. 'Compañía Inversora en Transmisiones Eléctricas Citelec S.A. y Dolphin Fund Management S.A. s/ notificación artículo 8 Ley 25.156 (Conc. 450)', Secretaría de Coordinación Técnica, Resolution No. 90 (28 Jul. 2004). It must be noted, however, that at the time this other purchaser – the Dolphin Group – acquired its stake in Transener, Petrobras was still a shareholder in the company (although not for very long).
446. 'Petrobras Energia S.A. y Compañía Inversora en Transmisión Eléctrica CITELEC S.A. s/ notificación art. 8 Ley 25.156 (Conc. 588)', Secretaría de Comercio Interior, Resolution No. 9 (9 Feb. 2007).
447. 'Petrobras Energía S.A. y otro', CNCiv. Com. Fed. [9007] LLO (2007).

Part II, Ch. 3, Concentrations

545. Finally, in *Suez/Gaz de France*,[448] the President of the CNDC and its remaining three members issued conflicting opinions, the former recommending to suspend the merger review process until Suez desisted from a claim it had brought against the Argentine Republic before the World Bank's International Centre for Settlement of Investment Disputes, and the latter approving the transaction without undertakings, as it ultimately occurred.

§5. Joint Ventures

546. As anticipated, there is no special treatment to joint ventures under the merger provisions of the Competition Act.

---

448. 'Suez S.A. y Gaz de France S.A s/ notificación art. 8 Ley 25.156', Secretaría de Comercio Interior (27 Jun. 2007).

Part III. Administrative Procedure

Chapter 1. Administrative Investigations

§1. INITIATIVE

I. General Sectors Inquiries

547. As anticipated in 197 above, sections 18 and 20 of the Competition Act provide for the power of the Secretariat and CNDC, as the case may be, to perform market studies and investigations; issue non-binding opinions upon competition matters as regards laws, regulations and other administrative acts, and issue recommendations on competition matters, including to, inter alia, the Executive and Congress.

548. As from the enactment of the 2014 Amendment the division of powers between the Secretariat and CNDC is clearer, thus making less relevant the holding of the Supreme Court's *Credit Suisse*[449] decision.

549. Section 50 sets forth that persons obstructing or impairing the investigation or not fulfilling other requirements of the competition authorities may be subject to daily fines of up to ARS 500. Whether this relatively low fine is enough to achieve its desired purpose or not (its application is not automatic as section 50 provides that the alleged infringer must be given the opportunity of providing explanations and offering evidence) will probably depend on the specific case, as for example, a continued lack of cooperation could expose certain infringers to an individual investigation, or – if the circumstances of the sectorial enquiry so justify it and is so ordered by a court – even a raid.

550. Even when the confidentiality of proprietary information is duly protected by the National Constitution and Argentine laws, said right is not absolute, and may be subject to the exercise of other constitutional rights. In addition, by application of criminal law principles,[450] investigations carried out by the CNDC are confidential for anyone but the parties involved. Consequently, in order for any attempt to refuse disclosing information or documents containing business secrets to be successful, the interested party should prove, at a minimum, not only its confidential

---

449. *Supra* n. 126.
450. CPPN, s. 204.

nature but also that it would, under no circumstance, be conducive to the investigation conducted by the CNDC. Also, as indicated under paragraph 575 further on, market participants that are requested to provide information or documents in the course of a market investigation are not made parties to the proceedings, so they do not have access to the relevant file.

551. Some of the foregoing issues were discussed in *Liquid Oxygen*,[451] where companies involved in a cartel investigation complained about the refusal of the CNDC to grant confidential treatment to the documents obtained during a raid on companies' premises. The Appeal Court confirmed the decision of the CNDC under the basis that, given that the documents referred to alleged anticompetitive agreements involving not only the company which owned the documents but also some or all of the other investigated companies, restricting access to them to the owner of the documents could affect the right of defence of the others.

552. A similar result was reached in *YPF*,[452] where the court refused to grant confidentiality to certain alleged confidential information filed by YPF in an abuse of dominance case, stating that plaintiff had provided insufficient arguments to justify a departure of the principle set forth in section 204 of the CPPN, which provides that the file (in this case, of an administrative nature) could be accessed by the parties, including the complainant in the dominance investigation.

553. As stated in paragraphs 198 et seq. above, the CNDC has carried out several sectorial investigations. A very brief reference will be made below.

554. *Health care (1997)*.[453] Due to the recurrence of competition issues in the health care sector, particularly of an exclusionary nature, the CNDC issued the following guidelines:

> *Guideline No. 1.* Providers' associations or groups of associations comprising more than 25% of providers of a given kind of specialists may not agree on minimum fees or fix prices for their services.
> *Guideline No 2.* Associations and groups of associations may agree on prices for their members' services and/or quotas when said prices arise from negotiations with administrators of resources to be allocated to health matters or their representatives. Prices may also arise from negotiations among said administrators (or their representatives) and independent service providers.
> *Guideline No 3.* Providers' associations and groups of providers' associations gathering more than 25% of providers with a given specialization in the relevant market shall not include exclusivity clauses stipulating the obligation of

---

451. 'Oxígeno Líquido s. Apelación Resolución Comisión Nacional de Defensa de la Competencia', CNCiv. Com. Fed., Sala III (12 Dec. 2002).
452. 'YPF S.A. c/ Comisión Nacional de Defensa de la Competencia s/ apelación Comisión Nacional de Defensa de la Competencia', Oxígeno Líquido s. Apelación Resolución Comisión Nacional de Defensa de la Competencia', CNCiv. Com. Fed., Sala I (21 Sep. 2004).
453. Available at http://www.cndc.gov.ar/biblioteca/Salud.pdf.

Part III, Ch. 1, Administrative Investigations

their members to enter into agreements with administrators of health funds through the association.

Guideline No 4. Administrators of health funds that, jointly or severally, represent more than 25% of the private demand in a relevant market must reach agreement with providers through the free election of their members or through competitive bid systems.

Guideline No 5. Agreements between providers' associations or groups of associations and administrators of health funds or their representatives shall not include exclusivity clauses that may prevent the association from entering into contracts with other parties demanding their services, or prevent the administrator from independently entering into contracts with other providers or providers' associations.

Guideline No 6. When an association comprises more than 50% of the providers in a given market and, due to facts related with the structure and dynamic of the same, not belonging to the association be an important barrier to the exercise of the supply of health care services, the association may not establish clauses impeding the affiliation of providers fulfilling the requirements of aptitude that may be relevant for the respective activity.

555. *Cattle and wholesale meat (1998).*[454] This report examined the impact of tax evasion on competition in the cattle and wholesale meat market, at a time of large idle capacity. Not surprisingly, it was concluded that tax evasion: (i) allowed inefficient competitors to stay in the market, and that by reducing it the idle capacity of the law-abiding competitors would be reduced; and (ii) was also a barrier of entry to law-abiding companies.

556. *LPG (2004).*[455] The Secretariat instructed the CNDC to investigate all stages of the LPG market, from production to the final sale to the internal market and its exportation. The CNDC requested information of about twenty-five market participants and held hearings with about twenty-two company executives, plus public officials, members of Congress and representatives of relevant trade associations.

557. The report thoroughly describes the international scenario and internal market, divided by sector (production, bottling and distribution), and concluded that:

(i) production was highly concentrated, mostly in Repsol YPF;
(ii) bottling was less concentrated, although subject to concern due to vertical integration in the case of Repsol YPF, which limited the potential growth of non-integrated bottlers; and
(iii) distribution was highly deconcentrated.

---

454. The Executive Summary of the report is available at www.mecon.gov.ar/cndc/htms_doc/docu3a.htm.
455. 'Estudios realizados por CNDC en el marco de denuncias', Comisión Nacional de Defensa de la Competencia, Report No. 456 (10 Aug. 2004) (available at www.cndc.gov.ar/dictamenes/dictamen967.pdf).

558. As regards prices, the CNDC pointed out that due to the fact that the market was unregulated, higher export prices would cause domestic prices to increase.

559. As anticipated, this last remark led to the passing of new regulation in the market in 2005.[456]

560. Granulated urea (2005).[457] As in the prior case, the Secretariat instructed the CNDC to study the granulated urea market, in particular at the production and distribution stages. Even when the report concluded that no anticompetitive conduct was observed, the CNDC observed that in the export contracts of one of the company's clauses prohibiting the re-importation of the products into Argentina had been included. Given that said clauses had been identified in the *YPF* case[458] as potentially anticompetitive, a separate investigation was opened to such effect.

561. Iron bars (2005).[459] The investigation encompassed all stages of production of iron bars, of common use in the construction industry, and was instructed by the Secretariat due to the notorious increase in the price of such products in 2003–2004. In particular, the focus was put on Acindar, the main competitor with around 50% of the market.

562. The report found that: (i) barriers of entry were low (for other type of iron producers); (ii) market concentration was observed worldwide and not only in Argentina; (iii) international prices had increased in the period of the study, mainly due to increased demand from China; (iv) even when Acindar had the largest market share, said share had been constantly declining, while that of its competitors had increased; (v) the market for distribution of iron bars was significantly de-concentrated; (vi) demand from the construction sector increased significantly, and so did iron bar production; (vii) most manufacturers were operating at around 90% of its installed capacity; and (viii) prices in the domestic market tracked those of the international market.

563. Probably given that essentially no major competition issues were detected, the CNDC pointed out to the fact that Acindar was modifying its distribution network, thus expressing its willingness to follow such process to examine its effects on competition.

564. Pay-TV television (2007).[460] This report was financed by the International Development Research Center of Canada, and carried out by then staff and former

---

456. Law No. 26,020, 8 Apr. 2005 [30628] BO.
457. 'Abastecimiento de urea para el sector agropecuario', File No. S01: 0263111/2004, CNDC report (available at www.cndc.gov.ar/dictamenes/dictamenfinal_urea.pdf).
458. 'YPF S.A.', *supra* n. 59.
459. 'Mercado de hierro redondo s/ investigación de mercado', Comisión Nacional de Defensa de la Competencia, Report No. 511 (8 Jul. 2005).
460. 'Problemas de competencia en el sector de distribución de programas de television en la Argentina' (*Competition problems in the distribution of televisión programs in Argentina*), English version of

Part III, Ch. 1, Administrative Investigations

staff of the CNDC with experience in pay-TV markets. It is worth noting that pay-TV distribution and programming have been among the sectors most frequently reviewed by the CNDC, both in the investigations and merger control area.

565. In particular, the ten years preceding the report saw an extraordinary change in the pay-TV industry, both in terms of development of new technologies and services and quality improvements, as well as in horizontal concentration (the Cablevisión–Multicanal merger having been announced by the date of the report) and vertical integration (in particular regarding programming rights over local soccer events, which was considered of substantial competitive importance). The main antitrust implications outlined in the report were the following:

> (1) Agreements to lessen competition among television system operators that operate in the same relevant market are particularly harmful for competition, since they increase the monopoly power of those operators and this can lead to an increase in the price that they charge their users or to a reduction in the variety of their contents. These agreements can either be price-fixing or market-division agreements, the effects of which being very similar. The same objections apply to most horizontal mergers among television system operators that are in the same relevant market.

566. Even when the first issue (horizontal agreements) is in no way surprising, the reference of the CNDC to the effects on mergers is interesting, especially as it can be regarded as an anticipation of some of the efficiency arguments in support of the Cablevisión–Multicanal merger,[461] expressed in the CNDC's and Secretariat's December 2007 decision:

> A similar phenomenon takes place when the horizontal agreement is carried out by means of a merger among the companies that compete in the same relevant market, with the exception that in this case the integration may bring about cost reductions (for instance, through savings in the distribution and marketing of the programmes) that in a way make up for the surplus loss induced by the disappearance of competition. That is why in these cases the analysis must take into account this additional element, as well as the possibility that the analyzed relevant market is a natural monopoly, and does therefore not allow for more than one supplier of the service.
> 2) Mergers among television channel suppliers that do not sell their products directly to the viewers could have a lower potential to affect the general economic interest than horizontal mergers among television system operators. This is due to the fact that, in general, there are a larger number of alternatives available in the market and a greater ability to replace a supplier's contents with another's. Besides, because of the way in which TV contents and channels are

---

the CNDC report (available at http://www.cndc.gov.ar/comp_television_eng.pdf). Note should be taken that this has not been a sectorial inquiry, but rather a white paper.
461. It refers to the welfare loss from collusive agreements, although surprisingly from a total welfare and not consumer standard, as advocated in Resolution No. 164/2001.

marketed, the effect of a greater market power in their provision can bring about changes in the distribution of profits between suppliers and operators, but less significant variations regarding the prices paid by the viewers.

567. The reference to 'the way in which TV contents and channels are marketed' points to markets where programming prices are in the form of fixed rather than unit (per subscriber) prices, and thus changes regarding the amounts paid by the distributors do not have a significant impact on the marginal cost of having new subscribers:[462]

(3) Vertical agreements between television content suppliers and television system operators are in principle harmless from the point of view of competition law. However, their potential anticompetitive effects appear in those situations in which there is a restriction to competition in one of the industry segments (which in general is the segment of retail television provision in a certain relevant market). The most important anticompetitive effect that can occur due to vertical agreements is undermining and eventually excluding a rival operator from the market. This kind of effect is also the one that deserves the most attention when analysing a vertical merger between a channel supplier and a television system operator.

568. This issue has frequently been studied in merger and conduct cases. In the former, it was mostly dealt with through 'non-discrimination warnings' included in the final decision,[463] although in one case where the merging parties were deemed to monopolize the relevant market upstream a divestiture was ordered.[464] In conduct cases, it has been commonplace that a pay-TV distributor would claim that its integrated competitor refused to sell (or sold at an abusive price) certain important content, as examined under paragraphs 454 et seq. above.

(4) Another potentially anticompetitive effect of vertical agreements and mergers between TV content suppliers and television system operators appears when those agreements or mergers help to extend the supplier's market power from the wholesale market to the retail market. The most important case is the one that occurs when the supplier imposes a marketing method for its channel or content (for instance, codified, pay-per-view) and the price at which such channel or content must be sold to the viewers. These practices can become

---

462. This practice was also the reason under which the predatory pricing case pointed out in paras. 419–420 was closed.
463. *See*, e.g., 'Telefónica S.A., Telefónica de Argentina S.A., International Equity Investments Inc., CEI Citicorp Holdings S.A. y Cablevisión S.A. s/ notificación art. 8 Ley No. 25.156', Secretaría de Defensa de la Competencia y del Consumidor, Resolution No. 245 (27 Oct. 2000), Art. 2; 'Nofal Sports Holding S.A., DLJ Offshore Partners C.V., DirecTV Latin America LLC, DirecTV Argentina S.A. y otros s/ Notificación Art. 8 Ley 25.156 (Conc. No. 709)', Art. 2, *supra* n. 277; and 'The News Corporation Limited, Hughes Electronics Corporation y General Motors Corporation s/ Notificación Artículo 8 Ley 25.156 (Conc. N° 0438)', Art. 2, *supra* n. 387, among others.
464. 'Adjunta Formulario 1 para la notificación de concentraciones económicas (Conc. 468)', Secretaría de Comercio Interior, Resolution No. 145 (29 Sep. 2004).

Part III, Ch. 1, Administrative Investigations 569–572

particularly harmful when they are used to lessen competition among operators, which stop competing with each other in a certain important dimension.

569. This point mostly refers to the practice known as resale price maintenance, and in particular the *Tele Red Imagen y Televisión Satelital Codificada* case.[465]

570. As regards national league soccer rights, which amounted to the majority of refusal to deal cases examined by the CNDC, it should be noted that as from August 2010 all related matches are broadcast over free-to-air television by the national government.

571. The report also included the following regulatory implications:

(5) The problems brought about by the existence of natural monopolies in the provision of television contents and services cannot be solved by means of usual competition policy mechanisms, since their solution generally involves the need to regulate prices and provision terms directly. This means that, if it is necessary to intervene in this kind of situations, it is more appropriate to do so using specific regulation and mechanisms, instead of applying competition law and its enforcement agencies.

572. This conclusion seemed largely theoretical, since the report clarified that:

The object of this work has not been to determine which segments of the distribution of television programmes are natural monopolies and which of them are not, since that issue must necessarily be analysed in each individual case and seems to be changing fast along with telecommunications technology.

In fact, this report was not even cited in subsequent regulation introduced to regulate prices in the pay-TV sector:[466]

(6) Certain interventions by the antitrust authority, however, can be useful in some cases to reduce the impact of specific problems that arise in the case of monopoly situations. Among those interventions, we can mention the prohibition to discriminate prices among customers, the obligation to give access to essential facilities, the prohibition to sell certain television contents in block, and the prohibition to fix resale prices regarding certain television contents.
(7) The last possible intervention by the antitrust agencies regarding regulatory matters can be the opinions given as competition advocacy. In the case of the sector of distribution of television programmes, those opinions can refer to the advantages to allow the broadcasting of such programmes through networks

---

465. *Supra* n. 147. The decision was reversed by the Appellate Court ('V.C.C. S.A. y otros', CNPenal Económico, sala B [2003-F] LL, 602).
466. Secretaría de Comercio Interior, Resolution No. 50/2001, *supra* n. 142.

other than cable television's, to enable direct competition among channel suppliers to capture the viewers' preferences, and to encourage the entry of new television system operators.

573. In particular, the report recommends in this point to study the convenience of changing the regulatory hurdles preventing telecommunications companies to provide 'triple play' services, in order to bring about more competition both in cable television and in fixed telephone services. This argument was central in the initial clearance of the Cablevisión–Multicanal merger,[467] as the regulatory change in that direction seemed almost inevitable. Further regulation in the media sector, while on the one hand aims to introduce drastic reforms in terms of fostering vertical disintegration and horizontal de-concentration, on the other specifically prevents the entering of telecommunications companies.[468]

574. *Fruit (2007)*.[469] The study was made due to the presumed existence of a buyer cartel. The CNDC concluded that the drop in prices was instead due to structural issues, such as a consumer oligopoly, dispersed seller structure and international aspects.

575. The description of the inquiries above may incorrectly suggest that third parties can also participate in sectorial investigations. In all cases above it was the CNDC who, under the empowerments granted by section 24 of the Competition Act, requested third parties to provide information or documents, or testify before the agency. As mentioned in paragraph 603 below third parties can request to be appointed party in investigations of prohibited conducts, but arguably not in the case of sectorial investigations, which are aimed at a different result (provide an overview of a certain market or identify potential or actual competition problems which *may lead* to a specific investigation). In fact, market participants which are enquired in the course of the sectorial investigation are not made parties to the proceeding, so adopting a different approach as regards third parties could affect due process.

575.1. In 2014, and in the context of increasing inflation, the CNDC launched four probes in the following markets: (i) food, beverage, toiletries and cleaning products; (ii) pharmaceutical and health insurance companies; (iii) inputs for the construction industry; and (iv) inputs for industrial companies.

575.2. Over 250 companies were issued information requests requesting specific information on products prices, market shares, costs, and commercialization

---

467. 'Grupo Clarín S.A., Vistone LLC, Fintech Advisory Inc., Fintech Media LLC, VLG Argentina LLC y Cablevisión S.A.', *supra* n. 152.
468. Audiovisual Communication Services Act 26,522, *supra* n. 388. This law, *inter alia*: (a) limits the possibility of a same economic group holding multiple broadcasting licenses, with an additional limit of 35% share of the national population or subscribers, as appropriate; (b) prohibits holders of radio, television or pay-TV licenses to control more than one programming channel; and (c) provides for the obligation of those infringing the foregoing provisions to divest the relevant assets.
469. 'Industria frutícola s/ investigación de mercado (c. 1033)', file S01:0157700/2005, CNDC report dated 20 Dec. 2007 (available at www.cndc.gov.ar/fruticola_rio_negro.pdf).

channels, among other items. No final report has been issued as of the time of this writing.

II. Ex Officio Investigations

576. Under section 26 of the Competition Act, an investigation may be initiated ex officio by the CNDC. The events leading to the opening of the investigation are generally two: (i) evidence collected by the CNDC in the course of other proceedings, or through third parties not willing to formally initiate a complaint; or (ii) a specific request made by the Secretariat or some other federal or local agency.

III. Complaints

577. Most commonly an investigation is initiated by a third-party complaint (section 26). Under section 28, the complaint must include the following:

(i) name and domicile of the complainant;
(ii) the purpose of the complaint, precisely described;
(iii) the facts on which the complaint is based, clearly explained; and
(iv) the legal provisions infringed.

578. The CNDC must summon the complainant to personally ratify the complaint. In the hearing in which this event takes place, the CNDC will normally try to complete any deficiencies the original complaint may have had, including details of the presumed anticompetitive conduct, the relevant market and the period in which the infringement took place.

579. Section 29 of the Regulation provides that the decision of the CNDC not to open the investigation may be appealed by the complainant under section 52 of the Competition Act. In practice, however, the CNDC rarely discharges a complaint, even in cases where neither the original complaint nor the subsequent ratification fulfilled the standard set forth in section 28.

§2. POWERS

I. Requests for Information

580. Under section 20 of the Competition Act, the CNDC is fully empowered to issue information requests to any person, including governmental agencies, in the course of an investigation. Requests are made in written form and a term is set forth for the replies. This method of collecting evidence has proved not to be very effective. It is common for the CNDC to issue repeated requests before obtaining the required information, which many times is not provided in the way the authority intended it to be. Part of this problem is caused by the lack of effective sanctions for the parties not complying with this obligation: as anticipated in paragraph 180, under section 50 of the Competition Act infringers are subject to a daily fine of only ARS 500.

II. Investigating and Search Powers

581. Under Resolution 359/2015 of the Secretariat, the investigating powers of the CNDC are limited to:

 (i) issue requests for information, as provided above;
 (ii) hold hearings;
 (iii) produce technical evidence over ' … *books, documents and remaining items that may be conducive to the investigation, control inventories, verify origin and costs of raw materials or other goods*'; and
 (iv) conduct searches on private premises, with the consent of the resident therein or upon obtaining of a search warrant from a competent judge which, as anticipated, must decide on the CNDC's request within twenty-four hours.

582. Searches on private premises, like company or trade association headquarters, have proved to be very effective in the past, with the two landmark *Cement* and *Liquid Oxygen* cartel cases.[470] Searches are conducted with the aid of the local police, and must be limited to the content of the search warrant.

583. Searches are conducted as in any white collar investigation, the authorities withdrawing documents, computers files, etc. Documents are sealed and opened in a judicial hearing with the presence of the parties, where a list is prepared. Unlike other jurisdictions, attorney–client communications (both from in-house and external counsel) are not outside the reach of the CNDC.[471]

584. In a few recent cases, the CNDC extended its powers to conduct investigations on-premise by appointing auditors to conduct long-term investigations. This was the case of the proceedings opened in connection with the *Cattle Market*[472] and the *Telecom Argentina Merger* case.[473] In the former, auditors appointed by the CNDC attended the Liniers cattle market to personally verify the bid process, which was subject to a cartel investigation. In the *Telecom Argentina* case, CNDC auditors visited the company's premises for a period of over six months, holding extensive interviews with key executives, requesting documents and attending board and shareholders meetings.

---

470. 'Loma Negra Compañía Industrial S.A. y otros', *supra* n. 107; and 'Oxígeno Liquido', *supra* n. 106.
471. CPPN, Arts 224 to 229.
472. 'Mercado de Hacienda de Liniers s/ investigación de mercado (C.1087)'.
473. 'Telefónica de España, Olimpia y Otros s/ diligencia preliminar Art. 8 de la Ley 25.156', Comisión Nacional de Defensa de la Competencia, Resolution No. 43 (30 Mar. 2009).

Part III, Ch. 1, Administrative Investigations

585. The legality of the actions mentioned in the preceding paragraph is questionable, given that they were made without a court order (in fact, in the *Telecom Argentina* case, the CNDC audit partially overlapped with one ordered by a court) and the Competition Act does not seem to allow for such powers.

586. As anticipated in paragraphs 219 and 549 above, persons obstructing or impairing the investigation or not fulfilling other requirements of the competition authorities may be subject to daily fines of up to ARS 500, evidently very low to achieve the desired purpose.

III. Cooperation with Other State Institutions

587. Given the secondary role reserved to competition policy in Argentina, it is not surprising that the opinion of competition agencies is not frequently requested by other agencies or branches of Government.

588. Interaction with other State agencies is normally carried out during merger review, where under section 16 of the Competition Act, the CNDC must request the opinion of the sectorial regulator, which nonetheless is non-binding. Other type of less frequent interaction can be found in the advocacy opinions issued by the CNDC, which were mentioned in paragraphs 199–203 above.

589. The legal dependence of the CNDC to the Secretariat causes the former to cooperate with the latter in ways that are perceived as alien to Competition Law. In particular, the CNDC has been ordered by the Secretariat, explicitly or not, to initiate proceedings in areas such as cattle, pay-TV, labour insurance, banking, fashion clothing, pharmaceuticals, construction materials, cleaning products, etc. Those investigations are sometimes described as cartel investigations, but by and large have evidenced a lack of substance, which has revealed that they were mostly addressed as attempts to tackle inflation concerns.

§3. RIGHT OF DEFENCE

I. Content and Notification of Opening Decisions

590. The period elapsing from the complaint or commencement of the ex officio investigation until the notification of the opening of the investigation is not regulated in the Competition Act. Presumably both acts should be relatively simultaneous, but in practice the CNDC may first gather some initial evidence, issuing requests for information or, in exceptional cases, holding testimonial hearings and/or requesting search warrants.

591. The decision notifying the opening of the investigation attaches either a copy of the complaint and ratification hearing or, in ex officio cases, a resolution by the CNDC setting forth reasons for the opening of the investigation, that is, identifying the prima facie anticompetitive conduct. In any case, the investigated party is requested to provide explanations to said conducts within ten business days (section 29).

II. The Proceedings: Hearings, Access to File, Briefs

592. Upon the investigated party providing explanations as set forth in section 29, or the term for doing so having expired, the CNDC must decide whether to formally open the investigation or not (section 30). At this point, the CNDC may also decide to close the case (section 31), although it rarely does so.

593. According to section 30 of the Regulation, the investigation must be carried out within the term of 180 business days. However, under criminal law principles, said term is not considered mandatory for the agency, and thus it is not uncommon for investigations to last several years.

594. Only the investigated parties have access to the file, which is unrestricted.

595. In the course of an investigation, parties may file briefs or present evidence as they deem fit, which generally will be considered by the CNDC even if filed outside the stages contemplated by the Competition Act.[474] For this reason, and considering that the CNDC rarely closes an investigation after the parties provided explanations under section 29, presentation of this last brief is not crucial, although advisable as a proof of the interest of the relevant party in proving its innocence.

596. A typical investigation heavily relies on testimonial hearings. The decision of the CNDC to summon a witness must be notified to the investigated parties in order that they may attend the hearing and question the witness. Pursuant to the CPPN,[475] the witness is first interrogated by the CNDC and then by the parties, which address their questions to the CNDC who then, if deemed appropriate, makes the question to the witness. A transcription of the hearing is signed by all parties and included in the file.

597. It is worth noting that lack of notification of a testimonial hearing has not been deemed invalid by the courts, insofar as they can be replicated during the course of the investigation.[476] If they are not, the hearings would still be valid, although its evidentiary value would be reduced.

---

474. Under criminal procedural law principles and regulations: (i) the CNDC should examine all facts leading to the decision of the case, with an aim to reaching the 'substantive truth' (*verdad material*). *See* Enrique M. Falcón, Tratado De La Prueba, Tomo 1 (ed. Astrea, 2003) at 594; and (ii) most limitations to the production of evidence provided for under civil laws do not apply in criminal proceedings (CPPN, Art. 206).
475. CPPN, Arts 203 and 249.
476. As provided for in Art. 200 of the CPPN.

Part III, Ch. 1, Administrative Investigations 598–603

598. The CNDC has no limitations as to the type of witnesses it may summon, and consequently may take depositions to company executives, competitors, clients, distributors, public officials, and whoever may be of value for the investigation.

599. In addition, section 38 allows the Secretariat to call for public hearings, through publications in the Official Gazette and nationwide newspapers with a minimum anticipation of ten days (pursuant to section 40 the investigated parties must however be notified of the date of the hearing with an anticipation of fifteen days).

600. The publication shall:

(i) identify the investigation;
(ii) describe the scope of the hearing and its objective;
(iii) include the date, time and place of the hearing; and
(iv) describe whatever requisites may be followed to attend and participate in the hearing (sections 39, 40 and 41).

601. Decree 1172/2003, approving inter alia the General Regulations for Public Hearings for the Federal Government, complements the foregoing provisions with procedure details.

602. There is no experience on public hearings under the Competition Law, although its usefulness can be easily appreciated. The CNDC could require the attendance of competitors or consumers affected by certain practice, for the purpose of gathering additional evidence. Even when opinions expressed during the hearing are non-binding,[477] parties can submit documents,[478] and the authority must prepare a final report with a detail of all opinions[479] and subsequently issue a resolution explaining what it did or did not do about them.[480]

603. In principle, only the complainant and the investigated parties are parties to the investigation. Third parties, such as trade associations, consumer associations or individual consumers can become third-party plaintiffs (*partes coadyuvantes*) only if expressly authorized by the CNDC. This possibility is not available in the case of merger reviews.[481] The decision to name assisting parties is an important one, because they may not only file briefs and present evidence but also appeal final decisions.[482]

---

477. Decree 1172/03, 4 Dec. 2003, [30291] BO 1, Annex I, Art. 6.
478. *Ibid.*, at Art. 31.
479. *Ibid.*, at Art. 36.
480. *Ibid.*, at Art. 38.
481. 'CASA ISENBECK s. apel. resol. Comisión Nacional de Defensa de la Competencia', CNCiv. Com. Fed., Sala III (29 Oct. 2002), LL 2003-E, 324.
482. CPPN, Art. 82.

III. Statement of Objections

604. Once the investigation is concluded, the CNDC may send a Statement of Objections to the investigated parties. This decision implies a formal accusation, where the CNDC enumerates all the evidence collected during the investigation leading to its conclusion that the Competition Act was affected.

605. The parties have fifteen business days to reply to the Statement of Objections and offer evidence. They are not limited to the type of evidence they may offer, insofar as it is reasonably linked to facts or statements included in the investigation.

606. Upon receipt of the reply to the Statement of Objections, the CNDC will first decide on the admissibility of evidence. Such decision cannot be appealed (section 33), although of course an unreasonable decision rejecting a certain evidence could be taken into account on appeal.

607. Once the evidence is produced, the parties must allege on their value within a term of six business days (section 34). At this last stage, the file is no longer available for the parties until issuance of the final decision.

IV. Final Hearing and Decision

608. According to section 34, once the evidence is produced and the parties are allowed to allege on them, the CNDC and the Secretariat have sixty business days to issue the final decision. Procedurally, the CNDC must write its opinion, send the file to the Secretariat for its review and issuance of the final decision, and once the file is returned from the Secretariat with the final decision, notify the same to the parties.

609. Until issuance of the final decision, the Competition Act allows the investigated parties to settle the case, under specific conditions.

610. According to section 36, the parties may agree to immediately or gradually cease with the investigated conducts or to modify certain aspects of them. If approved by the CNDC and Secretariat, the settlement suspends the investigation for a term of three years, upon which, if the settlement was complied with, the case is closed. The Former Competition Act contemplated similar provisions.[483]

611. It should be noted that a party is not required to acknowledge the existence of alleged anticompetitive conducts, although of course the decision to enter into a

---

483. Sections 24 and 25.

Part III, Ch. 1, Administrative Investigations 612–613

settlement could be taken as a presumption of liability in case the party were to breach it.[484]

612. Another issue worth considering for the applicant is that a rejection of a settlement proposal by the authorities is not subject to appeal, given that the agencies' decision is based on policy and not legal issues and, in addition, the party could appeal the final decision imposing a sanction.[485]

613. Case law has repeatedly stated that section 36 does not apply to conducts that have already been produced and which effects cannot be reversed, since its effect is the total exemption of liability. This principle, however, has in practice mostly applied to cases – particularly but not exclusively – of a collusive nature, where the CNDC considered that the conduct was reasonably proved and thus could apply a sanction,[486] but not to other type of conducts where the effects on competition were less clear and/or the evidence collected by the agency was weaker, including refusals to deal and discrimination,[487] several exclusionary acts,[488] exclusive distribution and dealing,[489] abusive[490] and predatory pricing.[491]

---

484. In fact, in some cases the CNDC has stated that the entering into settlement negotiations implied the acknowledgment by the party of a wrongdoing. *See* 'Colegio Médico de Corrientes', Secretaría de Industria, Comercio y Minería. Resolution No. 819 (30 Nov. 1998), point 5.11.3.
485. 'Papel Tucumán S.A. c/ Alto Paraná S.A.', CNPenal Económico, Sala A, LL 1997-B at 714–715.
486. 'Cámara Inmobiliaria Argentina', Secretaría de Comercio, Resolution No. 453 (2 Dec. 1983), 'Subsecretario de Industria y Comercio de la Pcia. de Corrientes (Empresas areneras)', Resolution No. 361 (26 Aug. 1983); 'A. Gas S. A. y otras c. Agip Argentina S. A. y otras', *supra* n. 214; and 'Cooperativa Entrerriana de Productores Mineros Ltda.', *supra* n. 222. On the contrary, in a few cases even cartel cases have been subject to a settlement, as the 'Lina Trippiccio de Pascuzzo' (complaint against Centro de Industriales Panaderos de Lanús), Secretaría de Industria, Comercio y Minería, Resolution No. 607 (27 Jun. 1997); and 'Organización de Investigaciones Privadas Argentina s/ denuncia c/ Control de Seguridad S.A. s/ Ley 22.262', Secretaría de Industria, Comercio y Minería, Resolution No. 565 (31 Aug. 1998) cases illustrate.
487. 'A.Z. Chaitas S.A.C.I.F.' (complaint against PASA Petroquímica Argentina S.A.I.C.), Secretaría de Comercio Interior. Resolution No. 406 (22 Sep. 1988), 'Cable Grande S.A.' (complaint against Empresa Distribuidora de Electricidad de Entre Ríos S.A.), Secretaría de Coordinación Técnica, Resolution No. 61 (7 Oct. 2003); 'Aceros Zapla S.A. s/ Infracción a la Ley 25.156 (c. 881)', Secretaría de Coordinación Técnica, Resolution No. 156 (19 Oct. 2004) and 'Pramer SCA s/ infracción Ley 22.262', Secretaría de Defensa de la Competencia y del Consumidor, Resolution No. 248 (1 Nov. 2000).
488. 'Colegio Médico de Corrientes', Secretaría de Industria, Comercio y Minería. Resolution No. 819 (30 Nov. 1998); 'Cooperativa de Trabajo Delta Villa Rosa Ltda. s/ Ley 25.156', Secretaría de la Competencia, la Desregulación y la Defensa del Consumidor, Resolution No. 36 (21 Oct. 2002).
489. 'Soda Fernández', *supra* n. 284; 'Miniphone S.A. y Compañía de Radiocomunicaciones Móviles S.A. s/ Infracción Art. 1 Ley 22.262', Secretaría de Industria, Comercio y Minería. Resolution No. 10 (11 Jan. 1999).
490. 'Directora de Comercio Interior' (complaint against Laboratorio Pfizer S.A.C.I), Secretaría de Comercio e Inversiones, Resolution No. 304 (Dic. 18, 1995).
491. 'AC Nielsen S.A. y AC Nielsen Company y otros s/ infracción a la Ley 25.156 (c. 934)', Secretaría de Coordinación Técnica, Resolution No. 92 (8 Jun. 2005).

614. In addition, the agreement proposed by the parties must have an appreciable effect on competition in the relevant market, and not only as regards the complainant.[492]

615. The relatively low enforcement record of the CNDC, coupled with the considerable length of the period in which the file is suspended but not closed, the lack of indications as to what would be required for the CNDC to resume the investigation and the risks stemming from unaccepted or breached settlements explain the few cases where this option has been used.

---

492. 'Dirección de Bienestar de la Armada', *supra* n. 255.

Chapter 2. Voluntary Notifications and Clearance Decisions Merger Control

§1. PRELIMINARY FILING OBLIGATIONS

I. Criteria and Thresholds

616. Section 6 of the Competition Act provides for the mandatory notification of certain economic concentrations. As regards the scope of this term, please refer to paragraphs 115 et seq. above.

II. Turnover Calculation

617. Section 8 provides that an economic concentration will only be notified when 'the sum of the total business volume of the group of affected companies exceeds in the country the sum of two hundred million (ARS 200,000,000) Argentine pesos'. Section 8 of the Regulation clarified that the term 'affected companies' means: (a) the company regarding which control is acquired (the target company); and (b) the company acquiring such control.

618. Section 8 of the Competition Act defines the term 'total business volume' as the sum resulting from the sale of products and the rendering of services by the affected companies during the last fiscal year related to their ordinary activities, after deducting any sales discounts, VAT and other taxes directly related to the business volume.

619. The requirement that said business volume be achieved in Argentina should be interpreted as including direct sales into Argentina of entities linked to the buyer or target (as explained below) but 100% of the turnover generated by local companies or branches, including exports.[493]

620. Section 8 also defines the group of companies for which local turnover must be taken into account for threshold purposes. Those are:

(1) The undertaking concerned.
(2) Those undertakings in which the undertaking concerned, directly or indirectly:
    (a) owns more than half the capital or issued capital;
    (b) has the power to exercise more than half of the voting rights;
    (c) has the power to appoint more than half the members of the supervisory board, the administrative board or bodies legally representing the undertakings; or
    (d) has the right to manage the undertakings' affairs.

---

493. Comisión Nacional de Defensa de la Competencia, Advisory Opinion No. 26 (1 Feb. 2000) and 'Henkel Argentina S.A. y otros s/ consulta interpretación Ley 25.156', Secretaría de Comercio Interior, Resolution No. 168 (25 Sep. 2008).

(3) Those undertakings which have in the undertaking concerned the rights or powers listed in (2).
(4) Those undertakings in which an undertaking, as referred to in (3), has the rights or powers listed in (4).
(5) Those undertakings in which several undertakings, as referred to in (1)–(4), jointly have the rights or powers listed in (b).

621. As can be easily seen, the above provision replicates the language of the EC's Merger Regulation,[494] although without including the numerous clarifications and exceptions listed therein. In particular, note should be taken that there are no specific exemptions as regards inter-group sales or joint undertakings.

622. The 'right to manage the undertakings' affairs' provided for in paragraph 620, item (2) (d) above, has been deemed as applicable to all situations where the relevant company exercises at least substantial influence over another, that is, the standard test to determine the existence of an economic concentration.

623. Section 10 of the Competition Act provides for a few specific exemptions to notifications, as follows:

(a) The acquisition of companies in which the acquirer already holds 50% of the shares.
(b) The acquisition of bonds, non-voting shares or debt instruments of an undertaking.
(c) The acquisition of a single enterprise by a single foreign enterprise not previously owning assets or shares in other companies in Argentina.
(d) Acquisitions of liquidated companies, defined as those that have had no activities during the preceding year.
(e) Economic concentrations where each of the amount of the transaction and the value of the assets located in Argentina being absorbed, acquired, transferred or controlled not exceed, respectively, ARS 20,000,000,unless in a preceding twelve-month term transactions were made in the same market which, on aggregate, exceed said amount, or that of ARS 60,000,000 in the last thirty-six months.

624. Save for the exemptions listed under paragraph 623, items (b) and (d) above, regarding which the author is not aware of any decision in which they were applied up-to-date, the remaining have been subject to several clarifications by the CNDC.

625. A typical procedure to obtain clarifications as to whether a certain economic concentration is exempted from notification is that of the request for an Advisory Opinion to the CNDC and Secretariat, which was described in footnote 42.

---

494. Council Regulation (EC) No. 139/2004 of 20 Jan. 2004 on the control of concentrations between undertakings, OJ L 024 (29 Jan. 2004), 1–22.

Part III, Ch. 2, Clearance Decisions Merger Control 626–629

626. Exemptions under items (a), (c) and (e) have been interpreted as follows.

627. *Item (a)*. A first line of opinions complemented this exemption as stating that the ownership of over 50% of the *voting rights*, and not the equity participation, had to be considered, and with this caveat applied the exemption literally; i.e., if a party owned over 50% of the voting rights of an undertaking it would not be subject to mandatory notification.[495] Another – more recent – line of opinions, however, also required that the party owning the majority of the voting rights *already had exclusive control over the undertaking*, that is, that the acquisition of the minority participation did not represent a change from joint to sole control.[496] This last line of opinion, however, has been challenged by the courts.[497]

628. *Item (c)*. The 'acquisition of a single enterprise' requirement has been extended to the acquisition of more than one legal entity, insofar as all of them are in the same business and develop their activity as a single group. However, the scope of the term 'assets' is more vague, since it may include direct sales to Argentina from entities of the acquiring group, insofar as title over the relevant goods is passed in Argentina, as opposed to the situation where local purchasers become the owners of the goods at the time they enter the country or purchase them from an independent local distributor, which has acquired title over those goods outside Argentina.[498]

629. *Item (e)*. The considerations made above as regards the meaning of the term 'assets' apply here as well. The 'value of the assets' is generally calculated by looking at a balance sheet of the relevant subsidiary or branch of target in Argentina;[499] where isolated assets rather than a company exist, an independent valuation would probably be required. The term 'amount of the transaction' is easy to apply when a transaction is a purely local one or, if of an international nature, the relevant agreement specifically allocates the price to be paid for the Argentinean operations. When none of the foregoing occur, but the relevant agreement determines the total price by the application of a formula (i.e., based on some EBITDA multiple), such formula could be applied for the Argentinean assets to determine their price.[500] When the agreement gives no reference as to the price paid for the local assets, the parties

---

495. Comisión Nacional de Defensa de la Competencia, Advisory Opinions No. 53 (18 Jul. 2000), 63 (28 Aug. 2000) and 72 (30 Oct. 2000).
496. Comisión Nacional de Defensa de la Competencia, Advisory Opinion No. 189 (19 Jul. 2004); 'ENEL S.p.A. y Acciona S.A. s/ consulta interpretación Ley 25.156 (OPI No. 172), Secretaría de Comercio Interior, Resolution No. 254 (3 Jul. 2009).
497. 'Enel S.p.A. y otros s/ apel. resol. Comisión Nacional de Defensa de la Competencia', CNCiv. Com. Fed., Sala II (21 Oct. 2010).
498. Comisión Nacional de Defensa de la Competencia, Advisory Opinion No. 218 (20 Mar. 2006); 'Element Netherlands Holding Cooperatief U.A. y Yakituri Holdings N.V. s/ consulta interpretación Ley No. 25.156 (Opi 189)', Secretaría de Comercio Interior, Resolution No. 289 (6 Aug. 2010).
499. Comisión Nacional de Defensa de la Competencia, Advisory Opinions No. 202 (16 Feb. 2005) and 204 (18 Mar. 2005).
500. Comisión Nacional de Defensa de la Competencia, Advisory Opinions No. 159 (25 Apr. 2002) and 171 (10 Oct. 2002).

should provide a reasonable, independent valuation. Failure to do so may result in the exemption not being granted.[501]

630. Even when the exemption does not refer to it, it is reasonable to assume that: (a) references to transactions in the last twelve and thirty-six months relate to 'economic concentrations', even if not subject to mandatory review; and (b) the parties should look at prior economic concentrations implemented *by the acquirer only* and not the target, since the value of those other transactions should be represented in the value of the target itself.[502] Also, it should be noted that a literal interpretation of Article 10(e) of the Competition Act might exempt purely foreign-to-foreign acquisitions where the target does not have assets in Argentina but nonetheless a substantial local market share, achieved through direct sales. Even when the CNDC has not directly addressed this situation, some advisory opinions seem to suggest that in those cases the CNDC would restrict the application of Article 10(e) to cases in which the target's assets are somewhat representative of its market presence, as otherwise the effects test mentioned in 87–89 above would still apply.

III. Market Share Calculation

631. Market shares are not part of the jurisdictional threshold of the Competition Act. The original language of said law, however, provided for a dual test involving both the turnover – as explained above – and the merging companies' resulting in a market share of 25% or more of the relevant market, or a 'substantial part of it'. This last language was vetoed by the Executive Power and is not part of the Competition Act.

632. As regards the calculation of market shares during the merger control review, it is made following the criteria set forth in the Guidelines, through a three-stage approach: definition of relevant market, identification of the companies participating in it and measurement of the market shares and market concentration.

633. The definitions of relevant product and geographic market contained in the Guidelines are purely of an economic nature.

634. The Guidelines explain that the definition of relevant product market includes:

> all other goods and/or services that are considered substitutes by the consumer, given the product and price characteristics, and the purpose of their consumption. If the good produced by the concentrated companies is substitutable by other goods, then their market power would be limited by the consumers'

---

501. 'Viña San Pedro Tarapacá S.A. s/ consulta interpretación Ley No. 25.156 (Opi No. 166)', Secretaría de Comercio Interior, Resolution No. 65 (31 Mar. 2009).
502. Comisión Nacional de Defensa de la Competencia, Advisory Opinions No. 127 (16 Jul. 2001) and 171 (10 Oct. 2002).

Part III, Ch. 2, Clearance Decisions Merger Control

behaviour. In such case, those companies will not be able to unilaterally increase the price of their product without experiencing a significant shift of their consumers to other alternative goods. In sum, goods that are substitutable between them compete to attract consumers' demand, as a consequence of which it is correct to include them within the same market.[503]

635. The following items will be examined to determine consumers' reactions vis-à-vis an increase of the relative price of the good or service:

(i) proof that consumers have shifted or may shift their consumption towards other goods in response to the change in relative prices or other relevant variables (i.e., quality);
(ii) evidence that producers prepare their business strategies on the assumption that there is substitution in the demand of different products upon changes in relative prices or other relevant variables; and
(iii) time and cost required by consumers to shift their demand to other goods.

636. The relevant product market is then defined as the smaller group of products regarding which a hypothetical monopolist of all of them would find profitable to impose a small but significant and non-transitory[504] increase in price (an SSNIP test).

637. By the same token, the relevant geographic market is defined as the smaller region in which a sole provider of a product may find profitable to impose a small, but significant and non-transitory price increase.

638. In defining the relevant geographic market, the CNDC will take into account, inter alia:

(i) evidence that consumers have shifted or may shift their consumption towards other geographic areas in response to a change in relative prices or other relevant variables;
(ii) evidence that producers prepare their business strategies on the basis that there is substitution in the demand of different geographic areas upon changes in relative prices or other relevant variables; and
(iii) time and cost to the consumer in shifting its demand towards other geographic areas.

639. The companies participating in the relevant market will be both those doing so at the time of the merger as well as those which may enter the market upon a favourable change of circumstances, such as a price increase (named 'immediate potential competitors').

---

503. Guidelines, s. II.1.
504. According to the Guidelines, an increase of 5% to 10% for a period of at least one year.

640. Entry is generally carefully examined to avoid reaching unrealistic results, so issues such as sunken costs and legal and other barriers of entry are carefully examined.

641. Once the relevant market is defined and its participants identified, market shares are calculated based on the most relevant data available, from public sources if possible.

642. There is no clear-cut rule as to what combined market share will be considered excessive, as market shares in themselves are not conclusive as to the effects any given concentration would have in the market. Issues such as the degree of concentration, whether a monopsony or oligopsony exists, barriers of entry, etc. will influence such conclusion.

643. In addition, the increase in market concentration will frequently be considered more relevant than the resulting market concentration in itself. Several mergers resulting in very high market shares have been approved just because the resulting increase in market power has been deemed minimal, even when the acquirer had substantial market power before the merger.[505]

IV. Other Relevant Notions

644. It is important to note that section 7 prohibits all mergers causing a substantially negative effect on competition, and not only mergers subject to mandatory notification. The CNDC would then be empowered to investigate non-reportable mergers and, potentially, impose divestment or other remedies, although we are not aware of any such action being adopted so far.

§2. STRUCTURE OF PROCEEDINGS

I. Preliminary Assessments and Full Investigation

645. An economic concentration is notified by both parties to the relevant transaction, that is, buyer and seller or merging parties, through the filing of Form 1 and, if required, Forms 2 and 3 as well. The contents of Forms 1 and 2 are detailed in Resolution 40, while Form 3 is tailor-made to the specific concentration. Form 1 is required for simpler transactions, while more complicated deals may require the filing of Form 2, together with Form 1 or at a later date, as required by the CNDC. In

---

505. *See*, e.g., 'BASF Argentina S.A. y Cynamid Argentina S.A. s/ notificación Art. 8 Ley No. 25.156', Secretaría de Defensa de la Competencia y del Consumidor, Resolution No. 154 (22 Aug. 2000) and 'Pfizer S.R.L y Pharmacia Argentina S.A. s/ notificación art. 8 Ley 25.156', Secretaría de la Competencia, la Desregulación y la Defensa del Consumidor, Resolution No. 19 (20 Feb. 2003), among others.

view of its status as an independent agency, section 25 of the Competition Act provided that the Tribunal could charge filing fees. However, this provision was deleted by the 2014 Amendment.

646. Form 1 requires basic information, inter alia:

(i) From the notifying party, its name and domicile, the identity of the representatives and persons in charge of the preparation of the notification forms and a list of shareholders with the participation of 5% or more.
(ii) From the affected enterprise, a description of its activities, copy of the last annual report and financial statements, group organizational charts, a description of the relevant and substitute products, geographic areas where those products are sold, their manufacturing processes and market size and the confirmation on whether the affected enterprises have been or are being investigated in Argentina or in any other jurisdiction for conduct infringing competition or anti-dumping laws.
(iii) From the economic concentration being notified, details of its characteristics, a copy of the final or more recent transaction documents, whether the notified transaction has been presented for review before any other foreign merger control authority, etc.

647. The information required by Form 2 is essentially focused on details regarding the relevant product, supply-side and offer-side substitution, the relevant geographic market, qualitative and quantitative market information, production costs and efficiency gains.

648. The structure of a filing is similar in all cases. Upon filing of Form 1, numerous follow-up questions by the CNDC are made and, if required, hearings are conducted with the parties, their competitors, suppliers and distributors, consumer associations, etc. in case they would be conducive to the review. On occasions public agencies are consulted; this request is mandatory in case of regulated industries, such as banking, telecommunications, media, insurance, energy, etc.[506]

II. Time Framework

649. A notification must be made, according to section 8 of the Competition Act, prior to or within a week as of the date of conclusion of the agreement, publication of purchase or exchange offer or acquisition of a controlling participation, whichever happens first.

650. As appears from the foregoing, the language of section 8 has been contradictory in adopting an *ex ante* or *ex post* approach as regards merger control, given that even when a filing can be made before the signing of the definitive agreement,

---

506. Competition Act, Art. 16.

and the publication of a purchase or exchange offer is to be regarded as a pre-closing event, the acquisition of a controlling participation clearly is not. Moreover, section 8 of the Regulation has interpreted the term 'conclusion of the agreement', as follows:

> The term of one week for the notification contemplated in Section 8 of Law No. 25,156 will be counted as follows:
>
> 1. In the case of mergers between undertakings, the date on which the definitive merger agreement is signed, in accordance with the provisions of item 4 of section 83 of Law No. 19,550 of 1984.
> 2. In the case of transfers of going concerns, the date on which the sale agreement is registered with the Public Registry of Commerce in accordance with the provisions of Section 7 of Law No. 11,867.
> 3. In the case of acquisition of ownership or any right over shares or capital participations, the date on which the acquisition of such rights be perfected in accordance with the acquisition agreement.
> 4. In other cases, the date on which the transaction be perfected pursuant to applicable laws.

651. However, section 8 of the Competition Act provides that:

> Acts shall only produce effects between the parties or vis-à-vis third parties once the provisions of Sections 13 and 14,[507] as appropriate, are complied with.

652. In spite of the above-cited language, that would prevent post-closing filings or at least oblige the parties to maintain the *status quo ante* until the acts mentioned in section 13 or 14 occur, in practice the CNDC interpreted it as a *condition subsequent*, meaning that the transaction produced effects until subjected to undertakings or prohibited.[508]

653. This interpretation was initially challenged by the Secretariat in the *LAPA* case,[509] where the CNDC recommended the Secretariat to prohibit the transaction more than one year after closing. The Secretariat, which ultimately authorized the acquirer to sell the airline to a third party instead of ordering the reversion of the original sale, criticized the CNDC in its decision for not preventing the effects of the transaction through the issuance of a cease-and-desist order.

654. References to injunctions in that case were not casual. Given that the Competition Act does not expressly envisage sanctions for closing a transaction before

---

507. As will be seen below, ss 13 and 14 refer to the adjudication of merger cases through, respectively: (a) a decision (i) approving the transaction; (ii) conditioning the transaction to the fulfilment of undertakings; or (iii) prohibiting the transaction; or (b) the passing of forty-five business days without a final decision being issued (tacit approval).
508. This position was also reproduced in Advisory Opinion No. 62 (29 Aug. 2000).
509. 'LAPA, Fexis S.A., Elenor S.A., Eduardo Eurnekian y Otros', *supra* n. 381.

Part III, Ch. 2, Clearance Decisions Merger Control

clearance[510] only an injunction would allow some enforcement of the suspensory obligation of section 8. Even then, as seen in paragraphs 225 et seq. above, section 35 would require serious injury to competition, so presumably most mergers would not face restrictions in closing before clearance.

655. In spite of *LAPA*, in the ensuing years the CNDC failed to suspend the effect of significant mergers under review, which prompted third parties to resort to the courts for similar remedies (i.e., in the Cencosud filing,[511] which lasted four years mostly due to the effect of interim measures of several kinds issued by the courts).

656. Attempts to issue injunctions as late as 2007 were faced with the judicial decision in re *Multicanal*,[512] ordering the CNDC to refrain from issuing cease-and-desist orders.

657. As anticipated above, however, the CNDC issued several such orders in the *Telecom Italia Internacional/Telefónica de España, Olimpia y Otros* cases,[513] most of which have been reversed by the courts. It is worth noting, however, that, diverting from its prior practice, the CNDC based those injunctions in the suspensory obligation contained in section 8 of the Competition Act and the potentially negative impact on competition that would occur were the transaction to have effects. In a more recent transaction,[514] however, an injunction was issued by the Secretariat based on a literal interpretation of section 8, that is, even when no impact on

---

510. A reasonable interpretation of this would be that, if the transaction were ultimately approved, the parties would have only committed a formal breach of the Act. However, if the Secretaríat prohibited the transaction, or cleared it subject to conditions, it is possible that sanctions under the Competition Act could be applied under s. 1, s. 7 or both, since any activity performed by the affected enterprises during that period would be deemed as though made by independent parties, although the foregoing would require the opening of a separate investigation. Sanctions in this case could amount to fines ranging from ARS 10,000 to ARS 150 million, plus the issuance of cease-and-desist orders or a request to competent courts to order the dissolution, winding-up, de-concentration or spin-off of the affected enterprises.
511. 'Cencosud S.A., Capital International Global Emerging Markets Private Equity Fund L.P., Capital International Private Equity Fund IV, L.P. y CGPE IV L.P., y Disco Ahold Internacional Holdings, N.V. s/ notificación artículo 8 Ley No. 25.156 (conc. 566)', Secretaría de Coordinación Técnica, Resolution No. 77 (24 May 2005).
512. 'Multicanal S.A. y otro c/ Conadeco', *supra* n. 153.
513. 'Telefónica de España, Olimpia y Otros s/ diligencia preliminar art. 8 de la Ley 25.156', Comisión Nacional de Defensa de la Competencia, Resolution No. 4 (9 Jan. 2009), pp. 145–146, among others.
514. 'Boldt S.A. y Ciccone Calcográfica s/ notificación art. 8 ley 25.156 (Conc. 847)', Secretaría de Comercio Interior, Resolution No. 538 (16 Dec. 2010). But in 'Recurso de queja en causa 'Boldt S.A. s/ Ley 25.156', CNPenal Económico, Sala B (24 Feb. 2011), the court decided that the appeal to the decision suspending the transaction stayed the application of the decision, on the basis that the latter was not one of those specifically enumerated in s. 52 of the Competition Act as not having such effects. By a later decision, Boldt was fined for not complying with the suspensory obligation (*see* 'Boldt S.A. y Ciccone Calcográfica s/ notificación art. 8 ley 25.156 (Conc. 847)', Secretaría de Comercio Interior, Resolution No. 82 (1 Jun. 2011)) but this decision was reversed by the courts and the judgment of the Court of Appeals confirmed by the Supreme Court (*see* 'Incidente de Recurso de Apelación de multa Resolución SCI N° 82/2011, en autos caratulados 'Boldt S.A. y Ciccone Calcográfica S.A. s/notificación Art. 8 de la Ley 25.156', Ministerio de Economía

competition occurred. Those decisions confirm that the authorities are well aware of the language and purpose of the Competition Act as regards preventing gun jumping, as well as the difficulties that would arise were they to regularly suspend the implementation of mergers being notified for the lengthy period of the review process, and are ready to enforce the former in specific cases.

658. As decided by the Supreme Court in re *Aeroandina y Fexis*,[515] a notification of a merger through means other than the standard notification forms will not be considered valid to comply with the filing deadline. The court did not consider whether an incomplete notification form would suffice to that effect, although in practice it is accepted, particularly given that practically all initial notification forms are considered incomplete by the CNDC.

659. Fines for late filing can amount to up to ARS 1 million per day of delay. The most significant fines in the merger arena due to late filing were imposed in the *Pirelli & C S.p.A.* case[516] to a number of firms involved in the acquisition of an indirect stake in Telecom Italia S.p.A.[517] Fines topped almost ARS 236 million, the highest to date. The case is a good example of the risks for private companies stemming from high-profile concentrations where a finding of change of control or acquisition of substantial influence is not evident. The parties involved in that merger did not believe a notification was required, even when the CNDC had initiated a preliminary investigation to such end. On the contrary, and possibly because they anticipated that the final outcome would be an outright prohibition of the transaction, strongly contested the findings of the CNDC, but ultimately – after over 300 days have elapsed in some cases – made the filing under protest[518].

660. Section 8 provides that economic concentrations must be approved in a term of forty-five business days. In addition, Resolution 40 divides such term into three stages, depending on whether Form 1, Forms 1 and 2, or Form 3 is required, and provide that clearance must be granted in, respectively, fifteen, thirty-five or forty-five business days.

661. Section IV of Resolution 40 provides that the reviewing terms will be suspended:

(a) from the date in which the authority requests the filing of the information contained in Forms F2 and F3 until such information be presented;

---

y Finanzas Públicas – Secretaría de Comercio Interior – Comisión Nacional de Defensa de la Competencia', CNPenal Económico, Sala B (3 Feb. 2012) and 'Boldt S.A. y Ciccone Calcográfica S.A. s/ notificación art. 8 ley 25.156 -causa 62.028' CSJN, B. 468. XLVIII (4 Jun. 2013).
515. 'Aeroandina S.A. y Fexis S.A. S.A. s/ apel. resol. Comisión Nacional de Defensa de la Competencia', 329 Fallos 972 (2006).
516. Secretaría de Comercio Interior, Resolution No. 2 (6 Jan. 2010), [31816] BO, 47.
517. Those firms were Pirelli & S.p.A., Telefónica S.A., Assicurazioni Generali S.p.A., Mediobanca S.p.A., Sintonía S.p.A. and Intesa Sanpaolo S.p.A.
518. As anticipated, even with the Court of Appeals revoked the fines for late filing imposed to all firms but Telefónica S.A., this decision was reversed by the Supreme Court, which confirmed all fines.

Part III, Ch. 2, Clearance Decisions Merger Control 662–667

(b) from the date in which the authority requests the filing of information missing from Forms F1, F2 or F3 until such information is presented in complete form, according to the provisions of section 14 of the regulation;
(c) from the time in which the requirement to the sectorial regulators is made until such requirement is answered or the term for doing so expires, in accordance to the provisions of section 16 of the regulation to Law No. 25,156;[519]
(d) when, in accordance with the provisions of section 24 (l) of Law No. 25,156, the authority so provides it by founded resolution.

662. With particular reference to the provisions of paragraph 661, item (b) above, it should be noted that the CNDC interprets that the information provided by the parties in response to an information request is not complete until the CNDC so confirms in writing.

663. In addition, it is standard CNDC practice to make repeated information requests under any of the three notification forms, with questions that may exceed the scope of the original form. As a consequence of all the foregoing, the statutory forty-five business day review period is extended to several months, commonly one year or more even in the case of simple transactions.

III. Right of Defence

664. Parties to the merger review process have full access to the file, and thus can easily verify whether any of the evidence collected by the CNDC may affect them. In spite of the fact that the merger review proceeding is mostly based on a Q&A format, there is no limitation for the parties to submit additional evidence or make presentations in order to contradict previous evidence collected by the CNDC.

665. Hearings with persons different from the parties must be notified to them in advance, so that they are able to attend it[520] and, once the interrogation by the CNDC is finished, question the witness regarding his or her statements, prior approval of the relevant CNDC official conducting the hearing.[521]

666. The parties may appeal any final decision of the Secretariat rejecting a merger or conditioning it to the fulfilment of undertakings.[522]

667. The principle stemming from the CPPN that any decision causing irreparable harm may be subject to appeal also applies to merger control; however, it is unclear what decision would fit into this category, given that final decisions are expressly subject to appeal, and so are injunctions suspending the effects of the merger.

---

519. Decree No. 89/2001 [29577] BO, 1.
520. CPPN, Arts 200–202.
521. CPPN, Art. 203.
522. Competition Act, s. 52 (c).

668. Doubts have been raised as to whether third parties may appeal a decision that they may perceive as unfairly affecting their interests. This issue was discussed by the Court of Appeals in relation to the *Ambev/Quilmes* beer merger case,[523] when a third party (Isenbeck, a competing beer company) requested that the CNDC granted the possibility to act as a third-party plaintiff in the merger proceeding. Though said petition was rejected (both by the CNDC and the Court of Appeals), the latter nonetheless suggested that the plaintiff might however challenge the Secretariat's final decision in case it caused the plaintiff a concrete injury. The Quilmes merger was approved subject to undertakings. This approval was then appealed both by the aforementioned competitor and a member of the National Congress, but said appeals have since been dismissed by the Court of Appeals for failure to prove irreparable damage. The Court of Appeals left open, however, the possibility of a third party initiating *amparo* proceedings which, as seen above, are currently being used by third parties in the context of merger control, the degree of their success from the perspective of the plaintiff is still uncertain.

669. In addition, it should be noted that section 15 of the Competition Act and the Regulation expressly contemplate the possibility of the competition authorities, ex officio or at the request of any third party, reviewing such approval if the same were based on false or incomplete information provided by the merging parties. It is worth noting that in case incomplete information was filed, the administrative approval would only be revoked if the authorities would not have approved the concentration based on the omitted information.

§3. CLEARANCE AND CONDITIONAL CLEARANCE

670. Under section 13 of Competition Act, a final decision must authorize, prohibit or subject a merger to the fulfilment of undertakings.

671. Section 14 of the Competition Act provides for a tacit approval in case that no decision is issued within forty-five business days. However, due to the way the CNDC interprets the application of suspensions to the reviewing term, rarely a transaction will lack a written decision and thus be considered as tacitly approved.

672. One exception to the foregoing is found in the *Monsanto Argentina* case,[524] where the National Chamber in Economic Crimes of the City of Buenos Aires reversed a decision of the Secretariat conditioning the approval of the acquisition to the fulfilment of certain divestiture undertakings, on the basis that it had been issued after the expiration of the forty-five business day term and, consequently, once the transaction was considered tacitly approved.

---

523. *Supra* n. 388.
524. 'Monsanto Argentina S.A. y otros s/ art. 8 Ley 25.156', CNPenal Económico, Sala A (22 Sep. 2009), [70057898] Lexis.

Part III, Ch. 2, Clearance Decisions Merger Control 673–678

I. Conditions and Undertakings

A. Content

673. Undertakings are generally of two types: divestment or behavioural.

674. Most divestment undertakings have been imposed in horizontal cases, where the degree of concentration in a specific relevant market was considered excessive. The authorities tend to apply this remedy in a way to restrict the original transaction as little as possible, and consequently have generally accepted relatively high degrees of concentration (i.e., above 50%) insofar as some 'workable' competition remained. Following the same policy, they have been generally willing to accept the divestment of the assets considered less valuable by the parties, whether they belong to the target or the acquiring company.

675. For example, in the *Ambev/Quilmes* case[525] buyer could choose to sell one of its own manufacturing plants and keep target's manufacturing facilities.

676. Under the Competition Act, the CNDC is not obliged to discuss the scope of the undertakings with the parties. This circumstance, coupled with the difficulty in finding a suitable purchaser for the assets to be divested, particularly in a context of recurring economic instability, makes the selection of divestments by the authority a crucial one.

677. For example, once again in the *Ambev/Quilmes* merger, the authorities decided that only a new entrant could purchase the assets. This decision was challenged by competitors of the merging parties on the basis that, given the acquiring parties' much stronger market position, it was preferable to allow the other incumbents to purchase the assets and become more competitive than to allow the entry of a new, smaller competitor.[526] Ultimately, a new company with no experience in the beer industry purchased the assets, and shortly thereafter sold them to one of the incumbents that could not purchase them in the first place because of the restrictions of the original divestment order.[527]

678. Earlier divestment decisions contemplated for the transfer of the divested assets to a trust fund, to be managed independently from the merging parties.[528] Subsequent cases have been more inclined to accept the implementation of 'hold

---

525. *Supra* n. 388.
526. 'Compañía Industrial Cervecera S.A. c. Estado Nacional -Secretaría de la Competencia, la Desregulación y Defensa del Consumidor- s/ Acción de Amparo -Medida Cautelar', *supra* n. 191.
527. 'CCBA S.A. y Cervecería y Maltería Quilmes S.A. s/ incidente de desinversión (en autos principales 'CCBA S.A. y Cervecería y Maltería Quilmes S.A. (Conc. 376) s/ notificación art. 8 de la Ley No. 25.156', Secretaría de Comercio Interior, Resolution No. 61 (12 Dec. 2006) and 'Inversora Cervecera S.A. y otros s/ notificación art. 8 Ley No. 25.156 (Conc. 655)', Secretaría de Comercio Interior, Resolution No. 45 (31 Mar. 2008).
528. *See*, e.g., 'Fresenius Medical Care AG', Ministry of Production, Resolution No. 6 (7 Feb. 2002) and 'Vigil Corp. S.A., Ambit S.A., Southtel Holdings S.A. y Telefónica Media S.A. s/ notificación

separate' agreements, while at the same time appointing an overseer to monitor the divestment process.[529]

679. The inconsistency of the Competition Act and the Regulation as to whether the competition regime is of an *ex ante* or *ex post* character was discussed in the context of a challenge by a competitor of the merging parties to the conduct of the latter as regards the divested assets pending their sale. This issue was discussed in the Quilmes merger, when competitor Isenbeck filed a complaint with the CNDC stating that the merging parties were voluntarily mismanaging the brands to be divested to impair their competitive value while at the same time acting as regards the other target brands as if the merger was already effective, something which, in Isenbeck view, could not take place until the divestment obligation was completed and approved by the competition authorities.

680. The Court concurred with Isenbeck and issued an interim measures[530] suspending the joint operation of the merging parties, although limiting the validity of said restriction until the date where the CNDC issued an order explaining how the merging parties were to conduct their business pending the approval of the undertakings.[531]

681. Behavioural undertakings can adopt many forms. The typical one involves the amendment of non-competition clauses, which are reviewed in all merger proceedings. Under current CNDC policy, such clauses are to be limited to a term of five or two years, depending on whether the seller transfers know-how to the buyer or not, respectively. As regards its geographic scope, they cannot exceed the areas where target was active before clearance.[532]

682. Whether imposing a non-compete obligation in a merger that is otherwise deemed as not infringing the Competition Act is subject to debate,[533] as there is no reference in the review made by the CNDC as to the effect on competition of preventing sellers from re-entering the market outside the time or geographic scope imposed by the authorities. Consequently, it could be argued that the authorities would be exceeding the scope of the Competition Act by *promoting* rather than *preventing restrictions* to competition.

---

art. 8 Ley No. 25156' and 'AC Inversora S.A. y Telefónica Media S.A. s/ notificación art. 8 Ley No. 25.156', Secretaría de la Competencia, la Desregulación y la Defensa del Consumidor, Resolution No. 8 (19 Mar. 2002).
529. 'P.R. Argentina S.A., Goal Acquisitions Limited y Allied Domecq PLC ', *supra* n. 427.
530. 'Cervecería Argentina S.A. Isenbeck S.A. y Estado Nacional s/ incidente de apelación', CNCiv. Com. Fed., Sala III (28 Aug. 2006), [7/17498] Lexis.
531. The CNDC had stated before the court that the joint operation of the undertakings was necessary to complete the divestment obligations.
532. 'Bayer Healthcare AG, Roche Holding AF, Roche Finanza AG, Roche Pharmhold BV, Roche Deutschland Holding GmbH, Hoffman-La Roche France SAS, Roche SAS y Laboratories Syntex s/ notificación art. 8 de la Ley 25.156 (c. 474)', among many others.
533. *See* Waisman, Agustín, *Cláusulas contractuales de no competencia*, LL, 2004-C, 1420.

Part III, Ch. 2, Clearance Decisions Merger Control 683–685

683. So far courts have considered the foregoing regulation of non-competition clauses in the context of acquisitions as reasonable, and have only been willing to apply limits in other circumstances. For example, in a case presented to the review of the CNDC, Adidas – the owner of the Reebok brand – and Vulcabras – a Reebok licensee and distributor – entered into a joint venture agreement for the manufacture of *Reebok* sports shoes, and agreed that: (a) until termination of the JV agreement, neither of them would independently compete with the JV products outside a specific list of products already manufactured by the parties; (b) upon termination of the JV agreement, the local distributor would not sell competing products for a term of six months; and (c) upon termination of the JV agreement, neither of the parties would hire employees of the other for a term of three years.

684. The Secretariat ordered the amendment of the JV agreement so that the parties could compete with other products immediately after the entering of the JV agreement, and no time restrictions were imposed to the distributor or the parties – as regards the hiring of employees – after the JV agreement ceased having effects.[534] On appeal, the court reversed the decision of the Secretariat on the first two issues but withheld the prohibition to restrict the hiring of employees, as they were regarded as third parties to the agreement which could not see their right to access to potentially more advantageous labour conditions restricted by the parties.[535]

684.1. In more recent decisions and following the line of the *Adidas/Reebok* case mentioned above, the CNDC and Secretariat stated that the term of the non-compete clause must be counted as from the closing of the concentration, and expire: (i) at the completion of the period accepted by the authorities (as stated, two or five years) regardless of, e.g., whether any of the sellers remains involved – in an executive capacity – in the target company as part of the deal conditions after the expiration of such term;[536] or (ii) in a pure JV context, upon one of the parties exiting the JV.[537]

685. Other typical type of behavioural undertaking involves non-discrimination warnings. These are normally found in vertical cases, where there may be the risk of restriction in the sale of a particular input to a competitor of the merging parties downstream. Warnings in other cases may also involve:

---

534. Secretariat of Domestic Trade, Resolution No. 169 (18 May 2010).
535. 'Vulcabras S.A. y otro s/ apel. resolución Comisión Nacional de Defensa de la Competencia', CNCont. Adm. Fed., Sala I (14 Jul. 2011).
536. 'Sheldrake Cooperatie U.A., José Luis Romero Victorica y Contax S.A. s/notificación Artículo 8° Ley 25.156 (Conc. 905)', Secretaría de Comercio Interior, Resolution No. 68 (6 Aug. 2012).
537. 'Corporación Azucarera del Perú S.A., Edgardo Alfredo García, Gerardo César Fernández y otros s/notificación Art. 8° Ley 25.156 (Conc. 927)', Secretaría de Comercio Interior, Resolution No. 67 (16 Jul. 2012).

(i) not carrying out tying practices (*Quilmes/Embotelladoras del Interior* and *Peñaflor/Coca Cola* filings);[538] and
(ii) not increasing the market share in the given market for certain period (*Carrefour/Promodès* and *Cinemark/Hoyts* filing).[539]

686. Behavioural undertakings sometimes have been drafted in very broad terms, even reaching areas other than competition law. This is problematic, since given that the application of behavioural undertakings effectively subjects the final approval of the merger to their fulfilment, it may become difficult to determine whether the undertakings have been fulfilled or not, thus subjecting the merger to a potential negative decision.

687. The foregoing issues are dramatically portrayed in the Cablevisión – Multicanal pay-TV merger described in paragraphs 474 et seq. above, which was approved in December 2007 subject to the fulfilment of several undertakings proposed by the merging parties themselves, which included several qualitative targets, some even of a social nature such as providing basic pay-TV services at no cost to hospitals and public health centres.[540] The undertakings were ultimately considered unfulfilled by the competition authorities two years later and thus the conditional approval was rejected.[541]

B. Timing

688. As anticipated, the Competition Act provides for a forty-five business day term for the issuance of final decisions, which in practice can be extended to one year or more for a number of reasons, including:

(i) an incorrect application by the CNDC of the legal provisions regulating the events which may grant a suspension of the reviewing term;
(ii) an abuse by the CNDC of the scope of the follow-up questions;
(iii) reluctance or lack of ability from the merging parties to provide complete information; and
(iv) an unreasonable delay by the Secretariat to adjudicate decisions ending the review process.

---

538. 'Embotelladoras del Interior S.A. y Cervecería y Maltería Quilmes S.A.I.C.A. y G. s/ notificación art. 8 Ley 25.156', Secretaría de Defensa de la Competencia y del Consumidor, Resolution No. 290 (7 Dec. 2000) and 'Peñaflor S.A. y Coca-Cola de Argentina S.A. s/ notificación art. 8 Ley 25.156 (conc. 429)', Secretaría de Coordinación Técnica, Resolution No. 27 (9 Mar. 2004).
539. 'Carrefour S.A. y Promodès S.A. s/ notificación art. 8 Ley 25.156', Secretaría de Defensa de la Competencia y del Consumidor, Resolution No. 57 (27 Apr. 2000). 'Hoyts General Cinema South America Inc. y Cinemark Argentina Holdings Inc. s/ notificación art. 8 de la Ley 25.156 (Conc. 938)', *supra* s. 532.2.
540. 'Grupo Clarín S.A., Vistone LLC, Fintech Advisory Inc., Fintech Media LLC, VLG Argentina LLC y Cablevisión S.A., *supra* n. 152.
541. 'Grupo Clarín S.A., Vistone LLC, Fintech Advisory Inc., Fintech Media LLC, VLG Argentina LLC y Cablevisión S.A.', *supra* n. 389.

Part III, Ch. 2, Clearance Decisions Merger Control

§4. RELATIONS WITH OTHER MERGER CONTROL AUTHORITIES

I. Other Authorities within the Local Jurisdiction

689. There are no merger control authorities in Argentina other than the CNDC and the Secretariat. As explained in paragraphs 97 and 206 above, section 59 of the Competition Act abrogated all empowerments previously granted to other agencies on competition law matters. This of course does not mean that other agencies cannot give their opinion on the impact of a merger in the market. In fact, section 16 of the Competition Act expressly contemplates the obligation of the CNDC to require the regulator its opinion on the compliance of the merger with the regulatory framework, opinion which on occasions include some competition considerations as well.

II. International Coordination

690. As regards the participation of the CNDC in international organizations, it must be noted that the CNDC regularly attends OECD and ICN meetings. In addition, training or rule harmonization efforts have been made through the visits of specialists from the EU, France and Spain, internships attended by CNDC officials with foreign agencies, or counselling given by the Argentinean authorities to delegations of the governments of Nicaragua, Bolivia and Uruguay.

Chapter 3. Challenging of the Administrative Decision

§1. COMPETENT COURTS

691. The original wording of section 53 of the bill that ultimately became the Competition Act provided that:

> Appeals must be filed before the Competition Defence Tribunal within a term of fifteen (15) days of notification of the resolution. Said Tribunal, within five (5) days of the filing of the appeal, must transfer the file to the National Appeal Court in Commercial Matters or the corresponding Federal Court of Appeals in the provinces.

692. In the same direction, the bill provided in section 56 that in the cases not expressly contemplated therein the CPCCN would apply in addition to the CPPN.

693. Through presidential Decree 1019/99 the President of Argentina vetoed several provisions of the bill, including the reference to the application of the CPCCN in section 56.

694. As regards section 53, the Decree deleted the references to the 'National Appeal Court in Commercial Matters' as well as 'in the provinces'. Section 53 was then left with the following wording when the Competition Act was passed:

> Appeals must be filed before the Competition Defence Tribunal within a term of fifteen (15) days of notification of the resolution. Said Tribunal, within five (5) days of the filing of the appeal, must transfer the file to the corresponding Federal Court of Appeals.

694.1. Finally, the wording of section 53 was again changed by virtue of the 2014 Amendment, which reduced the term from fifteen to ten days and provided for the deposit of the amount of the fine before appealing such decisions:

> Appeals must be filed and substantiated before the enforcement authority, within 10 days of notification of the resolution; the enforcement authority shall transfer the appeal and its reply to the National Court of Appeals in Consumer Protection Matters or the competent Courts of Appeals within 10 days, along with the file in which the administrative act were issued.
> In all cases, in order to file the appeal against the administrative resolution imposing a fine, the amount of the fine shall be deposited to the attention of the authority so deciding it, and evidence of the deposit shall be filed with the appeal writ, without which the appeal shall be rejected, unless compliance with the deposit could cause the appellee irreparable harm.

Part III, Ch. 3, Challenging of the Administrative Decision   695–700

695. In year 2000, in re *Imagen Satelital*,[542] the Supreme Court decided a conflict of jurisdiction between the Federal Court of Appeals on Contentious-Administrative matters and the National Court of Appeals in Economic Crimes to issue an interim measure under the Competition Act. The High Court decided in favour of the criminal court, given the Statement of Reasons of Decree 1019/99, which favoured such tribunals due to the nature of the Competition Act and the subsidiary application of criminal rules provided for therein.

696. A few months later, the Regulation expanded section 53 of the Competition Act as follows:

> The Federal Civil and Commercial Court of the City of Buenos Aires and the respective Federal Court of Appeal in the provinces will have jurisdiction to hear on appeals filed against decisions of the Competition Defence Tribunal.

697. This Regulation did not change the situation in the provinces, where generally only a single federal court exists, with jurisdiction on a number of different subjects. However, in the city of Buenos Aires – where most cases are heard – the change could entail that the Court of Appeals provided for in the Former Competition Act – the National Court of Appeals in Economic Crimes – no longer had jurisdiction.

698. The wording of section 53 of the Regulation was far from being accepted by the judiciary in the city of Buenos Aires. Two of the three chambers of the Federal Civil and Commercial Court of the City of Buenos Aires followed the aforementioned provision, while one of the chambers of said court[543] and the National Court of Appeals in Economic Crimes believed it was unconstitutional.

699. In addition, in 2006 the Supreme Court ratified the holding of *Imagen Satelital* in *Repsol YPF*,[544] but without referring to whether section 53 of the Regulation was unconstitutional or not.[545]

700. The issue was once again considered by the Supreme Court in re *Telecom Italia*.[546] Even when the decision was based on different grounds, the court in obiter dicta stated that, had the case only involved the issue of which court of the City of Buenos Aires Court had jurisdiction to hear on appeal decisions under the Competition Act, the answer would lie on *Repsol YPF.*

---

542. 'Imagen Satelital S.A.', 323 Fallos 2577 (2000).
543. 'Luncheon Tickets s/apel. resol. Comisión Nac. Defensa de la Compet.', CNCiv. Com. Fed., Sala II (22 Dec. 2006). This court changed its position though in re 'Telecom Italia S.p.A y otro s/ recurso de queja por rec. directo denegado' (27 Jul. 2009).
544. '*Repsol YPF GLP Envasado en la Ciudad de San Nicolás s/ recurso de queja* ', 329 Fallos 860 (2006).
545. Otamendi, Jorge, *Tribunales competentes en materia de aplicación de la ley de defensa de la competencia*, LL (30 May 2006) at 4.
546. 'Telecom Italia S.p.A. y otro s/ solicitud de inhibitoria'*, supra* n. 210.

701. Given that the *Telecom Italia* decision was ultimately decided on grounds other than jurisdiction, the dissenting opinion of one its Justices referred to in paragraph 280 above and that the decision is not binding on lower courts under the Argentinean legal system, it is likely that the existence of contradictory judgments will continue until a clearer Supreme Court is issued or legislative reform is implemented. This in spite of the fact that, as anticipated, the 2014 Amendment created the National Court of Appeals in Consumer Protection Matters, with jurisdiction in the City of Buenos Aires, as appeal court on competition matters in replacement of the Federal Civil and Commercial Court of Appeals and the Federal Court of Appeals in Economic Crimes, as such new courts have not been created as of the time of this report.

702. In addition, as anticipated under paragraph 263 above: (i) in the city of Buenos Aires, Contentious-Administrative courts would still have jurisdiction on issues other than the appeal of a decision by the CNDC or the Secretariat, as the *Multicanal* case[547] illustrates; and (ii) other courts may still hear on issues like injunctions or *amparo* proceedings.

703. As regards venue, interesting issues have arisen in two cases involving pay-TV company Cablevisión.

704. In one of them, a cartel case,[548] appellant argued that the courts of the city of Buenos Aires had jurisdiction over the matter given that the allegedly unlawful agreement, if existent, would have been entered into in the city of Buenos Aires, given that the main offices of both parties and most of the management were located there. The case ultimately reached the Supreme Court, which rejected that approach by application of the principle set forth in section 37 of the CPPN, deciding that regardless of where the presumed cartel had been devised, it had effects in a provincial jurisdiction only and thus the provincial courts had jurisdiction on it.[549]

705. A similar decision was reached in a price discrimination investigation involving the same company.[550]

§2. TIME LIMITS

706. The time limits to challenge an administrative decision will depend on the type of legal action that is being pursued.

707. Appeals based on section 53 of the Competition Act, as anticipated, must be filed before the Secretariat within ten business days of the issuance of the relevant resolution. The Secretariat, within ten days, must decide whether to grant the

---

547. *Supra* n. 154.
548. *Supra* n. 247.
549. 'Multicanal S.A. y otro / denuncia infr. a la ley 22.262.', 330 Fallos 1610 (2007).
550. 'Cablevisión S.A. s. solicitud de inhibitoria', CNCiv. Com. Fed., Sala III (9 Aug. 2005).

appeal – in which case it must transfer the file to relevant Court of Appeals – or reject it, in which case the parties may resort directly with the court for the same purpose.

708. Before the 2014 Amendment, appeals of decisions not included in section 53 followed the provisions of the CPPN (sections 449–455), and had to be filed within three business days. In this case, it was not necessary for the appellant to include the full reasoning of its arguments against the relevant resolution; those might be presented in writing, or orally before the Court of Appeals at a special hearing. A final decision would be made within five business days from the date of the hearing.

709. Likewise, decisions which the parties may consider unfounded may be subject to an appeal for reversal before the same agency that issued them, with the purpose that the same agency revoke the decision (CPPN, sections 446–448). This action must also be filed before the agency within three business days.

709.1. The replacement by the 2014 Amendment of the subsidiary application of the CPPN by that of the Administrative Procedures Law No. 19,549 would now prevent the application of the foregoing provisions, and instead the application of such law's own set of appeal provisions. Given the possibility of further changes in the Competition Act prompted by the new Administration that took office in December 2015 and the lack of precedents as of the date of this writing, we will not refer to the appeal provisions of Law 19,549.

710. An action similar to that identified in 709 above, but which is not directed at the reversal of the decision but its clarification, is contemplated in section 37 of the Competition Act. The term to file such action is also of three business days.

711. After the 2014 Amendment, no appeals suspend the execution of the appealed decision, including the application of fines. However, said suspension may be achieved in certain cases through the issuance of a court decision, as was anticipated in paragraphs 237 et seq. above.

712. Decisions by Courts of Appeals may be subject to an extraordinary appeal before the Supreme Court. The appeal must be filed before the Court of Appeals within ten business days from the notification of the appealed decision. Upon receipt, the Court of Appeals must notify the appeal to the appellee for an additional term of ten business days and upon said party having replied or the term for doing so having expired, the court will decide on the admissibility of the appeal. If the appeal is accepted, the file must be transferred to the Supreme Court within five business days, while if it is not the appellant may resort to the Supreme Court directly.[551]

---

551. CPCCN, ss 256 to 258.

§3. SCOPE OF JUDICIAL REVIEW

713. The judicial review at the appeal level is unlimited in scope, and consequently an administrative decision may be overturned based on procedural or substantive grounds alike.

714. Courts of Appeals have challenged many CNDC or Secretariat decisions based on procedural issues. Some had been declared null and void due to lack of legal reasoning,[552] failure to state a course of action[553] or due process considerations,[554] while others due to a defect in the passing of the administrative resolution by the CNDC (lack of quorum)[555] or the fact that the agency was not empowered to issue the decision.[556]

715. Courts are also empowered to review the substantive issues of a case, although they are more inclined to agree with the CNDC's position given its technical expertise. An exception can be found in the *V.C.C.* case,[557] where the Court of Appeals in Economic Crimes rejected the definition of relevant market adopted by the CNDC, replacing it for a broader one which diluted the potential anticompetitive effects of the conduct.

---

552. 'A. Gas S.A. y otras c/ Agip Argentina S.A. y otras', *supra* n. 216.
553. 'Monsanto Company' and 'Monsanto Argentina SAIC', *supra* n. 48.
554. 'Incidente de apelación contra Resolución SCI No. 483/09 (en autos principales: 'Pirelli & C S.p.A. y otros s/notificación art. 8 ley 25.156', *supra* n. 127.
555. 'Belmonte Manuel y Asociación Ruralista Gral. Alvear', *supra* n. 165, among others.
556. 'Recreativos Franco S.A.', CNCiv. Com. Fed., Sala I (11 May 2006), LL (23 Oct. 2006) at 11.
557. 'V.C.C. S.A. y otros', *supra* n. 465.

Selected Bibliography

Cabanellas de Las Cuevas, Guillermo. *Derecho antimonopólico y de defensa dela competencia*. Heliasta ed., 2005.

Cervio, Guillermo & Ropolo, Esteban. *Ley de defensa de la competencia, comentada y anotada*. La Ley ed., 2010.

Coloma, Germán. *Defensa de la competencia*. Ciudad Argentina ed., 2009.

Martinez Medrano, Gabriel. *Control de los monopolios y defensa de la competencia*. Lexis Nexis ed., 2002.

Quaglia, Marcelo. *Grupos de empresas, defensa de la competencia y derechos del consumidor*. La Ley ed., 2002.

Selected Bibliography

Index

The numbers here refer to paragraph number.

Abuse of dominance, 139, 140, 148, 159–168, 240, 244, 250, 383, 404, 406, 422, 424, 427, 429, 455, 552
Access to file, 592–597, 664
Administrative
　agencies applying antitrust rules other than the CNDC, 206
　injunctions, 225–231
　investigations, 547–615
Advisory opinions, 80, 88, 194, 630
Agrupación de Colaboración (ACE), 174, 176, 352–354
Amparo proceedings, 236–239, 268, 668, 702
Assets, 101, 115, 116, 124, 169, 170, 174, 176, 213, 311, 317, 351, 354, 388, 396, 467, 472, 523, 524, 623, 628–630, 674, 676–679

Balancing test, 132, 133
Barriers of entry, 108, 112, 151, 373, 416, 470, 473, 488, 533, 537, 562, 640, 642
Bilateral Agreement with Brazil, 68, 69

Cartels
　bid rigging, 296, 308, 345
　under the Criminal Code, 105, 155, 269, 270
　difference with concerted practices, 152
　draft leniency programme, 72, 220, 224
　group boycott, 329–340
　information exchange, 296, 346
　market/client allocation, 295–321
　price-fixing, 282–294
　production/innovation limitation, 322–328
Civil and Commercial Procedural Code, 113
Civil Enforcement, 237–268
　damages, 253–261

Comisión Nacional de Defensa de la Competencia (National Commission for the Defence of Competition (CNDC))
　agencies applying antitrust rules other than the CNDC, 206
　complaints, 102, 203, 244, 249, 259, 317, 328, 365, 419, 434, 576, 578, 579, 590, 679
　creation, 48, 179
　ex officio investigations, 512, 576, 590
　formation, composition, 178–190
　general sectors enquiries, 547–575
　investigating and adjudicating powers, 191–196
　other institutional tasks, 197–203
　relations with other merger control authorities, 689, 690
　right of defence, 590–613, 664–669
Companies Act (Law No. 19,550), 650
Competition Act (Law No. 25,156), 63
　congressional discussion leading to enactment, 32
　Law No. 11,210, 36, 37, 39, 41–43, 47
　Law No. 12,906, 42, 43, 45–49, 52
　Law No. 22,262, 44, 167, 392
　past competition law legislation
　　section (1), 37, 39, 42, 103, 106, 131, 132, 134, 154, 156, 157, 165, 167, 173, 213, 314, 351, 397
　　section (2), 37–39, 42, 43, 104, 153, 157, 165, 326, 329, 397, 446
　　section (3), 87, 88, 92, 99, 228
　　section (4), 107, 109, 139, 160, 242
　　section (5), 108, 431
　　section (6), 115, 118, 119, 124, 169, 616
　　section (7), 134, 473, 533, 644
　　section (8), 59, 230, 617, 618, 620, 649–651, 657, 660
　　section (10), 623

185

Index

section (13), 532, 651, 670
section (16), 96, 588, 661, 689
section (24), 60, 575, 661
section (25), 645
section (26), 275, 576, 577
section (28), 577, 579
section (29), 579, 591, 592, 595
section (30), 592, 593
section (31), 592
section (33), 606
section (34), 607, 608
section (35), 225, 228, 229, 231, 302
section (36), 610, 613
section (37), 704, 710
section (38), 599
section (40), 209, 599, 600
section (46), 213, 217
section (47), 218
section (49), 214
section (50), 219, 549, 580
section (51), 241
section (52), 579
section (53), 60, 279, 280, 691, 694, 696, 698, 707, 708
section (54), 248
section (55), 248
section (56), 60, 271, 278, 692
section (58), 187, 191, 227, 233
section (59), 97, 206, 689
Concentrations
as an anticompetitive practice, 310
behavioural undertakings, 511
clearance and conditional clearance, 670–688
conglomerate mergers, 539–545
definition, 169
divestment undertakings, 487, 501, 524, 532, 544
exemptions, generally, 630
horizontal mergers, 465–532
joint ventures, 546
market/product extension mergers, 536–538
market share calculation, 631–643
merger control notifications, 483
merger guidelines (Resolution No. 164/2001), 79
mergers prohibited by competition authorities, 472
Multicanal/Cablevisión merger, 475, 481, 488, 495
notification forms, 78
preliminary assessment and full investigation, 645–648
right of defence, 669
Telefónica/Telecom Italia merger, 489, 507, 508, 511, 513, 515, 516, 529
time framework, 659, 660
turnover calculation, 617, 622
vertical mergers, 533
Concerted practices, 148, 152–155, 273, 293.1, 364
Control, 116, 117, 170
Cooperation agreements, 68, 72.1, 173–175, 351–364
Cooperation with other State Institutions, 587–588
Criminal Code, 27
section, 54, 113

Damages, 253–261
passing on theory, 258
Decisive influence. *See* Control; Substantial influence
Decree
No. 89/2001 (the Regulation), 519
No. 396/2001, 63
No. 1019/1999, 25, 693, 695
No. 1172/2003, 601
No. 2284/1991, 228
De minimis exemption to notification, 77, 88, 100
Determining influence. *See* Substantial influence
effects test, 88
Discrimination. *See* Exploitative abuses of dominance
Divestment of assets, 523
Dominant position, 47, 106–109, 148–151.1, 164, 167, 330, 402, 419, 434–436

Efficiencies, 99, 136, 137, 468, 486, 487
Entry, 329, 374, 409, 441, 572, 640, 677
Excessive pricing. *See* Exploitative abuses of dominance
Exclusionary abuses of dominance, 139, 240, 330, 398
predation, 413–420
price squeeze, 460–464
rebates, 438–445.1
refusal to deal, 446–459
tying, 421–437
Exclusive dealing, 381–385, 438

Index

Exclusive distributorship, 365–380
Exploitative abuses of dominance, 159, 168, 406
  discrimination, 406
  excessive/unfair pricing, 397–405
  resale price maintenance, 408, 569

Fines, 48, 213–224, 255, 286, 290, 291, 371, 385, 580, 711
  guidelines, 216, 311
  late filing, 518, 659
Franchising, 387–388

General economic interest, 103, 106, 126–129, 131, 133–135, 137, 148, 157, 161, 166, 167, 283, 285, 289, 292, 381, 402, 412, 434, 447, 533, 566
General sector inquiries. *See Comisión Nacional de Defensa de la Competencia*
Government direct enforcement activities, 204–205
Group boycott. *See* Cartels

Health Care Guidelines, 333, 334, 338

Information exchange practices, 296, 346–350
Injunctions. *See* Administrative
Interim measures, 41, 192, 228, 234–236, 240, 262–268, 275, 294, 436, 524, 655, 680, 695

Joint venture, 120, 172–177, 327, 351–353, 363, 526, 546, 683
Judicial review, 56, 86, 340, 391, 713–715

Licensing
  compulsory (patents), 389, 391
  guidelines (telecommunications), 208-212
  technology, 389–396

Market power, 100, 108, 126, 133, 135, 136, 141, 143, 148–151.1, 159, 163, 164, 211, 314, 332, 333, 358, 359, 364, 394, 398, 416, 432, 447, 463, 483, 484, 493, 498, 499, 531, 538, 566, 568, 634, 643
Market shares, 59, 111–113, 151, 151.1, 414, 445, 466, 528, 532.2, 562, 575.2, 630–643, 685
  calculation, 631–643

Mercosur
  Committee for the Defence of Competition, 66
  Competition Agreement, 70
  Competition Protocol, 66
  Understanding on Cooperation between Competition Defence Authorities of Member States of the Mercosur for the Control of Economic Concentrations at a Regional Level, 69
  Understanding on Cooperation between Competition Defence Authorities of Member States of the Mercosur for the Enforcement of National Competition Laws, 69
Monopolization, 39, 160–168

National Constitution, 13, 30, 31, 550
Non-compete clauses, 469
Nullity, 251–252

Patent Law (Law No. 24,481), 390
  compulsory licensing (*see* Licensing)
Per se prohibitions, 126–131, 158
Predatory pricing. *See* Exclusionary abuses of dominance
Price-fixing. *See* Cartels
Professional associations, 140, 330, 383

Rebates. *See* Exclusionary abuses of dominance
Refusal to deal. *See* Exclusionary abuses of dominance
Relevant market, 59, 88, 96, 122, 126, 129, 135, 141–147, 151, 151.1, 201, 214, 284, 285, 314, 334, 337, 359, 369, 373, 374, 378, 394, 412, 420, 438, 440, 443, 470, 479, 481, 488, 525, 526, 539, 554, 565–568, 578, 614, 631, 632, 639, 641, 674, 715
  definition, 147, 151, 284, 374, 479, 632, 715
Resale price maintenance. *See* Exploitative abuses of dominance
Resolution
  No. 26/06, 80
  No. 40/2001, 78
  No. 70/2008, 180
  No. 100/04, 69
  No. 164/2001 (*see* Concentrations)
  No. 726/99, 136, 137, 142

187

Index

Right of defence, 551, 590–615, 664–669

Sanctions, 37, 42, 44, 48–50, 65, 97, 102, 105, 128, 155, 192, 193, 195, 212, 242, 251–270, 284, 301, 302, 307, 380, 383, 398, 401, 403, 455, 461, 580, 612, 613, 654
Secretaría de Comercio Interior (Secretariat of Domestic Trade), 75, 182, 193, 195, 196, 198, 204, 226–228, 252, 275–277, 576, 589, 608, 610, 625, 645, 653, 666, 688, 689, 716, 718
Substantial influence, 115, 117, 118, 120–122, 170, 174, 351, 477, 516, 622, 659

Supply Law (No. 20,680), 325

Tacit collusion, 152
Tribunal Nacional de Defensa de la Competencia (National Tribunal for the Defence of Competition), 65
Tying. *See* Exclusionary abuses of dominance

Unfair pricing. *See* Exploitative abuses of dominance
Unión Transitoria de Empresas (Transitory Union of Enterprises (UTEs)), 124

Vertical agreements, 365–396, 567, 568